Praise for

OH, *YOUR* god!

◆◆◆

"[An] excellent new book."

—**Hemant Mehta**, editor, The Friendly Atheist

"*Oh, Your god!* offers a devastating critique of today's organized religions and holds no punches in making an educated and rational case for why humanity would be better off without it. This book belongs on bookshelves next to the likes of Dawkins' *The God Delusion* and Hitchens' *god Is Not Great.*"

—**Dan Arel**, author, *Parenting Without God*

"Joshua Kelly offers a new and entertaining perspective on religion and the conflict that it has historically been responsible for. Kelly makes a strong case as he sets out to dispel the myth of the goodness of religion."

—**David G. McAfee**, author, *Disproving Christianity and other Secular Writings*

"Kelly has a voice that is important to hear. His book displays passion for a necessity to educate and understand."

—**Matthew O'Neil**, author, *What the Bible Really Does (and Doesn't) Say about Sex*

"Insightful, alarming, and convincing—Kelly will become a common voice among those leading the fight for atheism and secularism throughout the world."

—**J. D. Brucker**, author, *God Needs to Go: Why Christian Beliefs Fail*

"Striking and thought-provoking . . . a book that inspires people to think!"
—*Fourculture Magazine*

"Down to earth and to the point for theists and non-theists alike. Opens religious beliefs to the light of day in a fair and descriptive manner."

—**Dennis Erickson**, author, *God, Man and Moses*

OH, *YOUR* god!

The Evil Idea That Is Religion

—◆◆—

Revised edition

JOSHUA KELLY

PITCHSTONE PUBLISHING
Durham, North Carolina

Pitchstone Publishing
Durham, North Carolina
www.pitchstonepublishing.com

Illustration on page 203 copyright © 2012 by Callan Berry (www.mumblecity.com), used with permission

Library of Congress Cataloging-in-Publication Data

Kelly, Joshua, 1989- author.
  Oh, your God! : the evil idea that is religion / Joshua Kelly. — Revised edition.
    pages cm
  Includes bibliographical references.
  ISBN 978-1-63431-064-2 (pbk. : alk. paper)
  1. Religion—Controversial literature. 2. Atheism. I. Title.
  BL2775.3.K46 2016
  200—dc23
                            2015027508

Author photograph by Dustin Mennie

To My Family and Dear Friends,
In the ardent hope that some of them never read it.

To Ashley Trautwein, in memoriam;
To Christopher Hitchens, in memoriam;
Because sometimes the dead are the least silent of all.

"First, because it's based on a fantastic illusion. Let's say that the consensus is that our species, we being the higher primates, Homo sapiens, has been on the planet for at least 100,000 years, maybe more. Francis Collins says it may be 100,000; Richard Dawkins thinks maybe quarter of a million. I'll take 100,000. In order to be Christian you have to believe that for 98,000 years our species suffered and died, most of its children dying in childbirth, most other people having a life expectancy of about 25, dying of their teeth, famine, struggle, indigenous war, suffering, misery, all of that. For 98,000 heaven watches it with complete indifference and then 2,000 years ago thinks, "That's enough of that—it's time to intervene. The best way to do this would be by condemning someone to a human sacrifice somewhere in the less literate parts of the Middle East. Don't let's appear to the Chinese, for example, where people can read and study evidence and have a civilization, let's go the desert and have another revelation there." This is nonsense. It can't be believed by a thinking person."

—Christopher Hitchens

"A man's ethical behavior should be based effectually on sympathy, education, and social ties; no religious basis is necessary. Man would indeed be in a poor way if he had to be restrained by fear of punishment and hope of reward after death."

—Albert Einstein

"And if there were a God, I think it very unlikely that He would have such an uneasy vanity as to be offended by those who doubt His existence."

—Bertrand Russell

To the Prophets, All

O! the words of greater men
Are weaker, yes, by far
Than charmers—mystics wild-eyed,
If in the desert they espied
A burning bush or star.
Muhammad, in his wisdom great
For business may have been.
But if in deserts one has heard
An angel's voice with verse immured—
Can he then judge my sin?
A wandering, drooling madman then
Is such a prophet, he—
Who would partake in blank delight
The whimsy of an insane night
And then prescribe it me?
No farther in the dredge of time
Should we sojourn for truth.
Behind this merchant: bloody psalms
With screams and nail-impaléd palms
And men condemned in youth.
We are such things as dreams are made,
Though dreams shall not suffice—
When roused in mornings with a smile
The sun still rises all the while
Without a sacrifice.
So, foolish men who came before
With heads stuck in the sky:
Your heaven blurred your view of stars,
But I shall see despite your scars—
No Son for me did die.
And should such thoughts condemn me now,
I shall with patience go—
No frothy-mouthed advice most queer
Will fill my heart with empty fear
Or curse me with your woe.
I'll have a lived the life of love
You swore I could not know.

—**Joshua Kelly**

Contents

Preface to the Revised Edition

———————◆◆◆◆———————

When I first sat down to write *Oh, Your god!* in the spring of 2012, I was twenty-two years old—and it showed. My desperation to contribute to a vitally important conversation could barely be restrained, and that kind of brash enthusiasm made its way into my narrative. Such zeal is an excellent lightning rod that magnetizes people toward one's rhetoric, but it did, admittedly, make for some pretty bad writing in certain sections.

In this revised edition, I have made an effort to trim the rough edges of an earnest and authentic collection of observations on the evil inherent in religion. Rest assured that I have not editorialized my convictions, nor have I dampened the flames of a hot debate in which *parrhēsia* is sometimes necessary—but rather, I have taken this opportunity to clarify, correct, and calibrate my arguments in a more coherent fashion. The book you are now holding should be a much better submission of the previous edition, rather than a work displaying an entirely new character.

In the two years since *Oh, Your god!* first appeared on shelves, much has changed in my life. The maturational distance between twenty-two and twenty-five is, I think, a kind of evolution to which we all can attest. As a primary example: I've simply become a far better writer and scholar than I was—the academic effort of graduate school and the scholastic expectations of my Marxist theatre historian mentor have better trained me in the kinds of research methods, presentation of facts, and styles of rhetoric that make *Oh, Your god!* more concise, definitive, and engaging than my previous skills allowed. Most importantly, none of the personal sentiments you will read in this have been changed from the first edition without explicit notation as to why and how—I don't believe that going back and changing thoughts I had a few years ago without explanation would be entirely fair to the reader. Not many have evolved in any case.

I also desperately wished to discuss the Islamic State of Iraq and Syria (ISIS) further, but realized that anything more than a few cursory footnotes would have led to an entirely new book on its own. With such important moments in religious history as the establishment of the Islamic State, the imprisonment and execution of atheist authors in Bangladesh, the punishment of Raif Badawi in Saudi Arabia, the public beating of Farkhunda in Afghanistan, the Supreme Court decision legalizing same-sex marriage in the United States—all of these gave me more material than I could reasonably include in a book that had already been written. I have, in some places, attempted to comment on these events in order to keep the book relatively current, but these subjects merit an entire book on their own. If the reader is interested in my thoughts on these and other subjects, I hope they will consider reading my work on *Patheos*, where I write about current events and where these subjects make a much more substantial appearance.

Oh, Your god! has done better since its release than I ever hoped on a reasonable scale and has given me contact with many great authors and scholars of this subject. I have since been extraordinarily lucky (and equally grateful) to have been in correspondence and have worked on projects with notable men of the field like Dr. Lawrence Krauss, Dr. Peter Boghossian, Hemant Mehta, Dan Arel, and others. I was gifted with the opportunity to write a chapter on the philosophy of atheism for the book *666*, which contained the work of numerous voices in atheism and theism. I was graciously invited to write the argument against a moral god in the *Atheos* app, created by Peter Boghossian and sponsored by the Richard Dawkins Foundation for Reason and Science. As of this year, I became a frequent contributor to the Danthropology blog on *Patheos*, a wildly popular website for faith-based discussion. While the door has barely opened to my ambitious contributions to this subject, it is widening, and it may perhaps be submitted that I can write with a tad more authority in this field than when I first sat down to clack away at the keys in 2012. Some of you may have picked up this book because you are familiar with my work. Some of you may have grabbed the book because of its cover or description. Some of you may have opened the book because of its title alone. Regardless, I am pleased to be given the chance to share with you my thoughts.

In short, I have not altered this work in order to more broadly appeal, but to appeal *more effectively*, and to make the results of the message more fruitful. I also write this passage mere months after the atrocious attack on *Charlie Hebdo* in Paris—an event so heinous that it nearly drains me to continue commenting on it. But that and other attacks have been a brutal reminder, as were the mob riots after the *Jyllands-Posten* cartoons, that this debate is not (nor has it ever been) entirely philosophical. I feel that my voice is one among many (but still too few) that have been shouting against the ever-increasing danger of theism. In solidarity with this effort, the composition of the new edition of *Oh, Your god!* has been a reinvigorating process, a concrete reminder to myself that this is a battle of *ideas*, and that every last letter clicked into existence, whether in print or on the message boards, is vital to liberating ourselves and others from the bleak futures that theism envisions for us.

It is my sincere privilege to be a part of this discussion, and to lend a voice to the most serious and indispensable debate on our planet. In this, and in all other things, I remain humbly yours.

Joshua Kelly
Ellensburg, WA—2015

Introduction

WHO THE HELL ARE YOU?

This is the question I am asked the most often. And people expect an answer.

Ergo, it seems most fitting to answer it up front—get it out of the way. Incidentally, that leaves the marvelous freedom for those who do not care for my response to put this book down immediately and walk away (no doubt inspired to do so by the fear of being watched by The Invisible Sky Wizard, having picked it up in the first place). Sadly, the answer is absurdly simple and common, in that (much like god in one of the titles of the erudite and much missed Hitchens) I am no one great. At the time of this writing I am not a professor at a highly ranking academic institution—I do not yet even have an advanced degreee. And though for a time I was an ardent major in the field of clinical psychology with sincere hopes to continue on to what would eventually become a PhD in practice, admittedly that was a path I have since abandoned (some would argue that such a degree wouldn't qualify me to make the claims that I do within these pages anyway).

In fact, I am no one, academically speaking. I am a student of theater who just happens to be an atheist.

So how can you write what you do? people ask me. What credentials do you have to make your claims?

I would have to concede a point, there. I have no academic credentials. However, this gives rise to the argument that in order to be a good atheist, even a good *student*, all that is required is a decent respect for the empirical, for the known evidence; to have a healthy inclination for natural observation, to keep one's eyes open as much as possible, and to read continuously—especially all holy texts: therein the mirror up to nature lies. As Omar Khayyám wrote most elegantly in his *Rubáiyát*:

16 • OH, *YOUR* god!

The Koran! well, come put me to the test—
Lovely old book in hideous error drest—
Believe me, I can quote the Koran too,
The unbeliever knows his Koran best.

As well, expect nothing based on precedent. It has been the sad theme of the plot of my life to watch idiots graduate as valedictorians and geniuses work in common labors. (I would never deign to call myself a genius, though I think I can safely avoid being termed an idiot.) The moment we begin to judge a work based on the creator's quotidian servitude rather than on the creation's artistic or academic merit, we do injustice to any craft we seek to produce. There are few established degrees in atheism, and there are no Boards of Truth or Councils of Right or Scientific Bibles, nor (most importantly) does being an atheist make you an expert in evolutionary theory, biology, physics, neurology, astronomy, or theology. All one needs to do in order to have a point is to hypothesize and present evidence, and (hopefully) supplement with good nature. That is what I attempt to do here.

For those to whom this seems not enough justification for my publication, I will not express apology. You are very likely the kind of person with which the true message of this book seeks to connect. Those teetering on the edge of hope for these pages might be comforted in knowing that a good deal of my education in terms of atheism came from greats like Hitchens, Stenger, Dawkins, Dennett, Harris, Epstein, Russell, Kant and Spinoza, to name a few; it was born of knowing Darwin and seeing throughout the scope of my life the evils of religion on a global and intimate scale and the overwhelming stupidity of fundamentalists—the greed of "commercialigion" (a word of my own devising) that is sweeping the country. It is born from watching mega-churches built for the hundreds of millions of dollars that could have gone to feeding the very hungry vividly pictured in said churches' public relations campaigns. It came from seeing the bloodshed over Israel, Lebanon, Pakistan, India, and Bosnia, the attacks of September 11, and the political conflicts of Ireland and countless others, all in the name of feuding, god-incited idealism. It was spawned in a Mormon Church in Eureka, Utah, when, at the very tender age of nine, I was told I could not attend because my clothing was too poor. It emerged from watching in horror as hundreds of thousands of loving homosexual couples were torn in grief at the rise of Proposition 8 and the dissolution of their marriages for which they had fought so hard.

It was born at a military funeral where the children of Fred Phelps stood, waving signs painted in lurid colors screaming, "GOD HATES FAGS" and "THANK GOD FOR IEDS." My education in atheism came from directing a small troupe of young actors in *Romeo and Juliet*, and watching sadly as a young man stood from the group in isolation, unable to participate because his parents believed that Shake-speare was a tool of the devil. It comes from having, in such a short time in my relatively young life, seen religion destroy so much more than it ever created, more than ever could be imagined or explained within the scope of one lowly book.

And so, whoever you are holding this humble work in your hands now, perhaps this is enough to spur you on to my thoughts, my observations, and my arguments. If you are a fellow soldier of the anti-theism movement, perhaps you will learn nothing new from this, though I endeavor to supply this book with as much original thought as I possibly can, of course with acknowledgment of the powerful and far more worthy writers who came before me. If this is the case, then at the very least you will have discovered a like mind in this work, a hand extended in true friendship and in pursuit of logical hope. Whoever you are, we are friends and comrades of war—indeed, there is a war going on, and the frontlines are in every classroom where evolution is not allowed to be taught, or in every space where homosexuality is not allowed to be mentioned, or in every town where dollars are being spent on massive Christian theaters and not on charity, education, or progressive legislation.

The youngest generations are the casualties of this war, and for every new child born into a family where a mythical god is the only answer, where guilt and intolerance and hatred pervade a mind too young to decide for itself, another tally is added to the death count. Perhaps the metaphor is too harsh, but to me it feels fitting. I am moved to fury when I see a child of the Westboro Baptist Church holding up a sign of hatred and not being able to explain why. I am broken-hearted for that adolescent who stood outside of *Romeo and Juliet*, unable to know its poetry, majesty, and impact on the English-speaking world simply because he was unlucky enough to be born into a household where antiquated dogmas overrule common sense and objectivity. I am saddened for a young teen, impregnated and infected with AIDS by rape, who cannot receive a medical abortion to avoid serious complications because she is in a Catholic family. Indeed, the greatest failure of evolution was its inability to naturally select only those whose ideologies were based out of modern morality and not inane doctrine. (Actually, if the fanatically religious continue their relentless quest in killing themselves and their theistic enemies, natural selection might display itself after all.)

But why do you *hate* religion? people ask. If god doesn't exist, what does it matter to you? Can't you just leave it alone?

That is exactly the question this book tries to answer; to show that the *idea* of god when put into practice as it is done today is inherently evil, breeds conflict, and causes discrimination and pain on a global scale—put simply, that religion is divisive and deadly. I'll try to highlight arguments in terms of contradictions in the religions themselves and show how they promote violence overseas and at home; give way to teen suicides, mental illness, and hatred on a social level; deny greatly human and decently moral pleasures to an individual; and can in many ways be bad for your psychological and physical health. In the following chapters, I'll present as many pieces of my argument as I can in a cohesive manner to demonstrate the ways in which religion works as a cancer, overtaking the cells that would be happy in my life and the lives of others.

Also, I would like to dispel outright the painfully semantic debate that will no doubt arise from the use of my word "evil" in the book's subtitle. As we all know, there is no better tool than semantic debate to completely miss the point of an argument. One can readily understand what I mean to communicate by "evil," and it shouldn't have to be defined in a moral, existential, political, or etymological sense. The various influences that religion exerts are what I would describe as "evil" and thereby can be communicated in much the same way that murder, discrimination, racism, sexism, and rape are "evil," for these represent a grand portion of what religion is comprised. Therefore, if one picks up this book and finds that their first counterargument is indeed: "Well, what exactly does 'evil' *mean?*" you would do best to indulge yourself in other pursuits. I do not plan to be distracted by such rabbit trails, and if the crux of this argument for you depends on the definition of the word, you'll read on in vain. If you can readily identify my definition of the word and not become distracted by it, then you have the unparalleled luxury of focusing on the argument and not finding yourself lost on another tangent entirely, devoid of the point.

In these pages, I will seek to illuminate from a social and psychological standard many of the fallibilities of religion through use of anecdote, observation, and scientific study. My hope is to dispel the myth of the goodness of religion as much as I am able in the course of one book, while making it emotionally available for the reader. I do not seek to preach (ironically) or to impose from a pedestal the sometimes pedantic and pompous compendium of "higher thought." All I am trying to do is share my story and knowledge, such as it is, and illuminate the secular world's struggle against the voracity of theistic malice. We will pace through the Crusades and the current conflict in the Temple at the Mount and even to the doors of the Tabernacle and the debacle that was Proposition 8, and to the best of my ability, I shall pick at pieces of the Bible and the Koran and other texts in an attempt to highlight what actively reflects global and social policies from a religious standpoint today (though many monotheists argue these reflections are *not* part of *their* religion). We will, ultimately, attempt to uncover the idiocy of the absurd doctrines that, whether you are aware of them or not, very likely affect your thinking.

It might also serve of special note that this book does not attempt to disprove the theory of god's existence (a sadly unfalsifiable hypothesis—a note of thanks to Bertrand Russell), despite my very obvious and sometimes cruelly unbending atheistic voice. Many of my questions and some of my conclusions naturally favor an atheistic bent, but the overall question of whether or not god exists and the evidence that would be required to prove one thought or the other is nearly infinitely beyond my means at this time. I believe this question can be philosophically, logically, and scientifically answered, but that responsibility is for others to fulfill—as many already have. I would highly recommend reading Victor Stenger's *God: The Failed Hypothesis* or Dr. Peter Boghossian's *A Manual for Creating Atheists* if this is your aim. Also of note, I do find a very separate and identifiable difference between faith and religion, and while I find faith to be egotistical and foolish, I can only see in it the inherent potential for evil, especially when used in tandem with religion. The bullet of one is the gun to the other, as it were. There are many follow-up remarks I have on this subject, but again: that is for another book. And so, this work is much less atheistic than *anti-theistic*, a model most popularly coined by Hitchens, pointing out very real and observable flaws and evils in the *idea* of god and its enactment on earth, most especially by organized monotheisms and their "true" believers. Thankfully, the obviousness of that observation is clear enough that I should be able to do justice to it.

That is all I need to be. I don't need a divine creator at my back to validate me. All I need are a few good people and some simple science, a bit of morality evolved from human consciousness and not from magical mandate, and the hope that someday, somehow, the world will be a better place without the god of Abraham and the church whose only real spiritual motivation is the currency of whatever country in which it is housed. People don't need god and they don't need doctrine—that is the source of the great conflict in the first place (notice I did not use the phrase "all great conflicts"); what they need is the realization that being a good person, following your heart, knowing that right and wrong are uniquely *human* constructs and not godly, and seeking to better the world rather than perpetrating conflict through unfalsifiable mythologies are all that we need to create a comparative heaven on earth, devoid of the grander turmoil we see today. If this book can, to the smallest measured degree, accomplish that—even in the life of one person— then I will consider the work a success and well worth it.

That is who the hell I am. I'm ever so pleased to make your acquaintance.

1

The Grand Hypocrisy

◆◆◆

"Forbear to judge, for we are sinners all."
—William Shake-speare, *Henry VI*

*"One should examine oneself for a very long time
before thinking of condemning others."*
—Molière

It began in a garden—whether in the Middle East or in Jackson County, Missouri, is apparently up for debate.

The topic of hypocrisy naturally carries with it an element of subjectivity that I tend to avoid with as much enthusiasm as I do semantics or shark tanks. After all, aren't we all hypocrites? Haven't we *all* said one thing and done another? Why bring it up in regards to religion? Well, as put most definitively by Marcello Truzzi, extraordinary claims require extraordinary proof. And it can be readily supposed that since religion boasts the greatest claims within human philosophy, namely the purpose of the universe and its divine babysitter, it has much more to answer for than any other epistemological field. When dealing with such weighty proclamations, it's important to know that religion offers a bundle of incompatible dogmas that don't make sense in relation to each other, let alone aid in redeeming a globe of searching souls. In order to see the objective evils that it instills, it is important to find the impotence with which religion as a human organization stands and has stood in its incredibly tiny space in evolved primate history.

In a massive conference at Arizona State University in February 2012, renowned theoretical physicist Lawrence Krauss (in conversation with evolutionary biologist Richard Dawkins) said in reference to people who believe in fundamentalist religion: "When people say that to me, I not only get offended: I call them hypocrites—because, in fact, they are. If they drive a car, if they use a toaster, if they take drugs—if they do anything 'modern society': the chemistry, the biology, the physics that makes those things possible is completely inconsistent with a 6,000-year-old earth. So you cannot believe that and use a car or get in an airplane without calling yourself a hypocrite."[1]

Colluding with these examples includes a personal irritation of mine that illustrates the point: doctors who claim not to "believe" in evolution in favor of fundamentalist idealism. This example proves hypocrisy on two levels. Primarily, because evolution does not require belief—it remains validated as fact by the very scientific method on which their livelihoods are based. It is a poor investment in their belief for hundreds of thousands of dollars to be spent on their education and thousands of hours to be spent in internships, residencies, and fellowships, when they are all founded on the type of empiricism that corroborates both with atheism and explicable biology. Secondarily, the very facets of the process that they claim not to exist are the subjects of their routine, and it is evident in bacteria that evolve and adapt at a rate quickly enough to observe, ergo the continuous need to reinvent antibiotics as new strains of bacterial organisms learn to adapt in the manner of natural selection. Indeed, in a technologically advanced and economically aware world, the faux-reasoning of fundamentalist pseudo-science is an act of greatest possible ignorance.

As well, it comes with a marvelously supplemented double-standard that must be acknowledged: science *may* be wrong in any number of fields—it is continuously adapting to new evidences and observations, always allying itself with the empirical, regardless of personal offense or investment. Darwin himself was a scholar for the clergy at Cambridge (and was even lodged in the same room that William Paley, the concoctor of the well-used timepiece analogy, had been seventy years earlier). After coming across his grand and liberating theory, he waited twenty years to publish it, potentially due to the inner conflict that came between what he believed and what was true. If evidence existed that eliminated reasonable doubt over the existence of god and the relative truth of related spiritual claims, empiricists would be the *first* and most ardent supporters of the case—that's what objectivity *is*. Theists, sadly, have not allowed the opposition the same courtesy, for faced with all the potentiating evidence in the world they have remained not only ass-like in their stubbornness, but also volatile and extreme in their reactions. Secular society makes a myriad of indulgences for private belief, while theists continue to subvert the objective—and proven—in education and government. Such a lack of grace communicates infinitely more than a steadfast faith—it shows a willful blindness to reality.

Obviously, it bears great and heavy pains to a modern mind to look at the mythologies of both the Old and New Testaments and believe them—not even as a metaphorical poeticism into the histories of the world before, but as *literal* fact. And not only are there people who take the word of the Bible at its face without hesitation (i.e., Adam *really* was made of dust and an *actually talking* snake tempted Eve), but they also do so with such obstinate and often laughable stubbornness that they cannot be reasoned with at all. The late Jerry Falwell, noted fundamentalist and evangelical, said quite plainly: "The Bible is the inerrant . . . Word of the living God. It is absolutely infallible, without error in all matters pertaining to faith and practice, as well as in such areas as geography, science, history, etc."[2] The arrogance of this claim is unmistakable. When discussing a manuscript consisting of many authors, places, histories and even languages, jumbled together in an ancient court, edited, rehashed, and reworked over centuries, and translated into over 2,200 languages over the course of 2,000 years, the certainty that human error invaded at *some* point during this incredible process is almost definite, even if one were foolish enough to believe that Jesus was *literally* born of a virgin in the first place (a note which *none* of the Gospels deemed pertinent enough to talk about in astonishing detail and all have different ways of explaining how Mary and Joseph got to Bethlehem and that special unreferenced barn).

One only needs to look at the discrepancies or the translations of some rather interesting verses to see that the evolution (insert irony here) of the Bible was not without flaw:

Exodus (33:20)—[Says God,] *"Thou canst not see my face; for there shall be no man see me and live."*

The Alpha and Omega must have forgotten that sentiment:

Genesis (32:30)—*"So Jacob called the place Peniel, saying, 'It is because I saw God face to face, and yet my life was spared.'"*

To be followed by:

Exodus (24:9-11)—*"Then Moses went up, also Aaron, Nadab, and Abihu, and seventy of the of elders of Israel, and they saw the God of Israel. And there was under His feet as it were a paved work of sapphire stone, and it was like the very heavens in its clarity. But on the nobles of the children of Israel He did not lay His hand. So they saw God, and they ate and drank."*

But how could all this have been, when:

John (1:18)—*"No one has ever seen God; the only God, who is at the Father's side, he has made him known."*[3]

The potential that one has of seeing the face of god while alive seems to be ambiguous. If asked such a question, I would likely refer to the holy text of the god in question: but as we can see from the above example, I would be met with more than a nonanswer—I would be floundering over *conflicting* answers, some of them within the same book. This is merely one example of rampant biblical tangles, which exist whether the subject is of particular gravity in the nature of monotheism or in theological policy. Numerous other frustrating contradictions throughout the Old and New Testaments are happily highlighted in one witty website among several known as "the Holey Bible,"[4] where one can read a compiled list *en masse*. These are contradictions in text or ideas as opposed to hypocrisy of god or of god's chosen people in action, of which there are countless: such as in Numbers, when the lord, tired of the complaining of his followers because of their hunger and thirst, sent a swarm of venomous snakes to attack them. When they begged him for mercy, he instructed Moses on how they might be cured. (Complaining about food equals punishment. Complaining about punishment equals forgiveness?) Or, when Jonah was demanded to denounce Nineveh for the grossness of the city, Jonah turned away from the task, and god threw him in a tempest and was swallowed by a "big fish" as his comeuppance. Meek and subservient once more, Jonah returns to Nineveh to carry out his task only to discover that god has spared the city after all. Not to be outdone, even by himself, the god of Abraham begs to put forth more of his inadequacies:

Genesis (1:31)—*"And God saw every thing that he had made, and, behold, it was very good. And the evening and the morning were the sixth day."*

. . . and:

Genesis (6:6)—*"The LORD was grieved that he had made man on the earth, and his heart was filled with pain."*

The all-knowing creator of the universe had clearly confused the future (that he created) of the creature over which he has indomitable power and was left with an unforeseen pain. How could an almighty being be wrong? Clearly, some mistake has been made—for god has power over all, he knows all and sees all, or so I've been taught.

Genesis (18:14)—*"Is anything too hard for the Lord?"*

Apparently so. In the course of the Bible, man displeased god over and over again. So much so, it seems, that god had to wipe man out for his transgressions—not once, not even twice, but over 135 times, most with more than one casualty involved. From the flood of Noah (which god justified by saying "the earth is filled with violence . . ."[5] Priceless irony!) and the 185,000 soldiers killed by an angel of the lord laying siege to Jerusalem under King Sennacherib to the razing of Sodom and Gomorrah, god has been pissed off with his perfect creation almost too many times to count. Why? If perfection is within the grasp of the Omnipotent at a whim, the old approach of "if at first you don't succeed" seems slightly disingenuous. The ultimate fallibility of god may be the most frustrating contradiction for me to understand, simply because trying to believe in a god in the first place is difficult enough, but trying to believe in one so helplessly inept and unclear even in his own text is insane. One would have to literally have the faith of an angel or the stupidity of Jerry Falwell (or perhaps both) to take a text as backwards and self-contradicting as the Bible and praise it as indomitable, unfailing truth to the literal letter. And this is without remembering that Moses supposedly wrote the first five books of the Bible, yet he isn't mentioned in Genesis, refers to himself in the third person through Exodus, Leviticus, and Numbers, and describes his own death and funeral in Deuteronomy; or that the Ten Commandments appear three times with variations—twice in Exodus and once in Deuteronomy (the physical tablets of which, in one telling, Moses dropped and shattered like porcelain knick-knacks).

Furthermore, no product of man (or of god, if such were the case) is out of the realm of thoughtful inquiry. Consider it a side note if one must, but the Orwellian concept of an existing work that cannot be subject to criticism or Socratic examination is anathema to our cognitive liberation as evolved primates and the artistic precepts of freethinking people. Inconsistencies, banal mandates, and racial bias aside—the Bible being touted as an infallible work is an insult to the intelligences of anyone with the freedom to pick it up and actually read the damned thing.

The inconsistency of the Bible itself may prove to be incredibly disheartening, but it pales in comparison to the masses of people who claim to follow it. "Cafeteria Catholics" being only one of the monikers used to describe them, people who pick and choose which doctrines are important and which are obsolete in their minds run the gamut of denominations, not just Catholicism. Most notably, the subject of Leviticus 18:22 comes to mind, which in the King James Version infamously says: *"Thou shalt not lie with mankind, as with womankind: it is abomination."* This single verse can encompass the entire religious field of a biblically uneducated person and pervades the organizational as well as the individual mind-frame. Westboro Baptist Church, for example, uses this verse as the banner for their entire social mantra, conveniently forgetting such equally biblical creeds as:

Romans (13:8)—*"Owe no one anything, except to love each other, for the one who loves another has fulfilled the law."*

1 Peter (1:22)—*"Having purified your souls by your obedience to the truth for a sincere brotherly love, love one another earnestly from a pure heart."*

Galatians (5:13)—*"For you were called to freedom, brothers. Only do not use your freedom as an opportunity for the flesh, but through love serve one another."*

Contradictions, contradictions everywhere, but not a drop to drink. You could almost empathize with or pity those who flagrantly advertise one singular verse over another, simply because you are far more likely to find a verse that contradicts the one you chose than not. Still, the fact remains palpable that with over 31,000 verses in the Bible, many people are choosing specific ones to pursue and to disregard—almost invariably on the side of hatred. They seem to forget much of the time that their Jesus was supposedly a man of love and kindness, and his preaching was for tolerance and faith alone. How inaccurate this Word is to the Word of his father (allegedly the same being) who was bent on bloodshed and dominance:

Deuteronomy (13:12–16)—*"If you hear that in one of the towns of Yahweh your God has given you for a home, there are men, scoundrels from your own stock, who have led fellow citizens astray, saying "Let us go and serve other gods," hitherto unknown to you, it is your duty to look into the matter, examine it, and inquire most carefully. If it is proved and confirmed that such a hateful thing has taken place among you, you must put the inhabitants of that town to the sword; you must lay it under the curse of destruction—the town and everything in it. You must pile all of its loot in the public square and burn the town and all its loot, offering it all to Yahweh your God. It is to be a ruin for all time and never rebuilt."*

Exodus (22:20)—*"He that sacrificeth unto any god save unto the Lord only, he shall be utterly destroyed."*

Irate, jealous, vindictive, petty—these are not the emotions of an all-merciful, all-loving deity: they are the actions of a mortal man in power—further boosted after remembering that religion and all of its texts are *man-made*, not divinely emailed to the earth after celestial editing and ghostwriting, as is exemplified in the Thomas Hobbes line from his masterful *Leviathan*: "Seeing there are no signs, nor fruit of *religion*, but in man only; there is no cause to doubt, but that the seed of *religion*, is also only in man."[6] Indeed, the mandates and personifications of god (especially in the Old Testament, though the New Testament is not without its own pieces of ludicrousness) are so painfully childish and tribal that it's a wonder how any modern mind could be silly enough to look at it with a discerning eye and decide: "Yes, these are the laws for me. I'll keep my slaves on a tight leash and beat them with a rod (Exodus 21:1–20) and assuredly I shall never curse my father and mother or else I'll die (Exodus 21:17), but you can be *damned* sure I am not giving up my cotton-polyester polo shirts (Deuteronomy 22:11), or lobster and shrimp cocktails (Leviticus 11:10), and I am *definitely* keeping my haircuts (Leviticus 19:27) and my bacon and FOOTBALL (Leviticus 11:7)!"

This, of course, gives rise to the argument concerning the invalidation of the Old Testament with the coming of the New, the idea being that the actions of Jesus were so antithetical to the "laws" prescribed in Exodus and Leviticus that the modern Christian should base the standards of his doctrine on the teaching of the son of their god instead. There are several large flaws with this reasoning, my favorite being the most obvious: no one *does* it, and if they did, what would be the point of keeping the Old Testament? How many Christian sermons have been arched around Old Testament verses, or signs waved at protests and marches bearing Leviticus 18:22, etc.? Where stands the basis for the need to splash the Decalogue of Exodus in public parks and in school rooms, or the continuous reference of original sin and the holiness of the sabbath (which actually has two distinctly different definitions in the Old Testament)? A group of people as large as the Christian nation cannot possibly hope to avoid the negative reaction of Old Testament nightmares (e.g., genocide, rape, and infanticide, among others) by claiming it shares no part of their modern doctrine when, in actuality, it overflows with Pentateuch nonsense. Secondly, one must always remember that the New Testament is in constant coherence with proving the prophecy of the Old Testament, continuously referring to: "in accordance with the prophet," etc., etc., *ad nauseum*—the most important of which coming from the words of Jesus himself: "Do not think I have come to abolish the law or the prophets. I have not come to abolish but to fulfill. Amen, I say to you, until heaven and earth pass away, not the smallest part or the smallest part of a letter will pass from the law, until all things have taken place." (Matthew 5:17) And even *this* is hypocritical, considering how many times Jesus himself stood in the way of Mosaic law, most notably against the stoning of the woman taken by the Pharisees for adultery, the punishment of which should have resulted in her death by prophetic mandate of the Old Testament despite the guilt that Jesus inflicted upon her attackers (a story of which decent evidence has been discovered by Bart Ehrman and others suggesting that it wasn't originally in the Gospel of John in the first place [7]).

All of this, of course, is without taking into account the overwhelming pile of discrepancies that is the New Testament in whole, including the motivation for the holy family to have been in Bethlehem versus Nazareth in the first place (either census that put them there or the dream that came to Joseph urging him to flee); the first three Gospels claim that the Eucharist was invented during Passover, but the Fourth says it was invented well before, and Jesus' divinity is only seriously discussed in the Fourth; the fact that Herod died four years before the Current Era; the genealogy of Jesus in the line of David differs in two Gospels as does the minutiae of the Resurrection, Crucifixion, and the

Anointment—on top of the fact that the Gospels were written *decades* after the historical Jesus died, if he lived at all.[8]

The same observation quite commonly will back a theist into an ideological corner that has become one of my most despised arguments to encounter—namely, that there are so many pieces of the Bible that, even to them, are clear in their primal inaccuracy that they must be registered as "pieces of their time" or "no longer relevant." The moment one utters this true albeit contemptible observation, they show their blatant incapability to be a part of the discussion. For how should one acknowledge a text is outdated, tribal, and an illustration of our infant attitudes as a species and then claim it is an inerrant model for our deepest values? How can one admit that it is both flawed and divine, ancient and relevant? To me, this smacks of undiluted obstinacy. If our times and peoples have indeed changed (of course they have!) then it is decently time for a new book (or better, an entire literary compendium) that is consistent with our modern morality—one that doesn't require revelation in order for it to contain any merit.

The obviousness that modern theists transparently choose which mandates the Invisible Sky Wizard set for them are *truly* holy or not is incredible. Indeed, so much of the Old Testament is smeared by "moderate" or "progressive" Christians as exactly what it is—a convolution of tribal rites and inanities set down by clearly primal men—but some will still lour upon select pieces of it whenever convenience takes them. I, amused and horrified, witnessed a woman who was completely enraged by her "fellow Christians" for putting so much weight upon the Old Testament, saying, "It's just a bunch of prehistoric nonsense," then happily driving to a massive bonfire that night where numerous copies of the Harry Potter book series were collected to be burned for warping the minds of children and inciting them to practice witchcraft. When I asked her where in the Bible "witchcraft" (as if anyone with a merest study of pagan religions could say with confidence that Harry Potter represented true witchery) was condemned, she calmly said without missing a beat: "Exodus 22:18." I had to sincerely refrain from laughing.

Another superb example of this blatant hypocrisy is illustrated in an article posted by *The Advocate* on October 16, 2009, when 49-year-old Jack Price was assaulted by Daniel Rodriguez and Daniel Aleman outside of a deli in Queens, New York. The attack was wildly accepted as a hate crime by the local and national LBGT community, as the beating had come after Price had allegedly blown a kiss to his attackers. A friend of the accused, Mercel Gelmi, said that this kiss justified the attack, and that Price "deserved the beat down." He then proceeded to flash the camera a tattoo in English calligraphy on his right shoulder, proudly displaying the ever-so-lauded Leviticus 18:22: *"Thou shalt not lie with a male as one does with a woman; it is an abomination."*

What Gelmi clearly appears to have forgotten, however, is the point we have already made: you can't take a piece of the Bible and celebrate it without finding contradictions. And in this case, Mercel himself is in violation of his own religious fanaticism. For in Leviticus (19:28), not two chapters away from this verse that he so arrogantly totes about on his own skin, his god instructs him thusly: *"Do not cut your bodies for the dead, and do not mark your skin with tattoos. I am the LORD."*

And what is the spiritual punishment? Leviticus isn't specific. It does remark on the punishment for homosexuality: death—with the modern Christian addition of hell. (Though the idea of hell doesn't even arrive until the New Testament with the entrance of Jesus.) If one were to draw from the same biblical education as Fred Phelps or the rest of the sign-wielding, hell-mongering, inbred spawn of the same proclivity, we would have to assume that Mr. Gelmi would also be suffering an eternity of hell for the breaking of god's divine law. Perhaps next, the Westboro Baptist Church will be chanting "GOD HATES TATTOO ARTISTS"? It's doubtful—yet why do we know this? Because people with brains are conscious enough to the drama of the Religious Right to know that the Bible (and in equally as many cases, the Koran) itself is to blame for the institution of the evil paradigm, but the modern theist acts upon it with choice regard to his own prejudices. Gays are evil—tattoos are not, even though they sit in equal spots of the exact same book. This is cherry-picking at its finest, combined with prejudice, fear, and a healthy dose of hypocrisy.

Even in my beloved home town of Kalispell, Montana, the face of this claptrap is evident. Though blessed with a healthy liberal and artistic community, Kalispell remains home to one of the most petulant pieces of evangelism I have had to witness in the form of Skull Church (so named because of the reputedly skull-shaped hill upon which Christ was crucified), a mission of the Fresh Life multisite atrocity. Headed at the time of this writing by the desperate-for-lost-youth, Hot Topic faux-model Levi Lusko, the church seemingly seeks to breed a generation of fundamentalists without the rigorous practice of biblical adherence, namely in the form of rock-and-roll/screamo teenagers with piercings and tattoos and far more preppy youth with similar delusions of rebellion, who buy into the ruse easily due to the enormous quantities of money that Skull Church boasts and uses to bring in huge hit bands for concerts, such as Emery, Red, The Almost, and Family Force 5. And even though their mission statement is clearly fundamentalist in nature,[10] Lusko himself has broadcasted sermons depicting a grey area on getting tattoos, most especially in his "Eternally Tattooed" sermon, the audio of which is available to stream on various websites, where one can glean such backward and painfully hipsteresque observations as "if we wanted to put it this way, we could say the Gospel According to Body Modification. Jesus Christ was *pierced* so that the tattoos of sin could be removed."[11] Few pieces of more tawdry rationalization have ever been broadcasted.

Lusko also likens the followers of Christ to notch-eared sheep or bond-servants, who were slaves (apropos) bound to their masters through the identifier of a pierced ear. He even goes so far as to call modern tattooing an area of "Christian liberty."[12] This is all, naturally, while subjectively manipulating Leviticus 19:28—though, of course, the few times I have begrudgingly been forced to attend one of these rancorous sermons through circumstance, I have predictably heard the usual fundamentalist drivel on the ideas of a proper family life and the methods by which gays are going to hell and that abortion is a sin against god. Lusko pathetically imitates the sentiments of Jerry Falwell and also further condemns himself to hypocrisy in a gross verbal ejaculation in his sermon, "Soldier On," where he states clearly: "What do you do if, as you're reading the Bible, you come across something you don't agree with? *Change your mind,* for *you* are *wrong*, 'k? That's what it means to say, 'God's the boss.'"[13]

Obviously, Lusko didn't bother to change his mind when coming across passages forbidding tattooing or piercing, but instead jumbled together a weak ahistorical metaphor proclaiming the need to indulge instead, in order to potentially justify his own choices or perhaps to invite an untapped youth market of "lost" teens.[14] This is not to criticize tattooing (having one on my right arm of which I am especially proud,[15] and having dated people for whom tattoos were a particular passion), but once again my point is crudely obvious to the extent that I continuously wonder why it's not a matter of more discussion. Sadly, at one point in my life, I was romantically involved with a young woman whose father's family was entirely evangelical. Her uncle (brother-in-law to her father) was a staff member for Levi Lusko, and therefore her family was continuously in session for the pastor's pedantic foolishness, most notably for their massive Easter gathering (an event so inexplicably large the church would move for this one day from its normal venue to a massive arena north of town). Invariably, during Easter dinner we would sit around the table and the family (those who had gone, as I was thankfully spared) would prattle on in asinine detail about the greatness of the service and the brilliance of Lusko's moral intuition. As I am sure you can understand, I frequently lost my appetite.

On a side note, the Skull and Fresh Life churches occupy two historic cinema buildings located next to each other in Kalispell known as the Strand and Liberty theaters, as well as an adjacent office building that houses their administration (with more real estate rumored in the near future). I've always found it an unpoetic travesty that churches continuously find the means to take over and renovate buildings that were meant for (and should be put to) otherwise more gainful processes than brainwashing people with the insipid idea that the creator of the universe is at the other end of their personal telepathic hotline. Those buildings have the capacity to house marvelous examples of performance art, academic lecture, community event, or literary retail—but instead are revamped into evangelical eyesores. One also shudders at the obscene amount of money such an institution makes (see the first section of chapter two for the shamelessness of this enterprise). Indeed, it perturbs me so much that every time I pass a church while driving or walking in whatever town I am in, I habitually find myself cerebrally renovating the building into a theatre or a school for special needs or even a parking lot. On this note, there exists in Helena, Montana, a beautiful little theater known as the Grandstreet, which has turned a Unitarian church in the middle of town into a gorgeous, intimate performance facility. I often delight at this wonderfully backward turn of typicality, and, if for no other reason, the Grandstreet has become one of my personally favorite venues.

Back to the topic of hypocrisy, this type of isolated use of various passages of the Bible was most eloquently described by Richard Dawkins in his book *The God Delusion:*

> The fact that it has nothing else to contribute to human wisdom is no reason to hand religion a free license to tell us what to do. Which religion, anyway? The one in which we were brought up? To which chapter, then, of which book of the Bible should we turn—for they are far from unanimous and some of them are odious by any reasonable standards. How many literalists have read enough of the Bible to know that the death penalty is prescribed for adultery, for gathering sticks on the sabbath and for cheeking your parents? If we reject Deuteronomy and Leviticus (as all enlightened moderns do), by what criteria do we then decide which of religion's moral values do we accept? Or should we pick and choose among all the world's religions until we find one whose

*moral teaching suits us? If so, again we must ask, by what criterion do we
choose? And if we have independent criteria for choosing among religious
moralities, why not cut out the middle man and go straight for the moral
choice without the religion?*[16]

Unfortunately, it seems that many people do "cut out the middle man" but
insist on regarding their moral conclusion as consistent with their faith.[17] Mr.
Gelmi or Mr. Lusko, undoubtedly, think themselves as staunch a Christian as
any who walk the earth, despite their lack of acknowledgment for the Bible's
mandate of brotherly love and its prohibition against getting tattooed. And
again, while no literate mind could hold aloft the Old Testament as a necessity
of law (and *I* am certainly not suggesting to follow all the barbaric rules within
it), it cannot be denied from a simple observational point that many Christians
are swearing by mere *pieces* of their doctrine, and almost always choosing
wrongly. If Gelmi's friends had chosen to emulate the passage from Romans
13:8 instead of Leviticus 18:22, they might be on the softer side of the legal
system today. If one must choose, why choose hatred? Why opt for conflict and
enmity and social chaos? Yet the majority of theists invariably do.

This would be sufferable, even tolerable, for those of us without the
burden of biblical blindness on our hands if theists (note that I will endeavor
to illumine the same actions of all theists, not just Christians) would keep
their hypocrisy self-contained. Truly, if they wanted to argue inaccurately
about their fairy tales among themselves, I would see no reason to interfere.
I could care less if the Koran condemns me to a swift reckoning by god for
being an unbeliever[18] if followers of Islam didn't also read that they should
kill those who are of my particular vein.[19] It would bear no effect on me
whatsoever that millions of people think Jesus was born of a virgin, if many
didn't also equally believe that my lack of faith in the event was grounds
for my death.[20] Sadly, the monotheist mantra is expansion: it's simply not
enough that I am going to heaven, I need to save you from the bowels of hell
as well. This breeds a widespread campaign that endlessly seeks to enter the
realms of our philosophies, work places, and bedrooms in order to show us
the light of god—and even if they manage that, many fraudulent religious
leaders can't get their rhetoric right.

A mere twenty years ago, Pat Robertson said, "How can there be peace
when drunkards, drug dealers, communists, atheists, New Age worshipers
of Satan, secular humanists, oppressive dictators, greedy money changers,
revolutionary assassins, adulterers, and homosexuals are on top?"[21] This was

in the early nineties, when Republican president George H. W. Bush and vice president Dan Quayle were in office, both of whom openly and regularly expressed their strong Christian beliefs, with Quayle himself being associated with an interdenominational fundamentalist congregation.[22] And even though the Senate had a Democratic majority at the time, it was still presided over by Dan Quayle as U.S. vice president and Democrat Robert Byrd as president *pro tempore*, who, in early life had started his own chapter of the Ku Klux Klan,[23] favored racial segregation in office, voted against the rights of gays to enter the military under the Clinton administration,[24] and (though labeling himself as pro-choice) voted for the Partial Birth Abortion Ban Act in 2003. At this same time, Clarence Thomas was confirmed as a Supreme Court justice after a long history of conservative works and graduating from The College of the Holy Cross at Yale Law School. Robertson's statement is, of course, made barely one year before President George H. W. Bush vetoed S. 323, the "Family Planning Amendments Act of 1992," his justification being: "I have repeatedly informed the Congress that I would disapprove any legislation that would transform this program into a vehicle for the promotion of abortion."[25] As well, in 1987, Bush was quoted at an outdoor news conference in Chicago, Illinois, in response to a question from Robert I. Sherman, "No, I don't know that atheists should be considered as citizens, nor should they be considered as patriots. This is one nation under God."[26] Clearly, this was a nation run by the Christian enemy.

What Robertson was doing here was successfully using the weapon of fear to drive the Christian masses into further action (usually by throwing money at "the problem"), and it worked beautifully. His book *The New World Order* rose to the *New York Times* best-seller list that year. Robertson didn't need real-world enemies to incite faith, he simply needed the idea and the opposition came. Fear is a well-used tactic both by Robertson and his contemporaries. Robertson stood alongside Jerry Falwell as Falwell said, mere hours after the September 11 attacks, "The ACLU has to take a lot of blame for this," in addition to "the pagans, and the abortionists, and the feminists, and the gays, and the lesbians [who have] helped [the terror attacks of September 11] happen."[27] He also claimed that the September 11 attacks and Hurricane Katrina "were . . . connected in some way,"[28] a sentiment that presidential-candidate Michelle Bachmann would repeat ten years later in reference to Hurricane Irene[29]—not surprising, given that consistency is the sole virtue of the ineffectual.[30] Other chestnuts include claims that America harbors a country full of heathens and that these national tragedies were god's punishments for our gross society. If this were the case (as only an insane person could believe), it would only further the point of god being a zealous, petty child, and clearly not remaining within the confines of the Old Testament, as some "moderate" Christians implore one to consider. As if declaring that god "matured" over the last 4,000 years from the megalomaniac he was in the days of Moses into something more refined and cultured today is any defense. Still, being so almighty, he would clearly use his newfound morality and inestimable power to perhaps stop the Zionist feuding in the Middle East and end the homosexual discrimination movement and prevent the fear of Rapture being forced into our children like cafeteria food, no?

Clearly not. Discrimination continues in every monotheistic society in the name of god and god does nothing, which on a logical train of thought would imply: (A) god is in favor of a world of turmoil and pain in his name; (B) god ignores it for whatever reason, which is altogether as evil; or (C) god does not exist and the pains of the masses are as manmade as they ever were. Naturally, I am inclined toward the latter but with either of the former answers one can see my point. Not to border on cliché, but this example leads to an excellent and well-known adage by Epicurus (who was one of the figureheads for the scientific method) a few hundred years before the birth of Christ:

> *Is God willing to prevent evil, but not able? Then He is not omnipotent.*
> *Is He able, but not willing? Then He is malevolent. Is He both able and*
> *willing? Then whence cometh evil? Is He neither able nor willing? Then*
> *why call Him God?*

Needless to say, it is with rash and unfriendly reaction that the god-loving community takes to Epicurus; and in Dante's *Divine Comedy: The Inferno* one can find Epicurus and his followers in the Sixth Circle, known as the Circle of Heretics, trapped and tortured in flaming tombs, mostly for his insinuation that the soul goes no where after death, but dies with the body as mortal as the flesh surrounding it. As Canto X (1–18) reads,

> *Now onward goes, along a narrow path*
> *Between the torments and the city wall,*
> *My Master, and I follow at his back.*
> *"O power supreme, that through these impious circles*
> *Turnest me," I began, "as pleases thee,*
> *Speak to me, and my longings satisfy;*

The people who are lying in these tombs,
Might they be seen? already are uplifted
The covers all, and no one keepeth guard."
And he to me: "They all will be closed up
When from Jehoshaphat they shall return
Here with the bodies they have left above.
Their cemetery have upon this side
With Epicurus all his followers,
Who with the body mortal make the soul;
But in the question thou dost put to me,
Within here shalt thou soon be satisfied,
And likewise in the wish thou keepest silent."

This is not to imply that *The Inferno* (no matter how much better it may have been written than the "word of god") is to be taken as a holy text and truth, but once again we have a jealous tyrant painted for a deified leader: "Obey me unquestioningly or suffer." And even when posed the merest academic question, the softest inquiry as to whether or not the existence of god is possible in the face of so much evil, we see Epicurus cast to torment for all eternity. Heresy, clearly, is not something to be tampered with, and my only sincere regret at being an atheist comes in the form of two unfortunate events: (1) at the occurrence of my death there will be no afterlife in which to perform the proverbial "I told you so" dance, and (2) I will not be in the Circle of Heretics to clasp Epicurus by the hand and thank him for his candor.

The idea of "heresy," meanwhile, further perpetuates the hypocrisy of the monotheistic society. According to one online dictionary, "heresy" follows thus:

her – e – sy

1. opinion or doctrine at variance with the orthodox or
accepted doctrine, especially of a church or religious system.

2. the maintaining of such an opinion or doctrine.

We can see here an excellent problem, one that is clear and massive and utterly unfixable—the idea of "accepted doctrine." The brilliance of it comes from the idea of organized religion in the first place: how could a true and unwavering answer to the origins of the cosmos and the divination of a being and the interpretations of his/her/its/their word *ever* exist without discrepancies? And not to say that the peoples of monotheism haven't tried their hardest, but from the first insinuation of the Old Testament all the way through the far more modern doctrines of the Mormon faith and in every edition of the Talmud or Koran, *haddith* or Torah, everywhere we look there are errors. And not just annoying contradictions as I pointed out earlier in the chapter, but definitive dissents from the "accepted doctrine" of the time into something newer—more *convenient.* By this definition, any church evolved under the unorthodox heading of Roman Catholicism and the branches of Christianity are heretics, if not to say that the original Church didn't make some changes from whatever novel Sanhedrin venue it comes from itself, after Paul of Tarsus cast away Mosaic Law and Judaic dietary mandate, making itself equally as heretical.

For example, according to a report done by the BBC News on November 20, 2010, Pope Benedict XVI remarked that the Church may be able to condone the use of condoms in hopes of reducing the spread of HIV infection. He said: "She [the Church] of course does not regard it as a real or moral solution, but, in this or that case, there can be nonetheless, in the intention of reducing the risk of infection, a first step in a movement toward a different way, a more human way, of living sexuality." What a wonderful, progressive thought! A beautiful shift from the old-world paradigm of antiquated doctrine—which put millions of people at risk of HIV infection for fearing that the use of condoms would put them in the shadow of god's grace—into a modern, prohuman, antidisease mind-frame. Pope Benedict, unfortunately, was not able to see it entirely that way, continuing: "If the intention is to prevent transmission of the virus, rather than prevent contraception, moral theologians would say that was of a different moral order."

So, condoms are fine so long as they're meant for one thing and not another. Ratzinger has a gift for splitting pubic hairs, it would seem. However, this is only a few months after a visit to Cameroon, where the Pope also stated that the use of condoms could endanger public health and *increase the problem* of HIV/AIDS, rather than help to contain the virus.[31] Why would he change his mind? Why would the embodiment of Christ on earth have such a specific policy on a subject one month and change his mind the next? Is the Church so fickle? Is doctrine? We know that the intended purpose of marriage is for the procreation of god's children and that "contraception" or any method that prevents procreation is forcefully forbidden by several passages of the Bible, including:

Genesis (38:8-10)—*"Then Judah said to Onan, 'Sleep with your brother's wife and fulfill your duty to her as a brother-in-law to raise up offspring for your brother.' But Onan knew that the child would not be his; so whenever he slept with his brother's wife, he spilled his semen on the ground to keep from providing offspring for his brother. What he did was wicked in the LORD's sight; so the LORD put him to death also."*

Deuteronomy (23:1)—*"No one whose testicles are crushed or whose male organ is cut off shall enter the assembly of the LORD."* (This arguably includes vasectomies, an incredibly effective form of contraception.)

Malachi (2:15)—*"And did not he make them one? Yet had he the residue of the spirit. And wherefore one? That he might seek a godly seed."*

These are but three of a handful of related passages regarding sex without procreation in the Bible. Ever and anon god points his finger at those who have intercourse and decries that having children is the sole and single purpose for the action, no matter the consequences. What, then, does that make of Benedict's benevolence? Is it spiritually incorrect? Even though the purpose is to stop the infection of HIV/AIDS, the condom equally halts the machinery of reproduction and is thereby as punishable as these passages say. Not to criticize Pope Benedict's progressive stance on the subject (if for reasons devised of a dogmatic loophole), but here we have a very clear and honest act of heresy by the leader of the papal world, the Christ Incarnate of the earth! And, naturally, many Catholics remain divided about his purposeful remarks on the use of contraception, no matter the reason—but that in itself proves the point. Conflict bred over idiocy. Conflict over nothingness. So who was accurate in the first place? Which was the original "orthodox doctrine"? And how much "heresy" exactly has been committed in change since that first rule, that first mandate?

Answering these questions sincerely falls against the walls of impossibility—one would have to trace the furthest religious influences known in the world back through literally tens of thousands of years, establish that as the first known cause or revelation, and label every other religious claim following it as heretical.[32] Clearly, this is a useless ambition, theologically speaking. But for the purposes of the Christian time line, imagine a world where the use of a condom was not even forbidden but *encouraged,* and the respective health benefits seen the world over. Envisage a planet where HIV/AIDS might never have spread to epidemic levels for millions of people because they wouldn't fear the wrath of an unjust god for using simple protection. Perhaps Benedict took a step in the right direction, and for my part, I would say he did—but the residual anger and argument that came from this step is indicative of the original evil in the first place. The Catholic Church is only one major spiritual organization in the world that forbids the use of safety in sexual practice, presumably to garner more followers under its weighty dome. It places itself and the ideals of its mythology above the health and safety of its some 1.18 billion loyal followers. [33]

This in turn gives rise to a myriad of other conditions, solutions, and decisions made by leaders of religion from Martin Luther's *95 Thesis* to the publication of the Book of Mormon (of which an edition exists printed in Klingon[34]), all of which were, by definition, *heretical.* And, of course, let's not forget the grandest heretic of all—Jesus Christ himself, who, in a time before Catholic doctrine, had but one orthodox practice to adhere to: the followings and teachings of Judaism. His antidoctrine at the time was punished by death, an application that the Church became superbly adept at in the coming centuries. Yet the future Church could not see the irony of their later endeavors: the Inquisition, the Salem witch trials, the Crusades—how many millions fell upon the sword and the noose and the rocky bottoms of a lake on charges of "heresy" against the Church, an organization built upon the teachings of a heretic? More amusingly, what did Jesus have (empirically) that any of those thousands of innocent women burned at the stake as witches did not? If one of them had stepped forward and said that they were the daughter of god, or a new incarnate of the universe, would they have gathered a following, been martyred by the Catholic Church, and started a new religion all their own? Would people, decades after the death of this woman who had never met her, pen Gospels based on "eye-witness" accounts of the "miracles" she performed before her return to heaven? Perspective in these matters is everything, and it only takes one glorious death to turn a heretic into a martyr, and a few gullible people with "divinity" on their breath to turn it into something larger. Centuries from now, if HIV/AIDS is halted because the disease was stopped in transmission by the widespread use of condoms in predominantly Catholic countries, will we ever remember that contraception was forbidden by them in the first place, or will the Vatican be heralded as the grand orchestrator of world healing by the grace of god?[35] It is difficult to say. But almost every living follower of Christ and the Yahweh of the Jews before him and the many previous incarnations of the same stories of the Mediterranean religions before those has committed "heresy" in some way, unaccountable and unknown—and all poorly defined, ecclesiastically or otherwise.

"The Gods Are Just, and of Our Pleasant Vices Make Instruments to Plague Us"

—Edgar, *King Lear* (V.III.172)

In my pallet of religious topics, I try to cover theism as a whole in its general philosophies, but naturally Judaism, Christianity, and Islam have a grand monopoly on religious influence in the world, and therefore they vacuum in much of the global attentions. It's fitting, therefore, to give some very brief references specifically to thoughts that might occur involving less known religions, including polytheisms, if only for the sake of not ostracizing further aberrations where they are evident. Also of regard is the observation that the influential differences between polytheisms and monotheisms are not overwhelming, and may be practically nonexistent, save for popularity.

On this note, one should be aware of the fact that for religions that have only one god (only one away from the true number, as the old adage goes), that single god seems to take the back seat quite often and let other, lesser idols drive the universal automobile. Quoted in Bill Maher's decently pointed documentary, *Religulous,* a priest at the Vatican describes a poll given to Italians asking of whom they prayed to when in need—and Jesus came in sixth. Which really isn't too surprising, considering the veritable Pantheon of gods to choose from in the Catholic faith: not just god himself, but also the Son and the Holy Spirit of the Trinity; Mother Mary (an overwhelmingly popular one); nine ranks (or Choirs) of angels—Angels, Arch-angels, Principalities, Powers, Virtues, Dominions, Thrones, Cherubim, and Seraphim, among which are the overindulged St. Michael and St. Gabriel; thousands of named saints with more added to the list every year, including St. Francis, St. Christopher, etc.; the writers of the Gospels; the Patriarchs; any of the Prophets—the list goes on and on.

With such an impressive gaggle of godliness, it's no wonder that the carpenter didn't seem to have the panache to take the first spot. "What do you do?" Maher asked of the rather likeable Catholic priest outside of the very entrance to St. Peter's Square. "How do you bring people to the true faith?"

"Oh, you don't!" laughed the priest, throwing up his hands. "Forget it. They just have to live and die with their stupid ideas."

In Islam it is hardly different—even a few fairy tales of their own have been added for good measure. Islam is regarded by its followers as the final revelation that god has intended for the earth, making Muhammad the concluding prophet after Jesus. And rarely is it that you hear a Muslim speak of god before they speak of the prophet, following his name with "peace be upon him." Even his flying horse, Buraq, who bore Muhammad from Mecca to Jerusalem and whose hoof-print became the place of building for the Hauz-i-Shami reservoir by the Sultan Shamshudin Iltumish in 1250 CE, holds a place of special reverence.

So let us not pretend that a grand line has been drawn between the ancient practices of polytheism and the slightly-less-ancient indulgences of monotheism, even though the respective pantheons do come to a god-head—but, we will remember, so did Olympus and Valhalla, and Hinduism with Parabrahma and all its lesser demi-gods or incarnations beneath the divine leader. But do polytheisms in the traditional sense provide the same attitude and negative toxicity to the rest of the world as we see from Judaism and Christianity and Islam? It would be terribly easy to argue the contrary—when was the last time a suicide bomber shouted "Long live Aphrodite!" before detonating an explosive in a crowded square, or senators voted in detrimental legislation under the precept provided by Quetzalcoatl? Some of my closest friends are practicing—perhaps one might even use the term "devout"— pagans, who have never shown a single shred of their ideology that inflicts harm on other peoples, or debilitates the civil rights of others. Where, then, are the evils in these interpretations?

We will discuss several—e.g., the abuse of children in "satanic cults," the demoralizing influence of pagan morality myths, the ritual self-abuse of Aztec South America, etc.—in later chapters. It seems, though, one must indeed look at the wide scheme of the polytheistic or pagan world and say that *on average* the atrocity is not as vibrant or lurid as it is with monotheism, so description of it shall be summary. Is this a matter of statistic? Are there simply not enough pagans in the world to make the idea of a religious war a reality?

It wasn't always so, and not just in ancient times. As a matter of fact, modern fascism has its roots in deeply pagan origins—blood feuds, sexism, and general racism all being a part of the tribal mandates of old-world polytheisms (see Persia and Sparta or the Visigoths). Many times, the difference between one entire religion and another, complete with its own gods, rituals, and totems, was merely the span of distance between one tribe and the next. This observation leads us down the very common logical path that different gods made in the images of different races clearly point to the fact that gods were crafted from people, and not vice versa—but that's a separate subject. Deistic fascism might have been most clearly displayed in the Jacobins, with their dark, bloody leader Robespierre, who in the 1790s turned Notre Dame Cathedral into a temple for the worship of the Supreme Being, tearing down Christian statues and erecting his own deistic idol, a "goddess of reason," in their place. Cannibalization of religions has always been common—and Robespierre might have continued his spiritual empire with the French National Religion being the Cult of the Supreme Being for as long as possible had he not been imprisoned and executed by the National Convention. As well, pagan traditions regarding the privilege of blood is decidedly of Norse origin and inspired much of the "master race" tirade of the Third Reich and other fascist and racist regimes.[36]

With a wide panoply of charlatan psychics, bogus ghost-hunting television specials, and torpid mediums communicating with dead loved ones on day-time talk shows, we may not see as grand a miasma of evil in the world presented by polytheisms and other supernatural indulgence—not nearly as much as, perhaps, a car bombing—but one must ponder the lower implications of the false hope that comes from believing that not only is there Another Side, per se, but that you have stumbled across the extraordinary luck to find in a seedy, back-alley shop with a neon palmistry sign lighting up the stucco a person who can communicate with those who have passed—for merely $20 and a personal object to hold. On the subject of the supernatural, books fly from shelves at a stupendous pace, each one providing the next hopeful reader with a connection to the past, the future, or the dead. While there is nothing of this enterprise that I would say is harmful in the way I speak of monotheism—as in, no civil rights are blatantly violated to enact or perpetuate these inanities—it would at least merit the name of shameful to lead someone to believe a tarot card deck and a couple of sequined scarves can bend the rules of reality. Be that as it may, this waste of resource and of honesty is the worst that can be said for these kinds of supernatural enthusiasts, which is why I give them only slight notice in text—the argument lies in practices that cause entropy as part of their mandate, and not by virtue of their fraudulence.

As one can see, religion is nothing more than the idea of what I like to call the Ultimately Subjective—a field that bears no more relevance in truth than what varies from person to person. In order to be religious, a number of tenets of a single faith *must* be acknowledged, but it has clearly become the practice beyond that to accept all or none of those precepts in order to decide what constitutes a godly justification for life and action. If this is true of the common practice of religion, one must realize that it saps away all validation of religion's purpose. If one is allowed to make up the rules as they go, anything is possible—which is a fantastic turn of argument to theists who believe that the *lack* of god ascribes one the barbaric freedom to act with absolute impunity toward himself and fellow man. In truth, the very inverse is the correct assumption—one can only perform *any* task when they are under the belief that they are divinely backed, and if the mandates of that divinity come à la carte, the possibilities are as endless as they are cruel, subjective, and various.

Notes

1. "Something from Nothing: A Conversation with Richard Dawkins and Lawrence Krauss," Arizona State University, February 4, 2012.

2. Falwell, *Finding Inner Peace and Strength* (Doubleday Publishing, 1982).

3. Isaiah and Ezekiel are also thought to have seen god in their lifetime, according to Scripture.

4. "The Holey Bible," http://www.greenwych.ca/bible-a.htm.

5. Noah, being "perfect in the eyes of god," had an odd example of perfection. However, we are discussing the man who enslaved his grandson because his own son had glimpsed his genitals after Noah fell asleep, drunk, in an orchard. Some strange morality here.

6. Thomas Hobbes, *Leviathan*, chapter XII.

7. Bart D. Ehrman, *Misquoting Jesus* (New York: Harper Collins, 2005), p. 65

8. A. N. Wilson, *Jesus: A Life* (W. W. Norton & Company, 2004), pp. xiv.

9. Julie Boulder, "Hate Crime Suspects' Friend Blames Victim," *Advocate*, October 16, 2009, http://www.advocate.com/News/Daily_News/2009/10/16/Hate_Crime_Suspects_Friend_Blames_Victim/.

10. The Fresh Life Church's website reads: "We believe that the scriptures of the Old and New Testaments are the Word of God, fully inspired, without error in the original manuscripts, and the infallible rule of faith and practice." See "Statement

of Faith," http://www.freshlifechurch.org/3.0/about/doctrine.php, accessed May 6, 2012.

11.   Levi Lusko, "Eternally Tattooed," http://skipheitzig.com/teachings_view.asp?ServiceID=516&q=high.

12.   Levi Lusko, "Are Tattoos Bad?" YouTube, video, February 26, 2010, https://www.youtube.com/watch?feature=player_embedded&v=vuhB-2-pop4#!.

13.   Levi Lusko, "Soldier On," YouTube, video, November 8, 2010, http://levilusko.com/archives/soldier-on-a-faith-worth-fighting-for.

14.   The Skull Church's website reads: "We are specifically targeting a lost generation that doesn't know God, isn't necessarily 'into' church, and desperately needs Jesus." See "About: The Deal," http://skullchurch.com/3.0/about/index.php, accessed June 3, 2012.

15.   The tattoo on my right forearm is a band of Tolkien's Quenya Elvish written in the Tengwar that reads in English: "A single dream is more powerful than a thousand realities." I have always appreciated the desperately meaningful entendre in this.

16.   Richard Dawkins, *The God Delusion* (Mariner Books, 2006), p. 81.

17.   Solomon, easily of the loosest sexual morals in the biblical dramatis personae, was the author of the Proverbs, including those that look down on lust and adultery.

18.   Koran (3:19)

19.   Koran (9:73)

20.   Leviticus (24:14)

21.   Pat Robertson, *The New World Order* (Word Publishing, 1991), p. 227.

22.   "The Religious Affiliations of U.S. Vice President, Dan Quayle," http://www.adherents.com/people/pq/Dan_Quayle.html, accessed June 4, 2012.

23.   Eric Pianin, "A Senator's Shame: Byrd, in His New Book, Again Confronts Early Ties to KKK," *Washington Post*, June 19, 2005.

24.   Eric Schmitt, "Senators Reject Both Job-Bias Ban and Gay Marriage," *New York Times*, September 11, 1996.

25.   *Public Papers of the Presidents of the United States: George H. W. Bush* (1992–1993, Book II), http://www.gpo.gov/fdsys/pkg/PPP-1992-book2/html/PPP-1992-book2-doc-pg1655.htm.

26. Madalyn O'Hair, "Can Geroge Bush, with Impunity, State That Atheists Should Not Be Considered Either Citizens or Patriots?" http://www.positiveatheism. org/writ/ghwbush.htm.

27. "Falwell Speaks about WTC Disaster," Christian Broadcasting Network.

28. "Religious Conservatives Claim Katrina Was God's Omen, Punishment for the United States," Media Matters, September 13, 2005.

29. Nicola Menzie, "Michele Bachmann Quote about Earthquake, Irene Being Messages from God a Joke?" *Christian Post*, August 29, 2011, http://www. christianpost.com/news/michele-bachmann-quote-about-earthquake-irene-being-messages-from-god-a-joke-54702/.

30. A reference to a favorite quote of mine made by Oliver Welles in the Canadian TV series *Slings & Arrows*.

31. "Pope Condones Condom Use in Exceptional Cases—Book," BBC News, November 20, 2010, http://www.bbc.co.uk/news/world-europe-11804398.

32. Robert Roy Britt, "Scientists Find First Known Human Ritual: Archaeologists Discover Stone Snake Carved in a Cave in Botswana," MSNBC.com, November 30, 2006, http://www.msnbc.msn.com/id/15970442/ns/technology_and_science-science/t/scientists-find-first-known-human-ritual/#.UIBbtsXA-ks.

33. Francis X. Rocca, "Vatican: Number of Catholics Is Up, Still behind Muslims," USA Today, February 22, 2011, http://www.usatoday.com/news/religion/2011-02-23-catholic_vatican_22_ST_N.htm.

34. "The Klingon Book of Mormon," http://stfhe.jlcarroll.net/Klingon_BoM/, accessed July 1, 2012.

35. The waffling and disappointment of Pope Francis is in some ways an example of this. His first two years in office have been applauded wildly by believers and atheists alike, with his marginal acceptance of homosexuals and nonbelievers, a crack-down on corruption in the Church, etc. More recent events and statements, however, have revealed his return to conservatism on several of his primarily popular points. It is strange indeed that the world should repeatedly see the election of a new Bishop of Rome and without fail be despondent when he begins to perform his duties as though he were Catholic.

36. Jean-Michael Angebert, *The Occult and the Third Reich: The Mystical Origins of Nazism and the Search for the Holy Grail* (Macmillan, 1974).

2

Put Money in Thy Purse
and a Note on the Founding Fathers

———————◆◆———————

"So you think that money is the root of all evil?
Have you ever asked what is the root of all money?"
—Ayn Rand

"Money often costs too much."
—Ralph Waldo Emerson

The founder of Scientology, Lafayette Ronald Hubbard, was famously quoted as saying: "You don't get rich from writing science fiction. If you want to get rich, you start a religion."[1] His words could not have been more wretchedly prophetic. According to ReligionNewsBlog.com, noted fundamentalist Joel Osteen and his Houston based mega-church nets up to $43,000,000 a year from collection services; and though he does not ask for money in his broadcasts that reach another seven million viewers weekly, over $30,000,000 comes through the mail each year anyway[2]—and that is all before adding up the advance deals on his books, which are coming out at the religious rate of Stephen King novels. The ministry of his colleague, Billy Graham, reportedly earned $91,571,000 in 2010.[3] These are only two of the dozens of huge names in televangelism: the preaching of fundamentalist, evangelical, and Pentecostal values through television and radio media.

Why is it so profitable? And what do these great Christian benefactors do with these unimaginable amounts of money when they are deposited with open hearts into the collection plates? In the same year that Billy Graham's ministry garnered that $91,571,000, its reported expenses for the year tallied as follows: $74,223,000 on "Program Services," $9,598,000 on "Management and General," and $5,249,000 on fundraising for the next fiscal year; all of which left a mere $2,500,000 as "surplus," and a total of $127,945,000 in net assets from years before. Where did such a large amount of money go in outreach and community service? What happens to such an exorbitant amount of untaxed holy cash? Jesus certainly doesn't need it.

The first question is answered by the utilization of the rusty standard tool for religious leaders: fear. Time and again, these men use the name of the lord rather than the details of their needs to fuel the money-giving fires of conservative America. Too often, a televangelist will slobber: "God wants you to give until it hurts," or "The Holy Spirit wants you to use your credit card and give us $1,000—right now!" And who would be foolish enough to buy into such a scam, and let another man in a cheap suit and a bad haircut tell us the will of the almighty lord as he watches us sit on our couches *not* giving to his chosen church? Too many seem to. Humans appear to dread the possibility of retribution even if they see little justification for it. Knowing that Sally Mae down the street gave $500 to Joel Osteen and his ministry incites us to do it as well—not only because we want a piece of the heaven that these ministers have promised us over the magical picture box, but because *not* giving is against the lord, and earns us a ticket straight to hell. How do we know? The televangelist told us so.

This waste of resource isn't inherent in the cause—the idea of a very rich church could, in theory, be a massively beneficial thing to society. Visualize the food donations, charitable causes overseas, education, and benefits a church could provide when racking up almost $100,000,000 annually. Imagine the benefactions made to science to prevent and cure disease, the outreach to poverty-stricken countries, the genuine good that could be done on the face of this globe. The reality is far less immaculate. Primarily, donations go to funding leaders who insist on becoming anti-images of their own doctrine— such as Jimmy Swaggart, who led one of the leading televangelism ministries in the country at the time he was found (through the private investigations of another televangelist) to be having liaisons with a prostitute. Swaggart gave a televised, emotional apology in February 1988, begging for god's forgiveness, only to be found three years later in Southern California with another prostitute who admitted openly he had paid her for sex.[4] The apple doesn't fall far from the Tree of Knowledge, apparently—in 2011 the televangelist and founder of Glory House London, Albert Oduele, was charged with two counts of sexual assault on a 14-year-old boy and a 21-year-old man—charges that he denied until he eventually pled guilty. He is currently serving sentence at the time of this writing.[5]

Luke (16:18)—*"Whosoever putteth away his wife, and marrieth another, committeth adultery: and whosoever marrieth her that is put away from her husband committeth adultery."*

Exodus *(20:14)*—*"Thou shalt not commit adultery."*

How many of these Christian, super-funded leaders have broken their very own lauded Commandment? On February 1, 2012, wife of noted faith healer and televangelist Benny Hinn, whose TV broadcasts on the Trinity Broadcast Network (a Pentecostal broadcasting titan) and other networks are seen by millions of people around the world every day, filed for divorce in Orange County Superior Court.[6] This was shortly after allegations were made against colleague and fellow Christ-tycoon Ted Haggard, who in 2006 admitted to receiving drugs and massages from a male prostitute (though he denied that any legitimate sex had occurred).[7] Then, in September 2011, Pat Robertson officially condoned the employment of divorce if a wife is afflicted with Alzheimer's, saying: "I know it sounds cruel, but if he's going to do something, he should divorce her and start all over again, but make sure she has custodial care and somebody looking after her."[8] (Wonderfully sentimental advice considering that only months later Robertson advised husbands who have an itch to beat their wives to convert to Islam so that they could do so without shame.[9]) And how did Mr. Robertson reach this dogmatic conclusion? Did he find a lost verse of the Bible that said, "No adultery unless they're very ill—then it's okay," or did his vows before god and family at his wedding say merely, "Til debilitating mental illness do us part"? Not to sound overly cynical (nor to comment upon what hardship it must actually be to be married to a person who doesn't recognize you), but swearing "in sickness and in health" before a holy man of god sounds like an awfully weighty religious oath to me. This is without examining the sheer, heartless immorality it must take to leave the person you love and cherish because life gets tough, especially considering the age in which Alzheimer's usually sets in—does Robertson expect the elderly to hop onto some "Senior Lovin'" dating websites to, as he so brazenly put it, "start all over again"? The selfishness of the act and the pompous religious permission given by Robertson to perform it is nauseating.

The continued downfall in the perceived morality in the Christian Right has brought about the attention of more than a few, even among their own. J. Lee Grady, an ordained minister and editor of the evangelical magazine *Charisma*, published a book in April 2010 called *The Holy Spirit Is Not*

For Sale, chronicling (among other things) the continuing immorality of televangelists and other Christian leaders, and their fall from the power of their pulpits. Though his work is filled with the obscenely gilded rhetoric indicative of Christian writers, Grady makes some sharp, excellent points.

> *We have turned the holy fire of God into a circus sideshow—and naive Christians are buying this without realizing that such shenanigans are actually blasphemous.*
>
> *Greed has actually morphed into a virtue in some charismatic circles, where pastors take hour-long offerings and guest speakers require limousines and five-figure honorariums to maintain their celebrity lifestyles.*[10]

Of course, we all know that Jesus himself said (according to the Bible), *"Again I tell you, it is easier for a camel to go through the eye of a needle than for a rich man to enter the kingdom of God"* (Mark 19:24). In fact, we know that Jesus of Nazareth scorned worldly greed through several passages in his own words, including:

Mark (12: 41–44)—*"Jesus sat down opposite the place where the offerings were put and watched the crowd putting their money into the temple treasury. Many rich people threw in large amounts. But a poor widow came and put in two very small copper coins, worth only a few cents. Calling his disciples to him, Jesus said, 'Truly I tell you, this poor widow has put more into the treasury than all the others. They all gave out of their wealth; but she, out of her poverty, put in everything—all she had to live on.'"*

From where does this Christian greed stem? Clearly it was not in the teachings of the Abrahamic god nor his son.[11] Jesus preached from a rock wearing coarse wool—and reputedly changed the world. What right do modern priests have to carry golden and bejeweled crosiers and wear silken robes, swinging censers of solid gold and living in manors, preaching in churches whose estimated worth is in that of the hundreds of millions of dollars? What possible good do they think they can accomplish with billions more in resources than the man after whose behavior they claim to model themselves? In the fourth century, St. John Chrysostom wrote: "No one is ashamed, no one hides his face because he thinks that this [the Cross] is a symbol of an accursed death. Rather, we would prefer to adorn ourselves with the Cross than with crowns, or diadems, or necklaces of countless pearls."

Such humility should be the goal of all holy people—especially since their faith demands it. "Jesus was perfect," some would argue. "Jesus was the son of god." To which I reply: if one needs divinity to practice basic charity (i.e., to give the hundreds of millions to the homeless instead of building yourself big, shiny buildings), then there was no hope for the human race to begin with, with or without the need for a creator. In other words, to paraphrase a meme I found online recently: "If you can't be good without a god, that doesn't mean you need one. It means you're a shitty human being."

One can't help but think of the desiccated, rapacious bat Agnes Gonxha Bojaxhiu, better known by her erroneous moniker of Mother Teresa. Most aptly described as a "fat, Albanian dwarf" by Christopher Hitchens, the woman herself was a monolith of lost integrity. Above and beyond using a grand scope of the wealth she accrued to set up churches in her own name, the few charitable works she actually installed were ineffective—children's hospitals that she instituted were in poor condition with many shared beds among the virally contagious (she also refused to use proper medical care for most of them, instead preferring to let providence work its magical healing—the end result being too much death from otherwise very simple conditions), and she spent much of her public voice painting Calcutta to be a cesspool of poverty and disease, when, according to some of its own citizens, it also contains a garden of culture and a thriving spirit. Assuming for a moment that these were truthfully the vast enemies that the denizens of Calcutta faced, we remember that Agnes's grand proponents for its liberation were not for welfare and rehabilitation, but for a religious operation against birth control and other contraception.

In 1981 she was presented with a prestigious honor by the psychotic dictator of Haiti, Jean-Claude Duvalier, along with a good sum of money stolen from the Haitian poor. Her relationship with the crime family was long and even supported by the Vatican, despite the fact that it is estimated the Duvalier dictatorship is responsible for the embezzlement of between $300 million and $800 million from the people.[12] This is very much in tandem with her villainy alongside Charles Keating, the man who, after his arrest for the theft of $252 million from his famous savings-and-loan fraud, called on Mother Teresa as a character witness, trading her $1.25 million of the deceitful funds and a private jet for her blessing. When she was asked to return the money to the rightful owners that had been duped by Keating, she refused to respond, and not a penny of it escaped her withered clutches.[13] Yet, somehow, she escaped punishment in the end with both a beatification and the Nobel Peace Prize.

None of this is to say that only prominent monotheists are capable (or culpable) of immoral behavior—quite the contrary. Per contra, only monotheists and especially their leaders are hypocrites for committing the acts they damn others for. It is also simply to illuminate that the leaders to whom we devote so much time and energy (and most importantly, money) are no less human than we, and that the dogmas they regurgitate are not mandates from the divine. For even without their scandals and private jets, the obviously human motivations are vastly apparent. Televangelists and the Christian Right, with access to huge audiences in the public media, best-selling authors and politicians, and a grand portion of America's "faithful" preach a platform of hate on a regular basis:

"I've never seen a man in my life I wanted to marry. And I'm going to be blunt and plain: if one ever looks at me like that, I'm going to kill him and tell God he died." [14]

—Jimmy Swaggart

"Do you know that every unbeliever is filled with a demon spirit?" [15]

—Benny Hinn

"Morality as we know it cannot be maintained without Judeo-Christian religion." [16]

—Daniel P. Maloney

"We should invade their countries, kill their leaders and convert them to Christianity. We weren't punctilious about locating and punishing only Hitler and his top officers. We carpet-bombed German cities; we killed civilians. That's war. And this is war." [17]

—Ann Coulter

This is hatred. This is empirical discrimination against every walk of life not adherent to a Christian faith, which is made more absurd by their failures at emulating it. The face of this outright, unmitigated bigotry of the worst kind sells by nothing more than complete capital egomania suffused with the dollars of every American wanting to buy a piece of heaven through it. What does it ultimately do? Of course, we know that supporting these types of messages doesn't get one involved with the lord any more than purchasing an indulgence did in the 1500s (another time-honored piece of the Church profiting off the desperation of those who believe in it). Therefore, what does it breed? What do those *billions upon billions of dollars* create? The answer is simple: more hatred. Funding these ministries and buying these CDs and books and watching these television programs only serve to perpetuate them and the message they invoke: "We are the only way to god, and if you miss out on us, you miss out on heaven. Don't be one of those who do—they're damned. But with a credit card, you can avoid that." (Although I am sure that if an atheist or homosexual or a professed pagan sent them a check for any amount of money, they would happily cash it in.) Perhaps, however, these greed-mongers are more aligned with their faith than I give them credit for. After all:

> Proverbs (14:20)—*"The poor are disliked even by their neighbors, but the rich have many friends."*

> Proverbs *(17:8)*—*"A bribe is a charm to the one who gives it; wherever he turns, he succeeds."*[18]

> Ecclesiastes (10:19)—*"A feast is made for laughter and wine makes life merry, but money is the answer for everything."*

In 2012, the *Huffington Post* reported a scene in which an assembly took place in a public high school at Dunkerton, Iowa. A music band and moral activist group known as Junkyard Prophet (part of a team christened ominously on their website as "You Can Run But You Can't Hide") was scheduled to appear in the morning and give a motivational speech to students regarding the subject of bullying and drug and alcohol use. The speech turned into an inexplicable rant bashing the gay-equality statements of Elton John and Lady Gaga, and further spiraled out of control when the lead speaker said:

> *You can be judged and you do have control over it . . . Did you know the average age of death of a homosexual is about 42-years-old? Yeah, his actions actually kill him.*[19]

Naturally, this speaker failed to cite a source for his demeaning figures, or supply evidence that the "actions of a homosexual" are what led to the hypothetical homosexual's death. We don't need to Google it to discover that he is talking out of his hat. And while the superintendent of the school district involved said that the group had spoken before to great feedback, and that

Junkyard Prophet must have changed its message since its last performance, the question remains: why is a fundamentalist Christian groupperforming in a *public* school in the first place? This is an especially salient question given the group's mission statement: *"To reshape America by re-directing the current and future generations both morally and spiritually through education, media, and the Judeo-Christian values found in our U.S. Constitution."*[20]

Incidentally (and I confess myself to be driven slightly tangential, here), the idea that this country was founded on Judeo-Christian principles is a deplorable myth. Many of the Founding Fathers and the signers of the Declaration of Independence were no more Christian than I am. Thomas Jefferson himself in 1820 "wrote" his own version of the Bible, called *The Life and Morals of Jesus of Nazareth,* in which he used a razor to slice out any piece of the New Testament containing supernatural elements, including references to the divinity of Jesus and his resurrection, miracles, angels, prophecies, and the Trinity.[21] The purpose of this was to illustrate the humanity of a loving philosopher without a distracting fear of the jealous god hovering over him, or the necessity of a Middle Eastern magic show needed to convert those who couldn't tell the difference between right and wrong without a miracle or two. Jefferson wrote the Declaration in a deist philosophy, believing that there was a supernatural force that originated all things in the universe, but not in the ideal of an interfering deity as is inherent in Christian ideology. One could look at a comparatively pantheist god as similar to the Force in *Star Wars* (though, admittedly, without the addition of lightsabers, any temptation into the belief of pantheism is lost on me). Indeed, many of the dogmas and fictitious twaddle that compels Christians to think the way that they do was anathema to Jefferson, and he made it clear in several of his writings.

> *"Question with boldness even the existence of a god; because if there be one he must approve of the homage of reason more than that of blindfolded fear."*
> **—Thomas Jefferson, letter to Peter Carr, August 10, 1787**

> *"They [the clergy] believe that any portion of power confided to me, will be exerted in opposition to their schemes. And they believe rightly; for I have sworn upon the altar of god, eternal hostility against every form of tyranny over the mind of man. But this is all they have to fear from me: and enough, too, in their opinion."*
> **—Thomas Jefferson, letter to Dr. Benjamin Rush, September 23, 1800**

"History, I believe, furnishes no example of a priest-ridden people maintaining a free civil government. This marks the lowest grade of ignorance of which their civil as well as religious leaders will always avail themselves for their own purposes."
—**Thomas Jefferson, letter to Alexander von Humboldt, December 6, 1813**

"Christianity neither is, nor ever was a part of the common law."
—**Thomas Jefferson, letter to Dr. Thomas Cooper, February 10, 1814**

Not surprisingly, it would seem that Junkyard Prophet didn't bother to read (anything) before writing its mission statement with respect to the men who began our country, supposedly in the name of Christianity. But this was merely Jefferson, and he was quite young during the Continental Congress of 1776—perhaps the older, wiser men and their successors favored a more messianic bent?

"Lighthouses are more helpful than churches."
—**Benjamin Franklin, in *Poor Richard's Almanac***

"What influence, in fact, have ecclesiastical establishments had on society? In some instances they have been seen to erect a spiritual tyranny on the ruins of the civil authority; on many instances they have been seen upholding the thrones of political tyranny; in no instance have they been the guardians of the liberties of the people. Rulers who wish to subvert the public liberty may have found an established clergy convenient auxiliaries. A just government, instituted to secure and perpetuate it, needs them not."
—**James Madison "A Memorial and Remonstrance," 1785**

"I almost shudder at the thought of alluding to the most fatal example of the abuses of grief which the history of mankind has preserved—the Cross. Consider what calamities that engine of grief has produced!"
—**John Adams, letter to Thomas Jefferson**

"Religious controversies are always productive of more acrimony and irreconcilable hatreds than those which spring from any other cause. Of all the animosities which have existed among mankind, those which are

caused by the difference of sentiments in religion appear to be the most inveterate and distressing, and ought most to be depreciated. I was in hopes that the enlightened and liberal policy, which has marked the present age, would at least have reconciled Christians of every denomination so far that we should never again see the religious disputes carried to such a pitch as to endanger the peace of society."

—George Washington, letter to Edward Newenham

"So what about the Declaration of Independence?" Junkyard Prophets might cry. "What about the Pledge of Allegiance and 'In God We Trust' on our money? Where are your witty, book-learned answers for those pieces of holy awesomeness?" To which I must click my tongue and dolefully remind them that the first inclusion of a precursor to the phrase 'In God We Trust' was made on select coins during the Civil War as an idealistic notion to promote the existence of god on the side of the Union—incidentally, another horribly bloody conflict with the name of god smeared all over the face of the victor. (Ironically, this was an action President Lincoln purportedly objected to, saying: "Sir, my concern is not whether God is on our side; my greatest concern is to be on God's side.") The phrase wasn't introduced properly to all money until the Cold War, as an affront to the "godless" communists with whom we were at odds.[22] None of these motions were made by the Founding Fathers nor existed in the Constitution and certainly were not bred of devotion to Christianity, but instead were made as moves of desperation to fortify the idea that heaven stood with us against heathen enemies. The name of god was used only in the name of conflict—I'm sensing a pattern.

As for the Pledge of Allegiance, it was roughly influenced in the same way. President Eisenhower being a Presbyterian was amiable to the inclusion of mention of god for the spiritual unity of the nation and the further disassociation from Communism during the McCarthy era.[23] Even if the motives for the inclusion were based on an actually national love of god, the pledge itself was not written until 1892 nor officially adopted by Congress until 1942, with the addition of "under God" coming in 1954, a great deal of time after the death of the Founding Fathers and in no way included with the original plan for the spiritual inclination of this country.

Finally, the Declaration of Independence holds no allusion to the Christian god of Abraham and Moses. It refers to a spiritual likeness of a creator that originates freedom, and not a literal deity. Jefferson, as a deist, was inspired from those universally connected views and thence came the idea of "Nature's

God" mentioned in the Declaration, not Yahweh or any other incarnation of him. And even if one were to try to argue that point, the Declaration of Independence is not a legal document, nor does it bear any impact on the laws of this nation. Ergo, it cannot be cited as proof of a Christian rationale behind our country's founding, and by extension, as justification for inserting Christian dogmas in our credos. Christians are beyond stretching the truth at that point—they're submitting a puerile fabrication of it.

As a final thought, I would like to point out one last document known as the Treaty of Tripoli, a U.S. foreign affairs document written after the Declaration of Independence and the resolution of the Revolutionary War. Signed by President John Adams and ratified *unanimously* by the Senate in 1797,[24] it states quite clearly in Article 11:

> **As the Government of the United States of America is not, in any sense, founded on the Christian religion;** *as it has in itself no character of enmity against the laws, religion, or tranquillity, of Musselmen; and as the said States never have entered into any war or act of hostility against any Mehomitan nation, it is declared by the parties that no pretext arising from religious opinions shall ever produce an interruption of the harmony existing between the two countries* [bolded text mine].

How happy this governmental stance is in comparison to those of the bastard fathers of preceding establishments. What consolation we should take from a political institution that gives us the First Amendment and the Establishment Clause instead of the Church Building Acts of 1818 and 1824, which used bizarre amounts of government money to erect the Commissioners' Churches all over the United Kingdom (we should certainly expect no less from a country that facilitates incongruous amounts of its taxpayers' money per year to fatten its royal family). How noble in reason, then, was Thomas Jefferson in penning the Virginia Statute of Religious Freedom with its scathing and perfect observations:

> *That the impious presumption of legislators and rulers, civil as well as ecclesiastical, who, being themselves but fallible and uninspired men have assumed dominion over the faith of others, setting up their own opinions and modes of thinking as the only true and infallible, and as such endeavouring to impose them on others, hath established and maintained false religions over the greatest part of the world and through all time; . . . That our civil*

rights have no dependence on our religious opinions any more than our opinions in physics or geometry . . . That it is time enough for the rightful purposes of civil government, for its officers to interfere when principles break out into overt acts against peace and good order; . . . Be it enacted by General Assembly that no man shall be compelled to frequent or support any religious worship, place, or ministry whatsoever, nor shall be enforced, restrained, molested, or burthened in his body or goods, nor shall otherwise suffer on account of his religious opinions or belief.

And so, Junkyard Prophet and other illiterates of American history, I would like to leave these historic facts to your consideration on the impact of Christianity in the devising of the United States of America by its Founding Fathers. While I don't expect the information I have provided here to be the "be all and the end all" of the debate, I hope that it will illuminate your understandings to empirical pieces of history that highly descant upon your hypothesis. Furthermore, I wonder how someone who has so woefully misinterpreted the sentiments listed above by Thomas Jefferson et al. could ever manage to lead a speaking team to lecture on the Founding Fathers' thoughts in the first place. This argument is a long and sadly unending one, and others have displayed the evidence in much better structure and taste than I am able. Suffice it to say, the evidence of this section (as hopefully the rest of this book) in Newton's words "stands upon the shoulders of giants."[25]

"Time Shall Unfold What Plighted Cunning Hides: Who Cover Faults, at Last Shame Them Derides" —Cordelia, *King Lear* (I.I.302–303)

Hypocrisy, greed, and bias are the unfortunate conditions of men. We are vessels for incompetence, fear, mistakes, and confusion. We have been, for our sylvan and civilized history, subject to the evolution of our brains and physical capabilities, but error and mistake have always been constant. Humans are not perfect—nor is evolution. If we were, we wouldn't need the idea of a god, we would be living gods ourselves. Be that as it may, with conscience and with power come quandary, and when people abuse our faculties in the name of god, conflict arises inevitably and drastically. The purpose of these first two chapters has never been to point the finger of blame at monotheists and say: "Liars! Scoundrels! The troubles of the world are because of *you!*"

That would be foolish and impossible—and incorrect. However, there are remediable pieces of the world, great conflicts, hardships, dramas, and pains that are directly caused by religious and dogmatic quarrel, of turmoil over lost doctrines and dead gods. Knowing the fault of the people who follow them is integral to an understanding of the application of greater good. Realizing that religious organizations play a central role in the trials of homosexuals, supposed infidels, atheists, antizealots, women, and peoples of different faiths all around the world is the first step in understanding the evils of the people who seek to glorify it.

While the preachers of the globe condone war in the name of god, while great political leaders fear the fairy tale of an Invisible Sky Wizard, while billions of dollars are wasted in an effort to define the divine and demerit those not within the accepted standards based on 2,000-year-old fallacies, while children starve and disease runs rampant because those with the power to stop it instead cling to ill-earned wealth and meaningless covenants, the world will be a worse place for it—a dying place with no hope of redemption. A place where nineteen men will take their lives and the lives of nearly 3,000 Americans because they believe they will be eternally rewarded for it; or a place where we will get tied up in a war for more than a decade on the supposition proclaimed by our president it is our duty to mount a crusade,[26] where at the time of this writing almost 4,500 Americans have perished.[27] The time has come to view the monotheistic world as it is: a thing that seeks only to profit off your soul, and spurn the thinking world under its foot as it does so. And how can we follow it if it doesn't follow itself? What answers can it hope to provide on a sinking foundation, a culture at war with itself and between its own sects? The world is a kind of democracy where the majority rules; a few billion wrong people have the power to influence all, no matter the instability of their justifications.

Notes

1. Response to a question from the audience during a meeting of the Eastern Science Fiction Association, as quoted in a 1994 affidavit by Sam Moskowitz, November 7, 1948.

2. Mark I. Pinsky, "Televangelist Joel Osteen Shuns Lavish Lifestyle," Religion News Blog, November 29, 2007, http://www.religionnewsblog.com/20007/joel-osteen-5.

3.   See http://www.ministrywatch.com/profile/billy-graham.aspx, retrieved June 20, 2012.

4.   "Swaggart Plans to Step Down," *New York Times*, October 15, 1991.

5.   "Evangelical Pastor Odulele Sentenced for Sex Offences," Channel 4 News, March 31, 2011.

6.   Gillian Flaccus, "Benny Hinn Divorce: Wife Suzanne Hinn Files For Divorce from Televangelist," *Huffington Post*, February 18, 2010, http://www.huffingtonpost.com/2010/02/18/benny-hinn-divorce-wife-s_n_468296.html.

7.   Dan Harris, "Haggard Admits Buying Meth," ABC News, November 3, 2006, http://abcnews.go.com/GMA/story?id=2626067&page=1.

8.   Hannah Roberts, "Televangelist Pat Robertson Gives Blessing to Divorce . . . If Your Wife Has Alzheimer's," *Mail Online News*, September 15, 2011, http://www.dailymail.co.uk/news/article-2037606/Its-kind-death-Televangelist-Pat-Robertson-gives-blessing-divorce--wife-Alzheimers.html.

9.   Stephen C. Webster, "Pat Robertson to Humiliated Hubby: 'Well, You Could Become a Muslim and You Could Beat Her,'" Raw Story, September 10, 2012, http://www.rawstory.com/rs/2012/09/10/pat-robertson-to-humiliated-hubby-well-you-could-become-a-muslim-and-you-could-beat-her/

10.   J. Lee. Grady, *The Holy Spirit Is Not For Sale* (Chosen Publishing, 2010).

11.   This is a generalized understanding of the moderate version of god, as there are in fact a handful of biblical passages that indicate monetary greed is a virtue.

12.   Jon Swaine, "Haiti's Former Dictator Jean-Claude 'Baby Doc' Duvalier Charged with Corruption in Haiti," *Telegraph*, January 19 2011.

13.   Christopher Hitchens, *The Missionary Position: Mother Teresa in Theory and in Practice* (Twelve Books, April 2012).

14.   See "Evangelist Swaggart Apologizes for Remark," Associated Press, September 22, 2004.

15.   G. Richard Fisher and M. Kurt Goedelman, *The Confusing World of Benny Hinn* (Personal Freedom Outreach, 1995).

16.   "Scary Quotations," positiveatheism.org, retrieved June 2012.

17.   Ann Coulter, "This Is War: We Should Invade Their Countries," *National Review Online*, September 13, 2011, available at http://townhall.com/columnists/anncoulter/2001/09/14/this_is_war/page/full.

18. God himself isn't actually above bribery: in the book of Haggai he is constantly insinuating that the drought from which the people are desperately suffering might come to an end if the temple is rebuilt.

19. Laura Hibbard, "'Junkyard Prophet' Shocks Iowa School With Anti-Gay Messages at Assembly," *Huffington Post*, March 12, 2012, http://www.huffingtonpost. com/2012/03/12/junkyard-prophet-anti-gay-iowa-high-school_n_1340228.html.

20. See http://youcanruninternational.com/aboutus.html, retrieved August 3, 2012.

21. See "How Thomas Jefferson Created His Own Bible . . . after Taking a Razor Blade to Parts of the Gospels He Did Not Agree With," *Mail Online News*, January 17, 2012.

22. B. A. Robinson, *The U.S. National Mottos: Their History and Constitutionality,* ReligiousTolerance.org. August 13, 2000, http://www.religioustolerance.org/nat_ mott.htm

23. "God in America: God in the White House," PBS, October 11, 2010,http:// www.pbs.org/godinamerica/god-in-the-white-house/

24. *Journal of the Executive Proceedings of the Senate of the United States of America, 1789–1805,* Wednesday, June 7, 1797, U.S. Library of Congress.

25. Isaac Newton, in his letter to Robert Hooke, 1676.

26. Peter Ford, "Europe Cringes at Bush's 'Crusade' against Terrorists," *Christian Science Monitor*, September 19, 2001, http://www.csmonitor.com/2001/0919/ p12s2-woeu.html.

27. Margaret Griffies, "Casualties in Iraq," AntiWar.com http://antiwar.com/ casualties/, retrieved May 14, 2012.

3

My Brother's Keeper

———————◆◆◆———————

*"If a Christian should wrong a Jew, what should his sufferance be?
—by Christian example! Why, revenge."*
—William Shake-speare, *The Merchant of Venice*

*"A curse on him who is lax in doing the Lord's work!
A curse on him who keeps his sword from bloodshed!"*
—Jeremiah 48:10

Our present world is rampant with conflict and strife—and has been for as long as we have had recorded history. Even among our own peoples, sects, and cultures, fighting almost seems to be within the blood of man, making the idea of the milk of human kindness nearly ridiculous. In his book, *War on the Mind,* Peter Watson muses that "deviant behavior by members of our own group is perceived as more disturbing and produces stronger retaliation than that of others with whom we are less involved." Commenting further on this point in his masterful work, *On Killing,* former Army Ranger, paratrooper, and professor of psychology at West Point (and Christian) Lt. Col. Dave Grossman elaborates, "We need only look at the intensity of the aggression between different Christian factions in Europe across the centuries, or the infighting between the major Islamic sects of the Middle East . . . to confirm this fact."[1] It is for all this god-bathed violence that I am more than slightly wary when anyone shows up on my door exclaiming: "I have a message from God for you."[2] Continuing on the theme of religiously incited or religiously involved conflict, it should give some context to say that in my short time on this earth I have been alive to witness (albeit from afar) the Algerian Civil War, started in 1992 by the Islamic Salvation Army; the north Lebanon Conflict in 2007 where the Lebanese Army (supplied with weapons and ammunition from the

United States) began a siege against the militia group Fatah al-Islam (Conquest of Islam); the Northern Ireland Conflict, which took grand notice in 1969 and is under cease-fire today, where the Irish Catholic minority seeks to secede from the northern part of the island, causing an underground conflict with Protestant guerilla groups and over 2,500 deaths since its beginning; the Philippines Conflicts, also beginning in 1969 and continuing today, where Muslim rebels seek independence from Christian government; the Sudanese Civil War (1983–2005), a conflict between an Arab Muslim government and a black Christian population; the Hindu-Muslim conflict in India continuing since the release of the country by Britain in 1947, highlighted with the mob violence in 2002 that claimed between 800 and 1,000 lives; the Sulawesi Sectarian Violence (1998–present) between Christians and Muslims on the island of Sulawesi, fortified with thousands of fundamentalist Muslim militia known as Laksar Jihad; the Shiite Muslim Rebellion in Iraq that began in 1991 and whose aftermath is still occurring, where Iraqi Shiites rebelled against the government using guerilla warfare in the south; the Egyptian Muslim Rebellion (1992–2000), where fundamentalist Muslims sought to overthrow the Egyptian government, with over 1,200 deaths over the course of the rebellion; the current Syrian Civil War; and let us, of course, not forget to mention the religiously incited attacks on the World Trade Center in 2001 by Islamist militant group Al-Qaeda and the subsequent War on Terrorism, beginning in October 2001 and still continuing at the time of this writing—and surely there are conflicts merely from my birth in 1989 through now that were religiously motivated and endorsed and are not listed here, not to mention how many more before then? And while semantic debate exists as to whether or not the September 11 attacks and the following war were *actually* religiously motivated, I prefer to lean into the well-deduced bent of Sam Harris, who said in his book *The End of Faith*:

> *The answer to this question is obvious—if only because it has been patiently articulated ad nauseum by bin Laden himself. The answer is that men like bin Laden actually believe what they say they believe. They believe in the literal truth of the Koran. Why did nineteen well-educated middle-class men trade their lives in this world for the privilege of killing thousands of our neighbors? Because they believed that they would go straight to paradise for doing so. It is rare to find the behavior of humans so fully and satisfactorily explained. Why have we been so reluctant to accept this explanation?*"[3]

And what is the "literal truth" of the Koran that could have inspired these men to perform these atrocities? Stated plainly in the religious text and also quoted by Harris are the following verses:

Koran (4:95–101)—*"The believers who stay at home—apart from those that suffer from a grave impediment—are not the equal of those who fight for the cause of God with their goods and their persons. God has given those that fight with their goods and their persons a higher rank than those who stay at home. God has promised all a good reward; but far richer is the recompense of those who fight for Him . . . He that leaves his dwelling to fight for God and His apostle and is then overtaken by death, shall be rewarded by God . . . The unbelievers are your inveterate enemies."*

Koran (9:73)—*"Prophet, make war on the unbelievers and the hypocrites and deal rigorously with them. Hell shall be their home: an evil fate."*

Koran (9:123)—*"Believers, make war on the infidels who dwell around you. Deal firmly with them. Know that God is with the righteous."*

Ironic, isn't it—that these would be the commands, "to make war on the . . . hypocrites," from a faith whose primary alleged mandate is peace? And Harris's remarks prove to be intrinsically true even when taking into account the entire political or socioeconomic motivations for the same attack. What did Al-Qaeda seek to gain otherwise? They had no invested hope of winning a war with the United States of America. They were not psychopaths or sadists in the clinical sense. The only reward they had to reap from such a scheme was the eternal gratefulness of god (notice, I refrain from using the words *their* god, for Allah is also the god of Abraham, a prophet whose holy place is the same for Jews, Christians, and Muslims—whether the subsequent saints and prophets and myths of the three monotheisms are radically different or not, the founding god is still the same, despite the conflicting arguments over it). Their motive was to purge the world of unbelievers, and to feel the joy of instantaneously martyring themselves.

This, perhaps, is what fuels our patriotic American drive to see Islam as a religion bent on world domination, on spiritually cleansing the living world of all nonbelievers, and our patriotic argument that Christianity would never afford such barbarism. On the contrary, however, apart from the verses that I quoted in chapter one which clearly illustrate a similar demand by the

Christian god to wipe our nonbelieving neighbors away, there follows this little gem from Deuteronomy:

> Deuteronomy (13:7–11)—*"If your brother, the son of your father or your mother, or your son or daughter, or the spouse whom you embrace, or your most intimate friend, tries to secretly seduce you, saying "Let us go and serve other gods," unknown to you or your ancestors before you, gods of the peoples surrounding you, whether near you or far away, anywhere in the world, you must not consent, you must not listen to him; you must show him no pity, you must not spare him or conceal his guilt. No, you must kill him, your hand must strike the first blow in putting him to death and the hands of the rest of the people following. You must stone him to death, since he has tried to divert you from Yahweh your God."*

Try to conceive if the average American Christian had the same volition in the belief of the "literal word of god" as do these Muslims. Would they strap bombs to themselves and blow up mosques and trade centers? Would they hijack planes and use their grand military power to destroy the heathen world? The truth is, we wouldn't want to think these things of ourselves (I use the term generally) *personally*, and thereby decry those of other faiths with a mighty enough conviction (or in my opinion, delusion) to enact these events by calling them *extremists*. The sad reality, as Sam Harris also says, is that there is no such thing: a Muslim who believes the word of his god and prescribes it to the letter is merely a devout follower of his lord, no different than a true fundamentalist. Christians who executed the penalties of Deuteronomy, Leviticus, and others would be the same—not to say it's any less evil to be *extremely* deluded than *moderately* deluded, but a cynic would argue it is less hypocritical. And ultimately, the Christian world is *not* naïve to what we would label another fanatic religious act as 'extremism,' especially given the Judeo-Christian advocates' call to arms in similar actions and enterprises. One could hardly forget the peaceful and innocent cities of Jericho and Laish that god allowed the Israelites to massacre in order to make room for his chosen people.[4]

In what *should* accurately be labeled as an act of terrorism, on September 15, 1995, Larry Gene Ashbrook walked into Wedgwood Baptist Church in Fort Worth, Texas, where a youth rally was taking place, carrying two guns and a pipe bomb. He shot into the crowd, killing six (four of whom were teenagers) and wounding eight, before trying and failing to detonate the explosive device. It was later found that Ashbrook was a member of a U.S.

Christian Identity Group known as the Phineas Priesthood, widely known to be violently opposed to homosexuality, interracial intercourse and conception, abortion, and Semitism (during the time of the shooting, Baptist churches in Fort Worth were praying for the conversion of the Jews to Christianity during the High Holy Days).[5] This led to the speculation on the motivation for his attack. What seems semantically interesting, on the other hand, is that *if* this man were led to his actions by spiritual justification yet was a Christian, the surrounding Christian culture deems it necessary to label him and his cause as the sad and unfortunate whim of a schizophrenic.[6] The pastor of Wedgwood, Al Meredith, even went so far as to pity him, saying: "We must forgive. I hold no rancor in my heart for the family of Larry Ashbrook. The poor man was deranged. His mind has been twisted by heaven knows what."[7] Whether or not he sadly was is not the subject of this argument, yet if a man of another faith—whose holy text exacts the same mandate toward the extinguishing of "incorrect" doctrine as the Bible does—commits the same heinous act, we[8] would refer to it as an act of "terrorism," if not a sign and justification of religious war, no matter what the status of his mental health. Forget that he was diagnosed with, for example, dissociative identity disorder—he was a *Muslim* and therefore it was a *terrorist* attack.

Similar events with clearly indicated Christian motivation run rampant in recent American history, including the myriad of lynching, riots, and crimes executed by the Ku Klux Klan,[9] the attacks on abortion clinics and doctors by the Army of God,[10][11] and the bombings of a lesbian dance club, an abortion clinic, and Centennial Olympic Park in 1996 by Eric Robert Rudolph.[12] This is without mentioning the attempted plots abroad by Christian "extremists," such as the failed scheme in 1999 by the group Concerned Christians, who were deported from Israel after having targeted several holy places in Jerusalem, thinking their actions, like those of the Muslim hijackers on September 11, would bring them to god.[13] All of these were acts of *terrorism*.

These killings and others are intimately linked with even more recent tragedies. In 2011, Oslo was contracted in one brow of woe over the work of Anders Behring Breivik, who bombed government buildings then moved on to conduct a mass shooting at a summer camp. The Christian Right of America and religious sympathizers in the rest of the world were quick to spurn the suggestion that the attacks were made in an effort of Christian extremism, despite Breivik's 1,518-page manifesto that was emailed to thousands of people hours before the bombing and expressed support for Zionism, the eradication of multiculturalism, and a hatred of Marxism and Islam. A summary of his thoughts are found in his statement: "I believe Europe should strive for: A cultural conservative approach where monoculturalism, moral, the nuclear family, a free market, support for Israel and our Christian cousins of the east, law and order and Christendom itself must be central aspects (unlike now)."[14]

This subject has led to a tangled debate over the difference between blaming the perpetrator and blaming the religion. Ben Affleck, on an October 2014 episode of *Real Time with Bill Maher*, called Sam Harris's remarks on fanatical Islam "racist," making the now-classic mistake of conflating the criticism of a series of ideas with bigotry toward the people who advocate them—hating the believer and not the belief, in other words. This is a discussion in which I and many of my colleagues have been fiercely entrenched and can be further read in my posts on the *Patheos* blog hosted by Dan Arel. In short, it is desperately important for the reader to note that in all instances where I condemn or criticize religion, I am not in the same way condemning a group of people who follow it. This is the difference between hating Islam and hating Muslims, to be specific. In earlier and in future events described in this work, such a distinction will be necessary.[15]

The fighting in Syria begins to take more and more world notice as the bodies pile up. Between Syria's continuing state of war with Israel, the conflicting gangs of Shiite and Sunni Muslims, the revolution to end government corruption, and the rise of ISIS, death has become almost commonplace in this Middle Eastern country. In the earliest days of of the conflict, campaigners for human rights were labeled terrorists by President Bashar al-Assad,[16] such as Ghassan Mohammed Najjar, leader of the Islamic Democratic movement. Sadly enough, Najjar's hometown of Aleppo was the site of a chaotic bombing of a bakery that occurred in October 2012—a reported 20 victims (mostly children) were mangled by the explosion in the early hours of reporting. A video accompanied the report as posted by the *New York Times* that was sickening to watch, but demonstrated the fearful and inhumane consequences of religious conflict in the images of decapitated young ones, shredded corpses, pools of blood and men and women in agony calling for help through the smoke, dust, and rubble of the bakery's remains.[17] This grim haze, which darkens ever more today, reflects the cost of a government willing to do anything to maintain power and an opposition that includes those willing to do anything to create a new caliphate.

There are reams of religious justification pointing the finger at Islam for the attacks on September 11 (and all would be correct when saying that they *were* spiritually motivated, especially after the *fatwa* issued by Osama bin Laden in 1991), and one should look at the paper *The Global War on Terrorism: A Religious War?* by Laurence Andrew Dobrot to get a good idea of that side of the argument. What of the American retaliation for those same attacks? No one (myself least of all) would deny that an overwhelming element of our decision as a nation to invade Afghanistan and liberate Iraq was the memory of our families and loved ones burning in wreckages of metal and fire in New York City, at the Pentagon, and in a field in Pennsylvania at the whim of Al-Qaeda, partnered with the extremely social view of those attacks as a human evil and a need for recompense—despite the fact that such motivations were, delicately put, not honestly presented to the American people. More importantly, in my opinion, the tyranny of the Taliban and Saddam Hussein and countless other ruling parties were belligerently poisonous to the civil rights both of people in their own countries and in their foreign policies—and thus, an intervention was sorely needed on behalf of the civil rights of those people under the whim of a tyrannical psychopath in Iraq and a shadow government in Afghanistan.

But did religion play a part in the American decision to go to war? Was 9/11 a catalyst for a religious feud that had been brewing between two monotheistic nations for much, much longer? After all, George W. Bush himself said in August 2003 to the Palestinian foreign minister: "God would tell me, 'George, go and fight those terrorists in Afghanistan.' And I did, and then God would tell me, George, go and end the tyranny in Iraq . . . And I did. And now, again, I feel God's words coming to me, 'Go get the Palestinians their state and get the Israelis their security, and get peace in the Middle East.' And by God I'm gonna do it."[18] Later both the White House and Mahmoud Abbas denied that Bush had ever made this remark. (This is only two years before he appeared on ABC's *20/20* and said: "I'm also mindful that man should never try to put words in God's mouth . . . We are in no way, shape, or form should a human being, play God.") In his term of office through the years of the war he also said: "And I just—I cannot speak strongly enough about how we must collectively get after those who kill in the name of—in the name of some kind of false religion,"[19] and "It's also important for people to know we never seek to impose our culture or our form of government. We just want to live under those universal values, God-given values."[20] Let us not disregard his statement to French president Jacques Chirac in 2003 at the Coalition of the Willing: "This confrontation is willed by God, who wants to use this conflict to erase his people's enemies before a New Age begins." As a justifying metaphor for the U.S. invasions in the Middle East, he went on to reference the biblical battle in the Middle East in the Book of Revelation prophesy involving Gog and Magog, two forces of the Apocalypse.[21]

Either way, it seems that at the very least the *President* felt that the war in Iraq was religiously sanctioned (I mean, god himself *did* tell him to do it), so at some level, America's involvement in the Middle East was driven by faith and divine mandate—and probably on a much, much larger level than I have just described. More than half a decade after the war began, government leaders still touted god's name in justification of war. For example, in 2008, Sarah Palin (reading off of notes on her hand, no doubt) stood before a graduating class and stated: "Pray for our military men and women who are striving to do what is right. Also, for this country, that our leaders, our national leaders, are sending [U.S. soldiers] out on a task that is from God."[22] Lt. Gen. William Boykin, meanwhile, Donald Rumsfeld's deputy secretary of defense for intelligence and an evangelical who often spoke publicly in front of prayer groups and churches, said that America's adversary in the Middle East was not political or social, but Islam itself: "The enemy is not the terrorists . . . The enemy has come against us in a spiritual realm."[23]

In her book *Grace (Eventually)*, Anne Lamott keenly states: "You can safely assume you've created God in your own image when it turns out that God hates all the same people you do."[24] This thought gives way to the beauty of hindsight through the eras—for which holy conflict done in the name of any deity, supernatural force, or worshipers of the same ideological vein was ever spured on without personal bias? It's easy enough to say "god hates so-and-so," but when pressed to the point, how many would ever muse: "Well, *I* don't mind these people so much, but *god* hates them, so grab your torch and pitchforks!"? This reasoning may be circular, as if to ask: do people hate others because they do intrinsically and use the holy texts to validate their hate, or do people not hate others intrinsically and the holy texts inspire them to hate? To this, I answer: does it *matter*? Both answers use doctrine and dogma as catalysts for conflict that are based entirely within faith. Without religion, the conflict would not exist—or would at least relate only to lesser temporal matters—in either case. As the Nobel Prize–winning physicist Steven Weinberg said, "on a balance of moral influence religion has been awful . . . with or without religion, good people can behave well and bad people can do evil; but for good people to do evil—that takes religion."[25]

Perhaps, if one believes the holy text is merely the green light to produce this violence on our neighbors—the vindication that god is with us and therefore justifies whatever hatreds we might have harbored anyhow, it gives rise to the question: if the universe is so infinitely large and a supreme creator masterfully crafted it all, what cares he of the trifling struggles of men over a patch of soil—or *anything*, for that matter? As Russell Brand comically pointed out in his stand-up performance in 2009: "Interesting to me, the relentless gratitude to God . . . but I kinda think it's a complex idea, God; and that if there is an omnipotent, omniscient being controlling all from the infinitesimally small to the inconceivably large . . . I don't reckon he cares what happens at the MTV VMA Awards."[26] The suggestion that a seemingly infinite being could, in honesty, listen to our individual thoughts, motives, needs, and wants is beyond childish—it's selfish; and to further brand the name of that *impossibly unimaginable* creature onto *any* endeavor of humankind, no matter the scale, is an act of utmost possible ego (this includes how well you play football, Mr. Tebow). But that is nothing new for theists—keeping in mind that *man* set down the words to every holy or spiritual text ever written, it is clear that humans have attempted to divine the will of whatever almighty creators they have believed in for millennia.

So where is the line? How do these knowers of the desire of the celestial graces figure out that god hates homosexuals and that touching pig skin is an abomination and that women's faces should be covered at nearly all times? Unfortunately, if asked this question of a theist, the answer is self-serving: because [insert god here] told/sent a messenge to [insert prophet here]. "But there was no proof!" we would cry. "Where is the evidence that such a thing occurred?" That's obvious, replies the theist. The [insert holy text here] says so. Unfortunately, a theist may go one step further down the rabbit hole of inanity and seem to think a proper justification to their argument is the response: prove it *didn't* happen, or prove god *doesn't* exist. The helplessness of this argument is expounded upon in Bertrand Russell's "teapot" analogy so well that it seems silly to try to better it—and other, greater writers on this same subject have used it to a fine point. I will instead present the equally as effective and comical argument by fellow atheist Ricky Gervais, who said: "It annoys me that the burden of proof is on us . . . It should be: 'You came up with the idea. Why do you believe it?' I could tell you I've got super powers. But I can't go up to people saying 'Prove I can't fly.' They'd go: 'What do you mean "Prove you can't fly?" Prove you can!"[27]

It would seem a self-perpetuating book justifies itself through self-perpetuating dogma—and this leads to the crucial actions of the horrible conflicts listed earlier (and later) in this chapter. This line of thought is absolutely criminal, and it takes an unhealthy mind to give into it willingly. Be that as it may, using a holy text as a justification for bloodshed, bigotry, violence, and even war is an evil that in over 6,000 years of recorded human history has yet failed to be bred out. Each and every time these zealots forget that somewhere, the same holy tome necessitates love and forbids killing—the hypocritical contradictions are as extreme as the consequences.

Fairly recently, we have seen outbreaks of religious violence erupt like herpes over the state of Orissa in India, where mob riots and clashes between Hindus and Christians have taken much world focus. Hindus there have eyed Christian missionary work with suspicion and have set fire to churches and triggered riots. In one such riot, twenty lives were lost as a few hundred Hindus cheered on.[28] This was one of many conflicts between the two religious factions in Orissa, one of which led to the torching of Christian homes, leaving approximately 5,000 Christians homeless in the jungle.[29] I feel a pang in my heart for people—*any* people, theists or not—forced to run from burning houses and into homelessness. Orissa may be a primarily Hindu state run by caste where Christian interference or conversion is a huge point of conflict, but how different would events be if Islamic missionaries set up mosques and organizations in, say, Kansas—preaching the Koran and inviting converts into their doors. How would militant citizens react? Would Baptists or fundamentalists of a different breed start torching mosques?

Everything comes back to the expansionist principle of theism—your way isn't right, let me slide right in and start teaching you mine: the inevitable result being retaliation. Orissa is a most unfortunate portrait of that very phenomenon, and only a small facet of the greater example of the same feud throughout history—and one of the least bloody. Arguably, the institution of the foul paradigm might be attributed even as early as Constantine, whose dubious baptism was heralded by his incredible military prowess that spread his influence all over the Eastern Mediterranean and erected the glory of Constantinople, giving Christianity a safe haven in its early infancy that was protected fiercely by the might of his armies.[30] "Hey, if you read history, God's one of the leading causes of death—has been for thousands of years! Hindus, Muslims, Jews, Christians, all takin' turns killin' each other 'cause God told 'em it was a good idea. The sword of God, the Blood of the Lamb—vengeance is mine. Millions of dead motherfuckers!"[31] Carlin undoubtedly had a gift not only for speaking perfect truth but also for making us consider the seriousness of it once the laughter had died away.

Consider for a moment the toll of the Holocaust, in which an estimated 5,860,000 Jews were killed between January 30, 1933, when Hitler became chancellor, and May 8, 1945.[32] Anyone with the merest understanding of world history knows the atrocities that occurred in the concentration camps during this time: the starvation and gas chambers and ovens in which millions of Jews and homosexuals were crammed, a mere piece of the graphic and hellish imagery that emerged from that time. And while some vague descriptions of the man who orchestrated it all are true, namely that he was a painter and a vegetarian, rumors seem to abound that Hitler was an atheist and his lack of faith is what allowed him to have the evil tenacity to brook the obscene as he did.

As it stands, we of the atheist community cannot claim credit for Hitler. In actuality, Hitler grew up in a Catholic family, and while he leaned toward a Protestant viewpoint, he was outspoken about his Christian faith. He even believed in the farcical idea of an "Aryan" Jesus that battled the Jews.[33] One can discover that the belts of the soldiers of the Third Reich were emblazoned with the German phrase: "*Gott mit uns!*" or, "God is with us." Surprisingly, Hitler so strongly believed that his work was the will of god that he professed it to horrifying degrees in his famous work, *Mein Kampf.*

I believe that I am acting in accordance with the will of the Almighty Creator: by defending myself against the Jew, I am fighting for the work of the Lord.

The personification of the devil as the symbol of all evil assumes the living shape of the Jew.

A folkish state must therefore begin by raising marriage from the level of a continuous defilement of the race, and give it the consecration of an institution which is called upon to produce images of the Lord and not monstrosities halfway between man and ape.

Of course, the latter made no secret of his attitude toward the Jewish people, and when necessary he even took the whip to drive from the temple of the Lord this adversary of all humanity, who then as always saw in religion nothing but an instrument for his business existence. In return, Christ was nailed to the cross, while our present-day party Christians debase themselves to begging for Jewish votes at elections and later try to arrange political swindles with atheistic Jewish parties—and this against their own nation.

So much for the lack of faith of Adolf. In addition to the many notable quarrels performed perhaps exclusively in god's name, here lies one of the greatest genocidal travesties the world had known since the Old Testament and done expressly, without irony or sardonicism, in the name of the Christian god. What gave Hitler the conviction that this was his creator's will? What drove him in the name of "truth"? Pathetically, nothing more than drove Ashbrook or Concerned Christians or Al-Qaeda—a horrific idea, and promise of a divine reward for a job well done. We know Hitler's hatred of Jews came from a myriad of motivations, economical and political, but given his religious tenacity it could be believed that their supposed role in the killing of Christ may have had something to do with it as well. (Pope Benedict XVI finally exonerated the Jews for this act in his book, *Jesus of Nazareth: Part II*, forgiving them for the laughable crime of 'deicide,'[34] though that human gesture was quickly overshadowed by his acceptance of the hugely anti-Semitic gaggle known as the Society of Pope Pius X back into Catholic circles.) We might find biblical motivations for the Nazi treatment of homosexuals as well.

Just behind Hitler in the genocide death count is Leopold II of Belgium, who occupied the Congo and attempted to set up colonies there, erecting widespread Catholic missions where natives were eventually trained in military action after being kidnapped—only if they had also escaped torture, flogging, and rape. In his time ruling the Congo between 1885 and 1912, the exact number of natives killed under his command (primarily by severing of the hands and genitals) is unknown, but is estimated somewhere between three and thirty million.[35]

Of course, blatant racism has hardly been weeded out with the advent of newer monotheistic religions. The Mormon faith, for example, is convinced that those people with darker skin pigmentation are suffering from a curse laid upon them by god—if only so their former fairness would not tempt his good and loving people. This became the basis for the refusal to properly acknowledge members of the faith who were of African descent until around 1978. (A pathetic thing considering that we are *all* of African descent.) The Book of Mormon chronicles this division of the saintly Nephites and the wicked, charcoal-toned Lamanites:

Nephi 5:25—*"And he had caused the a cursing to come upon them, yea, even a sore cursing, because of their iniquity. For behold, they had hardened their hearts against him, that they had become like unto a flint; wherefore, as they were white, and exceedingly fair and delightsome, that they might not be enticing unto my people the Lord God did cause a skin of blackness to come upon them."*

There Is Some Soul of Goodness in Things Evil, Would Men Observingly Distil It Out —Henry, *Henry V* (IV.I.6–7)

We all know that violence needs not the wide world as a stage in order to be seen, nor for the deaths it causes to number in the hundreds or thousands for it to provide an impact. Disagreement breeds and delights itself in the small venues as well as the large, and too often has it preyed upon the lives of our teens and neighbors. Monotheism has used this platform of micro-discrimination as an outlet for the enmity it breeds—a useless fight within our borders as well as those overseas in the name of nothingness.

In early 2012, young Eric James Borges committed suicide after his Christian parents found out about his homosexuality and tried to cure it by performing an exorcism—and then banished him from their house once that failed. This was shortly after he was allegedly physically assaulted by several students in his class while his teacher stood by and did nothing. In his suicide note, Borges stated quite plainly:

> *My pain is not caused because I am gay. My pain was caused by how I am treated because I was gay.*[36]

My greatest wish is that Eric's story was a sincerely unique, tragic event, orchestrated by a few bad people who learned their lesson well after his demise (or that it hadn't happened at all, obviously). Unfortunately, Eric is one of the more recent tragedies of a long line of similar suicides, assaults, and even homicides where religious discrimination played a clear and key factor in the resulting violence and death of innocent young men and women.

According to a study done in 2007 by the Massachusetts Youth Risk Survey, lesbian, gay, and bisexual youth are up to four times more likely to attempt suicide than their heterosexual peers, and in another study we see that LGB youth who come from highly rejecting families are more than eight times as likely to have attempted suicide than LGB peers who reported no or low levels of family rejection.[37] (We can't help but propose with that sobering figure that had Eric Borges's family been more supportive of him, as opposed to ostracizing him after subjecting him to a medieval ritual, he would still be alive today.) Charles Robbins, director and CEO of the Trevor Project, the leading organization promoting awareness and prevention of teen suicide amongst the LGBTQ community, has seen firsthand how religious influence greatly attests to this amount of social entropy:

> *I think that the fact that so many young people are so tormented—so ostracized by their family, peers, school, and society in general—that rather than engage and participate in life, they choose to end their life, says a lot about the Christian values that everywhere inform our culture. I think each and every one of us needs to look inside of ourselves and examine those values for both the good and the harm they're doing. What I would also very much like Christians to know is that being gay isn't a choice that anyone makes. It's not a switch you can turn off and on. Gay people were born into creation just like anyone else, and to devalue who they are by insisting God didn't really make them as they are is to deny them the right to a rich and loving relationship with God, and that's a terrible, terrible thing to deny anybody. No one should ever use scripture to justify removing another person from the spiritual process. If you're a Christian, as I am, you should look to Christ for how to live and act toward others. And what does the Great Commandment of Jesus say but that we're all supposed to love our neighbors as we love ourselves? I wish more Christians would remember what Jesus himself told them to do.[38]*

While many staunch Christians throw up their hands and (understandably) refuse to take the blame for the lives of these depressed and fear-filled teens, it raises an interesting argument of perception. Many Christians may indeed believe that the bullying of homosexuals is wrong and the results are ethically negligent. I appreciate and empathize with these objective concerns deeply, and I hope they will be grateful for this acknowledgement of their opposition to violence in text. However, their tolerance parallels much the same argument as the disassociation of global conflict from what people identify with as "*their* religion"—so what? It's a very lovely thing that one can sit on their couch and see the latest string of suicides on the television and say to themselves:

"Well, that is just awful. I wish *other* Christians wouldn't deface how *I* see the Bible and cause this sadness," but it does absolutely nothing in the face of it. If all Christians thought tolerance was key, it would be a far more beautiful institution—but no amount of "moderation" in religion edits the precepts of hatred from the holy text.

Organizations like True Tolerance decry the antibullying policies put in place in schools to protect homosexuals:

> *Unfortunately, many homosexual advocacy groups have been quick to capitalize on all of the national attention—turning the movement into a campaign for more inclusion of controversial sexual topics in public schools.*
>
> *As a result, many parents have discovered that programs promoted to them as "anti-bullying" or "tolerance" lessons actually turned out to include teaching on things like gay marriage—sometimes against parents' will—and what it means to be "transgender" for kids in elementary school.*[39]

This is the standard to which Christian activist groups have modeled to prevent the tolerance of gay life and culture in schools, and to revoke the very few protections currently in place: "We don't like gays, etc. We don't want our children around them, or to know about their cultural existence. Allowing gay culture to be taught/protected in public schools is an infringement on our religious rights." This drivel is further propagated by similarly activist groups like Focus on the Family, which held its 10th Anniversary Conference in Colorado Springs, Colorado (which has one of the highest concentrations of evangelicals in the United States) in 2008. At the event, Melissa Fryrear, director of the organization's Gender Issues Department, said: "We are ministering to Christian families. They are devastated when a loved one is living homosexually. They can't condone what falls outside biblical truth."[40] When such massive organizations holding the "inerrant" word of god in their hands condemn young minds with words like "devastated" or "outside . . . truth," it's a small wonder many turn to suicide to escape the emotional and social persecution. How strong would one have to be to look at their families and their ancient credos and rebel for the sake of their own health? Or to face religious organizations numbering in the millions and stand against all their pointing fingers, both in the media world and in real life? When the pope dribbles from his golden throne that homosexuals are a defect in nature, undeveloped, and a threat to human dignity and the future of humanity itself,[41] how best should young gays ignore this slander and the billions of ears that hearken to it? Honestly, they simply *shouldn't have to.*

And let's not forget the grand human travesty that was Proposition 8, which was a bill passed in Southern California that eliminated the rights of same-sex couples to marry shortly after that very right was granted to the California people by the California Supreme Court. While, arguably, the passing of the bill was done by the voting of in-state citizens, the vast majority of public awareness ads, protests, and campaign funds were provided by the Mormon Church, whose "prophet" announced over the radio that a call to arms was required of all devout Mormons to put their time and means into the passing of this bill. Almost overnight, the support for Proposition 8 exploded with Mormon advocates staging protests and making house calls, and the bill became the highest-funded campaign on any state ballot and more expensive than any other state campaign with the exception of the presidency. Families sold their possessions to donate money in the *millions* for the campaign, not including the alleged vast quantity of money the Church itself put in illegally. This went forward to pay for such despicable pieces of public awareness as the "Storm Is Coming" commercials—where oily-acted "concerned" citizens were afraid that their children would grow up in a world where same-sex marriage was acceptable (. . . the horror). Tragically, Proposition 8 was passed in 2008, effectively making the right to have a same-sex marriage invalid.

The controversy stirred by the blatant involvement of a tax-free organization in the funding of a political campaign, thankfully, was not unnoticed, and a brilliant documentary titled *8: The Mormon Proposition* was released in 2010, chronicling many of these details with a surprising amount of documentation and vividly portraying the widespread heartbreak of the results. As well, witnesses from the Church itself began to step forward and make statements in print, including a proclaimed descendent of Joseph Smith and a leader amongst the Church, Cary Crall, who explained how Church meetings had been specifically devised to initiate action against the bill, inspiring him into activism against the Mormon faith.[42]

Of course, these well-meaning Christians were likely only following their biblical inspirations who led the way for the example of good marriage. Let us consider, of course, that Moses allowed Pharaoh to sleep with his wife (who was also his sister); Jacob married two of his first cousins, Leah and Rachel (only one of whom he wanted, anyhow), and they in turn both curried his favoritism by giving him maids of their own to sleep with; King David (ancestor of Jesus, no less!) committed adultery with Bathsheba; Solomon had over 1,000 wives and mistresses—all very fine visions of a moral union among straight couples who love each other.

I cannot get into the ethical and scientific mud-pit of whether or not homosexuality is a naturally biological occurrence and the subsequent ramifications thereof, so I will do my best to keep my point on the subject as simple as possible: *this reaction to a community of people based on religious ideology is resulting in conflict and death*—pure and simple. Who cares if homosexuality is a choice or not (incidentally, I'm inclined to think not)? What does it matter what your book says or what his test says about the subject? The sobering, unfortunate observation is that the influence made by this very specific, admittedly religiously motivated society is causing young people to *die*. Where is the divinity in that? Where is the goodness in it? By common definition, these are evil influences with catastrophic results. I often wonder (less than quietly to myself) if Fryrear or the people at True Tolerance ever feel a sting of regret for the lives lost every year, with written word, testimony, and witness all signifying that Christian intolerance (at the very least) contributed to their ultimate decision? How holy they must see themselves for spreading the idealism of their "loving" god. This reverts very easily back to an earlier point—if god exists and this is his will, then he is an evil and petty child. If this is not his will, then he allows it to happen in his name for no justifiable reason. Thousands of years after the fact, Epicurus still rings true to form.

On a personal note, I hedge upon the subject of young homosexual discrimination for two distinct reasons: because it is an honest and open debate where evidence is abundant and blatant and the consequences are sorely impactful; and because the *only* point of discrimination in writing against homosexuals *anywhere* in human history is religiously motivated. This is one of the few very unfortunate conflicts that *would not exist* without the idea of god. Arguers to earlier and later topics (quite rightly) imply that said conflicts would happen for human reasons if religion didn't exist anyway—violence over money or territory or tribal feuds, etc. But this singular subject is religious discrimination all on its own. If no holy text had ever said, in essence, that homosexuality is wrong, we would *never,* in the course of human history, have seen its conflict. All the lives that have ever been lost on the subject, including Matthew Shepard and Brandon Teena and thousands of others—all that blood is specifically and unequivocally on the idea of god and its followers. That is an unanswerable crime and eternally lacking recompense. I am rather reminded of a demagogic zealot who was fond of traipsing around the University of Montana campus in September 2012 shouting from an unintimidating plastic step-stool (but a self-imposed pulpit nonetheless) the hellish fate of those who committed the crime of homosexuality. I engaged in rather heated debate with this fool for only a short time before he cut me off with the justified (if absurdly meaningless) observation that my argument was disrespectful and not worthy of notice. To which I replied that applauding torture of gays in a public square and declining criticism for it was the very definition of disrespect and, furthermore, hypocrisy.

Most sadly, persecution for some of these teens does not stop even after their death. Westboro Baptist Church, after protesting the funeral of Matthew Shepard in 1998, dedicated a page to him on its website, titled "Perpetual Gospel Memorial to Matthew Shepard,"[43] sadly and excruciatingly addressed at www.godhatesfags.com, where one can read every new day how long Matthew has "been in hell."[44] The page painfully expounds upon the punishment WBC members "know" he is receiving for all eternity. This is, of course, with barefaced insensitivity to a young man who not only died, but who also was brutally tortured and murdered. They also frequently show up to picket productions of *The Laramie Project,* a play chronicling the widespread pain of his murder, no matter where it is performed in the country.

WBC members are responsible for infinitely more sting and confusion to the living homosexual and heterosexual alike. In February 2012, for example, WBC, in its standard "love thy neighbor" Christian familiarity, announced its intention to picket radical slanders at the funeral of two small boys, Charlie (7) and Braden (5) Powell, who had been murdered by their father in Tacoma, Washington, after the father purposefully blew up their house with explosives—a tragic murder-suicide that sent grief across the country. WBC proclaimed that the boys had died as an act of god's anger in response to the state legislature's support of gay marriage. Margie Phelps (daughter of Fred—most of the church population are his descendents), tweeted the collective view of the WBC, saying their protest was to remind Governor Christine Gregoire that "they died because of her rebellion. . . . This is why God's cursed you w Josh Powells blowing up kids."[45]

The above are just two of the self-proclaimed 30,000 protests they have conducted since their inception—every single one offering prophetic descriptions of punishment for those who protect or treat homosexuals equally—often at funerals, including those for former Mormon Church president Gordon B. Hinckley and Apple CEO Steve Jobs. In the latter case, the *Washington Post* wrote a beautifully scathing article making fun of the fact that Margie Phelps announced their plans to picket Jobs' funeral via Twitter by *using her iPhone.*[46] This is what we could call, in the modern Internet lingo of the world today, an epic fail.

I'll leave most of my WBC stories and comments to silence, simply because it is a commonly accepted topic of sorrow among theists and atheists alike that the actions of this wayward church (including the protesting of military funerals and the admonition that those soldiers are now suffering in hell on account of their service being in deference to a country where some states allow homosexual marriage and tolerance) are a social depravity and not a lot needs to be said. I will confess without hesitation that a tear is being shed even as I type these words for the horrors that this group have inflicted on non-Christian and Christian alike.

But mention of it is important (and not because I necessarily wish to lump their actions in with that of far less fear-mongering or pain-spreading people of the same ideological origins), but because it would be remiss of the point of this entire work not to elaborate that WBC exerts the same mental terrorism that previously mentioned others do physically, based on the same standards. Where would WBC exist without the origins of religion, or the outdated laws of a primal Testament? Without a god and without a Bible, their miseries would be beyond the scope of imagination because the possibility of their enterprise would be nonexistent. Without a god, without religion, Fred Phelps and his atrocities would be a distant nightmare, as would *all* of the other subjects I have listed. And again, too many well-meaning people will step backward tentatively and say, "That is not *my* god," or "That is not *my* reading of the Bible." Again, to which I must reply—so what? Clearly, *your* redacted version of Christianity or Islam or whatever else doesn't rise up to influence the world. *Your* god sits silently, while the consequences of his revealed text play havoc with the world. While the original god of action that moves upon this planet and is characterized in your holy text is the one exerting violence, the idea of peaceful religion in whatever context is wholly destroyed. And for those just tuning in: *that's* the god that wrote your Bible and your Koran. Without that god, these pains would not be realities, whether they are stoning gays to death in the Middle East or blowing up abortion clinics.

Most of us remember the haunting cover of *Time* magazine on August 9, 2010, depicting the horribly mutilated face of Bibi Aisha, who had been married by arrangement at the age of twelve to another man in accordance with *baad,* which works as a type of payment system in some Muslim countries. When she suffered continual abuse at the whim of her husband over the course of six years, she fled—only to be caught by the Taliban and returned. Her in-laws then took her to a remote place in the desolate mountains, cut off her nose and ears, and left her to bleed out over the scorching, disconsolate sand. Barely alive, she was found by U.S. military and saved, and became the literal face of domestic abuse in the Middle East. The *Time* article spoke not only of Bibi, but also of the continuous abuse women suffer in Islamic countries and especially under Taliban rule:

> *Under the Taliban, who ruled Afghanistan from 1996 to 2001, women accused of adultery were stoned to death; those who flashed a bare ankle from under the shroud of a burqa were whipped. Koofi remembers being beaten on the street for forgetting to remove the polish from her nails after her wedding. "We were not even allowed to laugh out loud," she says.[47]*

The same article illuminates how these atrocities are allowed to occur, in that the Taliban necessitated its own judgments without regard for the Afghanistan Constitution, which has several articles protecting the rights of women. Article 3 of the same document, however, says that no law overrides *sharia*, or Islamic law—much of which is in heavy debate over the righteousness of punishing women for divorce, refusing to wear the burka or hijab, or for fleeing abuse—just as Bibi did. It is this religiously protected grey area that allows Taliban officials (and indeed, many male citizens) to evoke the violence they do upon their innocent spouses. When it again comes to this pivotal discussion of basic human rights and the hope that another soul on earth could live without daily torment, the voices at the forefront of the argument are the ones with the weight of antiquated dogma on their breaths. The article goes on:

> *Abdul Hadi Arghandiwal, the Minister of Economy and leader of the ideologically conservative Hizb-i-Islami faction, for example, holds that women and men shouldn't go to university together. Like the Taliban, he believes that women should not be allowed to leave the home unaccompanied by a male relative. "That is in accordance with Islam. And what we want for Afghanistan is Islamic rights, not Western rights," Arghandiwal says.*

The *sharia* breeds just as much contention surrounding it and the supporting texts of the Koran and the *haddith* as does any other religious scripture—somehow, no one can seem to figure out what their own holy book means in simplicity, not even insofar as: "Should we beat our wives and throw rocks at them until they die if they break any of these rules?" For such an important yes-or-no question, I would wish my divine manual would have a clear-cut answer, for her sake. Of course it doesn't—and the ones who pay for it are as innocent as any social class tortured physically and emotionally for the sake of clarity in fantasy-fiction.

The same is true with Muslim unions in the United States, as with the marriages of Pakistani Shamim and Turkish Shireen, both living in arranged marriages to Muslim husbands in the United States. The *Washington Post* reported both of their continual abuses with graphically honest quotes such as:

> *"My husband beat. He show knife. I am scared for him, for all family,"* said Shamim, 21, the Pakistani bride, who was rescued by police. She is being sheltered and tutored in English at a private home. "They say no money, no call mother at home. I cook for all, I not eat. I not know 911 what is. I think I go crazy."[48]

Shireen, when she finally took her husband to court, was abandoned by her family and social circles, and many U.S. Muslims do not know that there are laws protecting their civil rights and can be liberated from the abuse situation if they can provide evidence of mistreatment. Shamim, despite her broken English, possibly sums up the place women hold in Islamic countries most effectively:

> *"Now I am freedom,"* Shamim said, grinning broadly as she took a tea break recently from her English studies. "I stay America. Not go home. In home, everyone blame woman, it is my culture. Everyone blame me."

Thankfully, some small hope remains for reason and civility. In March 2012, the *New York Times* reported that Tunisia had developed a new Constitution after the revolution that would not include *sharia* as a source of its legislation,[49] making a progressive step not only in favor of the rights of women but also in the division of religious idealism from politics in the Eastern world, despite the ultraconservative Salafis claims that this move is blasphemy. (A victimless crime, as the saying goes!) But such victories feel small when remembering the millions of women, a large number of them young teens, suffering from the brutal retributions of their husbands under divine law in other countries—such as the eleven-year-old girl in Yemen, who, according to ABC News in 2010, was hospitalized with genital injuries that occurred when the girl was forced into intercourse by her husband against the agreement of the marriage (to wait until she reached puberty). This was in the same week that a thirteen-year-old bride there perished from her injuries as the result of a sexual assault from her husband. Despite a local activist's efforts to change government and pass a minimum marriage age, conservative Islamists claim child marriage is ordained by god, and those who oppose it are apostates to the faith.[50]

Beyond this madness, how many other victims are there? How many innocent women stoned and beaten and killed because a self-validated holy text says so? Furthermore, how can an objective human being condone the use of such action with only that justification? This ideology, as so many others, gives us nothing but pain—but is clung to in the name of god with obstinate resolution. Keep in mind that while sexual discrimination is not a legal or widespread practice in the Western world, its mandate is still very clear in Christian texts—beginning with Eve, who was cursed with painful childbirth for giving in to temptation (women in the Greek Orthodox Church are not allowed to attend mass while menstruating). Woman are categorized as property with oxen and other chattel all through the Torah; Ephesians (5:22-24) notes: "Wives, submit yourselves unto your own husbands, as unto the Lord. For the husband is the head of the wife, even as Christ is the head of the church: and he is the saviour of the body. Therefore as the church is subject unto Christ, so let the wives be to their own husbands in everything"; Peter similarly commands women to submit to the will of their spouses; and Lot offers up his daughters to a sex-crazed crowd rather than letting them have the angels he harbored within his house (of course, his girls got their comeback later, didn't they?). And let us not overlook the heinous verse of Exodus, which gives permission for a man to sell his daughter, like an animal, into sexual slavery:

> Exodus 21:7–11—"*When a man sells his daughter as a slave, she shall not go out as the male slaves do. If she does not please her master, who has designated her for himself, then he shall let her be redeemed; he shall have no right to sell her to a foreign people, since he has dealt faithlessly with her. If he designates her for his son, he shall deal with her as a daughter. If he takes another wife to himself, he shall not diminish her food, her clothing, or her marital rights. And if he does not do these things for her, she shall go out for nothing, without payment of money.*"

Without a doubt, Christian ideology is equal (at least in its precedents) to Islamic culture in regards to the demoralization and inequality of the fairer sex.

Nor is that radical, Christian political agenda kept only to the low and voiceless and without mirror to Eastern groups such as the Muslim Brotherhood—not with presidents, such as George W. Bush, and powerful presidential candidates, such as former Republican senator Rick Santorum, standing on highly religious platforms. In 2011, Santorum said: "The American Left hates Christendom. They hate Western civilization," and "This nation was founded as a Christian nation . . . there's only one God and his name is Jesus. I'm tired of people telling me that I can't say those words . . . If you don't love America and you don't like the way we do things, I've got one thing to say—Get out! We don't worship Buddha. I said we don't worship Buddha. We don't worship Muhammad. We don't worship Allah. We worship God. We worship God's son Jesus Christ." Santorum has made religion a forefront of his campaigns, just as pseudo-political factions of the Middle East do. Just because Americans do it democratically doesn't mean the influence is not absurdly tangible. Nor do we differ from our "radical" Eastern brethren in terms of building our younger religious armies with the mission to ultimately destroy the separation between church and state—while institutions like Patrick Henry College exist, America plays host to the exact same kind of theocratic revolution.

Women, homosexuals, people of other faiths, people of no faiths, even people among their own creeds—but above all, *people* are primary victims of religion. The use of religion in the justification of discrimination and violence is paramount, and while the conflicts in the Middle East are still occurring, we should be aware of the motivations today better than ever—especially in a society where such information is so easily available. And again, *none* of this violence is turned against people within their *own* faiths who have performed the same transgressions. Woe betide the day the Mormon Church funds millions for the campaign against getting tattooed based on a Leviticus law, or against football for touching of pigskin! Or the day the Catholic Church makes an organizational attempt to stop pedophilia in the world.

What of the day that militant Islamist groups punish those within their own sects for enacting violence on innocent peoples in the name of a religion whose alleged primary mandate is peace? These are fantasies—and thin ones at that. My only hope for the salvation of theism will occur when these events come to pass, but I am not holding my breath any more than I am waiting for the Seattle Mariners to win a World Series. This is what occurs when people align themselves with coarse mantras like what is emblazoned on the front of Patrick Henry College: *"For Christ and For Liberty"*— A clear and hollow mixture of priorities, to put the concept of liberty behind *anything*.

There comes a time to fear the possibility that such religious factions, or countries dominated by such factions, may eventually (if not already) have weapons of mass destruction (such as Pakistan)—especially when considering the havoc they have wreaked with arms of a much lower impact. Not to sound apocalyptic, but my fear of nuclear war has never been questioned when a decently secular body was in control of a WMD (and is not entirely alleviated thinking that the United States could, in theory, be driven to such resource by the same motivation)—it is only sparked when those of the same radical delusion it takes to believe that god loves you for killing others obtains the tools required for global destruction. It is thoughts like these that make the focus on the conflicts over Israel and Palestine, Iraq, Afghanistan, and Iran so important. If Al-Qaeda had somehow had possession of a WMD in 2001, the *exact* same motivation would have driven them to use it rather than hijacking planes. Obviously, I jump on hypothetical and hyperbole, here, considering I am no expert on international affairs, nuclear weaponry, or the details in which Al-Qaeda managed to highjack those planes in the first place—but the reasoning stands to, at the very least, consider. What could have happened if someone who believed that god spoke in his ear had his hand on the big red button?

Arguably, since the inconceivable guilt and global shame that occurred from Nagasaki and Hiroshima, the idea of detonating another weapon of the same or higher caliber in an act of war is an unthinkable notion to the common senses of most peoples—ergo the continuous pissing match that was the Cold War. So-called "moderate" theists and secular individuals would have a difficult time deciding on using nuclear weaponry as a legitimate response to any encounter (though that is not to say they are incapable). Therefore the only people predictably who would actually detonate a nuclear device in attack would be someone religiously vindicated—who believed that the mandate was divine.

Israel is capable. Iran is coming closer every day. But one can see the train of thought, here. It's not difficult—and it should be damnably scary. For this reason and many, many others, I have had doubts about people of extreme faith holding public office, because it is somewhat likely they feel they will be compelled to make one action or other by the literal voice of god, but more commonly because they will almost always be motivated by religious prescription rather than objective observation and circumstance. While, naturally, there are exceptions, the examples of the point are far more numerous—and do not have to entail nuclear warfare in order to be devastating.

We may not be divinely ordained, but we are naturally so. We are the most dominant species on the planet since the dinosaur. Yet how is it that after 250,000 years on this earth, after all the struggle and fighting and learning in order to become bipeds; to utilize tools; to create social interaction and communication—even language; to become literate; to develop art and economics; to birth industry and architecture and politics; to spawn into something greater than the history of this insignificant rock in this tiny corner of space has ever known and perhaps will ever know; to achieve nothing in the known history of the universe to be rivaled or paralleled—that we still haven't learned civility, that we still haven't accomplished peace, or basic humanity, and that for whatever reason—religious or otherwise—we cannot transcend the boundaries of imaginary lines or imaginary friends? For this failure, we are weaker than we could ever imagine, and it would take far more than a failed god to justify our state. We have failed ourselves for this calamity.

Notes

1. Dave Grossman, *On Killing* (Back Bay Books, 1995), p. 26.

2. These are the words passed from Ehud to Moab just before slamming a blade into his viscera in Judges.

3. Sam Harris, *The End of Faith: Religion, Terror, and the Future of Reason* (Norton & Company, 2004).

4. Jericho, it seems, was prized so highly that god made the sun stand still so Joshua would have light by which to murder all those within the city (Joshua 10:12–14).

5. Kim Cobb, "Church Massacre/Small Phineas Priests Group Tied to Other Acts of Violence," *Houston Chronicle*, September 16, 1989, http://www.chron.com/CDA/archives/archive.mpl/1999_3165256/church-massacre-small-phineas-priests-group-tied-t.html.

6. *"Fort Worth Gunman Called 'Paranoid Schizophrenic,'"* Baptist Press, September 19, 1999, http://www.mcjonline.com/news/news3421b.htm.

7. "Politicians Don't Count Wedgewood Shooting as a Hate Crime," Baptist Press, September 11, 2000, http://www.layman.org/news.aspx?article=10489.

8.   I use the word 'we' as a generality of American mind-set, being an American myself. I sincerely hope I could never characterize myself as one of the semantically deluded people I am describing. The same proverbial 'we' may be used several times in the course of this book, before and after this note.

9.   Aref M Al-Khattar, *Religion and Terrorism: An Interfaith Perspective* (Praeger, 2003), pp. 21, 30, 55, 91.

10.   Frederick Clarkson, "Kopp Lays Groundwork to Justify Murdering Abortion Provider Slepian," National Organization for Women, December 2, 2002.

11.   "'Army Of God' Anthrax Threats," CBS News, November 9, 2001.

12.   Alan Cooperman, "Is Terrorism Tied to Christian Sect? Religion May Have Motivated Bombing: Suspect," *Washington Post*, June 2, 2003. "'Based on what we know of Rudolph so far, and admittedly it's fragmentary, there seems to be a fairly high likelihood that he can legitimately be called a Christian terrorist,' said Michael Barkun, a professor of political science at Syracuse University who has been a consultant to the FBI on Christian extremist groups."

13.   "Cult Members Deported from Israel," BBC News, January 9, 1999.

14.   *2083: A European Declaration of Independence*, archived by the Federation of American Scientists, April 24, 2012, p. 650.

15.   This paragraph was added on February 16, 2015.

16.   Iyad Al-Sayegh, "Arrest of Leader of the Islamic Democratic Movement in Syria," Elaph, retrieved October 23, 2012.

17.   Rick Glastone, "Massacre at Syrian Bakery Dims Hopes for a Holiday Truce," *New York Times*, October 23, 2012, http://www.nytimes.com/2012/10/24/world/middleeast/syria.html?ref=global-home.

18.   Ewen MacAskill, "George Bush: 'God Told Me to End the Tyranny in Iraq,'" *Guardian*, October 6, 2005, http://www.guardian.co.uk/world/2005/oct/07/iraq.usa.

19.   As cited in Christopher Cerf and Victor Navasky, *Mission Accomplished!: Or, How We Won the War in Iraq* (Simon & Schuster, 2008).

20.   George W. Bush, *The Public Papers of the Presidents of the United States: George W. Bush*, 2002, p. 1783.

21.   Clive Hamilton, "Bush, God, Iraq and Gog," Counterpunch, May 24th, 2009, http://www.counterpunch.org/2009/05/22/bush-god-iraq-and-gog/

22.   "Palin's Church May Have Shaped Controversial Overview," *Huffington Post*, January 14, 2011, http://www.huffingtonpost.com/2008/09/02/palins-church-may-have-sh_n_123205.html#postComment.

23.   Remarks at the Installation Prayer Breakfast Club Dix, February 6, 2003, dix.army.mil.

24.   Anne Lamott, *Grace (Eventually)* (Riverhead, 2007).

25.   Quoted by Ron Csillag, *"Math +Religion = Trouble,"* *Toronto Star*, January 26, 2008, http://www.thestar.com/.

26.   *Russell Brand in New York City,* Comedy Central, 2009

27.   Dominic Cavendish, "Ricky Gervais on Atheism and More," *Telegraph*, blog, December 4, 2008, http://blogs.telegraph.co.uk/culture/dominiccavendish/5893767/Ricky_Gervais_on_atheism_and_more/.

28.   "20 Feared Dead as Hindu-Christian Riots Spread in India," *CNN World News*, September 16, 2008, http://articles.cnn.com/2008-09-16/world/india.riots_1_christian-minority-hindu-leader-kandhamal?_s=PM:WORLD.

29.   Hari Kumar,c"Thousands Homeless after Hindu-Christian Violence in India," *New York Times*, August 29, 2008, http://www.nytimes.com/2008/08/29/world/asia/29iht-29india.15727169.html.

30.   Daniel Rancour-Laferriere, *The Sign of the Cross: From Golgotha to Genocide* (Transaction, 2011), p. 17.

31.   George Carlin, *Back in Town*, MPI Home Video, 2003.

32.   During which Pope Pius XII not only remained largely silent and took no proactive movements toward the liberation of the Jews but instead made agreements with both Hitler and Mussolini and later was nominated to canonization for his deeds and marked for sainthood.

33.   Richard Steigmann-Gall, *The Holy Reich: Nazi Conceptions of Christianity, 1919–1945* (Cambridge University Press, 2003).

34.   Pope Benedict XVI, *Jesus of Nazareth*, Part II (Ignatius Press, March 2011).

35.   B. A. Robinson, "Mass Crimes Against Humanity and Genocides: The Congo Free State Genocide: Circa 1895 to 1912," ReligiousTolerance.org. May 25, 2001, http://www.religioustolerance.org/genocong.htm.

36.   Christian Piatt, "Christian Exorcism Leads to Gay Teen's Suicide," *Father, Son and Holy Heretic, Patheos* blog, February 2, 2012, http://www.patheos.com/blogs/christianpiatt/2012/02/christian-exorcism-leads-to-gay-teens-suicide/.

37.   C. Ryan et al., "Family Rejection as a Predictor of Negative Health Outcomes in White and Latino Lesbian, Gay, and Bisexual Young Adults," *Pediatrics* 123, no. 1 (January 2009): pp. 346–352.

38.   John Shore, "Gay Teen Suicides: Bullying and Christianity: A Talk with the Trevor Project Director," *Huffington Post*, October 5, 2010, http://www. huffingtonpost.com/john-shore/a-talk-about-gay-teen-sui_b_745912.html.

39.   "Bullying Issues," True Tolerance, a project of Focus on the Family, https:// www.truetolerance.org/latest-issues/.

40.   Electa Draper, "Focus on the Family Focuses on Homosexuals," *Denver Post*, October 23, 2008, http://www.denverpost.com/breakingnews/ci_10788844.

41.   Joe Morgan, "Pope Says Gay People Are Not Fully Developed Humans," GayStarNews.com, September 28, 2012, http://www.gaystarnews.com/article/ pope-says-gay-people-are-not-fully-developed-humans280912

42.   "The Unlikely Prophet," *Advocate*, April 13, 2011, http://www.advocate. com/Politics/Prop__8/The_Unlikely_Prophet/.

43.   http://www.godhatesfags.com/memorials/matthewshepardmemorial.html.

44.   Use of quotes because, despite my lack of belief in a hell in the first place, I very much doubt Matthew would reside there if it did exist.

45.   Michael Winter, "Anti-Gay Westboro Church to Protest at Powell Boys' Funeral," *USA Today*, February 9, 2012, http://content.usatoday.com/communities/ ondeadline/post/2012/02/anti-gay-westboro-church-to-protest-at-powell-boys-funeral/1#.UH41K8XA-ks.

46.   Elizabeth Tenety, "Westboro Baptist Church Uses iPhone to Announce Protest at Steve Jobs Funeral," *Washington Post*, October 6, 2011.

47.   "Afghan Women and the Return of the Taliban," *Time*, August 9, 2010.

48.   Pamela Constable, "For Some Muslim Wives, Abuse Knows No Borders," *Washington Post*, May 8, 2007.

49.   Kareem Faheen, "Tunisia Says Constitution Will Not Cite Islamic Law," *New York Times*, March 26, 2012, http://www.nytimes.com/2012/03/27/world/africa/ tunisia-says-constitution-will-not-cite-islamic-law.html?_r=1&ref=shariaislamiclaw.

50.   Laura Setekian, "Yemeni Bride, 11, Hospitalized with Genital Injuries," ABC News.com, April 13, 2010, http://abcnews.go.com/Health/International/ yemeni-bride-11-hospitalized-genital-injuries/story?id=10362500#.T3ouVKtrNak.

4

The God Epidemic
or Damage to Health and Psyche

◆◆◆

"Our remedies oft in ourselves do lie, which we ascribe to Heaven."
—William Shake-speare, *As You Like It*

"Every human being is the author of his own health or disease."
—Hindu Prince Gautama Siddhartha, Founder of Buddhism

Imagine if you will that you have suffered from a horrible accident at seventeen years of age. Pretend that you have been blind-sided by a bus, unexpectedly, while riding your bike to class, or to a friend's house, or to meet the person you love for a picnic in the park. The day is sunny, the breeze is minimal—and out of nowhere you are flying through the air, aware of every broken bone before you even hit the asphalt, blood pooling around your face as jagged splinters of what was once your femur stick brazenly through a cleft in your skin. Your vision swims in a hazy fog. You are concussed, hemorrhaging, and quickly lose consciousness even before the nearest person can run to check your vitals—but you are alive.

You are transported to hospital and are declared to be in a coma, and subsequently placed on life support. Just as the doctors are taking care of your rather serious injuries, your parents burst in, shouting for doctors to stop treatment. They are Christian Scientists—as are you: devoted to the idea that healing occurs spiritually and not through man's medicine. Your parents explain that they will pray for you, and that is all the healing you require. If you were a resident of one of forty-four states that, for a time, handed the right to religious practice over the health concerns of a minor, your doctors would have counseled against it—explaining that your cranial injuries may have devastating effects—but they would resign the battle or face litigation.[1]

91

During this time, you suffer a formidable brain hemorrhage that might have been detected by an MRI. Unchecked, you bleed into your brain until you eventually die.

This kind of story is not that uncommon (though, arguably, the incidence of it happening even *once* is too common for moral comfort). Using their First Amendment Rights, those Christian Scientists acting as medical proxies for loved ones suffering injury have been responsible for a myriad of otherwise preventable deaths—such as David and Ginger Twitchell, a Massachusetts couple who were convicted of involuntary manslaughter for the death of their two-year-old son, Robyn, who suffered merely from a bowel obstruction and perished in great pain. According to the *New York Times* article which reported the incident, that was the latest in a series of convictions on the same premise, and naturally stirred huge controversy over the subject of the First Amendment.[2] In many places, the debate still continues heatedly. We *should* notwithstanding be able to see that while religious right is protected by the First Amendment, the life of a person who cannot fend for themselves should be the most important concern of the situation—and whatever treatment has *proven* to be most effective should be immediately prescribed for the safety of the injured (objectively, that seems like common sense). In a different world where prayer was proven to have more healing effect than a cast for a broken leg, I would implore the masses to pray away for every scrape and bruise! Unfortunately, we know this can't be done—and not just from inference. We've *tested* it.

Already noted by Richard Dawkins, but more than worthy enough to bring up again, is the truly laughable subject of the Great Prayer Experiment,[3] funded with a *staggering* $2.4 million by the Templeton Foundation (one can't help but think of the rat of the same name from E. B. White's *Charlotte's Web*). This was done in careful adherence to the scientific method using control and experimental groups, monitoring the course of just over 1,800 patients who had all received coronary bypass surgery: a random third strategically receiving prayers and knowing it, a second receiving no prayers and knowing it, and third receiving no prayers and not knowing it. All prayers were done from distant churches in separate states, all with exact and specific medical goals to be prayed for in terms of speedy and uncomplicated recoveries. The result was childishly predictable—there was not a jot of difference between those prayed for and those not (who were unaware of being prayed for). As a matter of fact, those who *knew* they were being prayed for suffered many more setbacks than those not—with various conjectures as to why. The greatest victory this experiment *did* accomplish was draining over $2 million from the Templeton account, which I would argue was well worth the effort.

Even if more money was to be wasted in testing like this, we could at least infer one crucial bit of information simply by observation—a Band-Aid or stitches will close and heal a cut far more quickly and more effectively than a prayer (or, indeed, thousands of prayers from churches in different states), and a prayer will not have more remedial effects on a myriad of other afflictions more successfully in any one case than approved medicinal treatment for the same malady will. So why—ever—subject someone who cannot decide for themselves to an inferior process at risk of their life? Beyond protection of religious rights, this then becomes an abject disregard for the necessary medical need of the patient. Arguably, those conscious and of an age to be their own medical guardian can suffer themselves however they see fit—muttering incantations to a god who will never hear them while cancer eats away their internal tissues—but *children*? In the wide, ghastly mural of religious suffering, children take up too much of the fresco.

In April 2000, the *Independent* published an article announcing that Britain's Department of Health was releasing a report confirming the abuse of children in satanic cults and the experience of fifty victims[4] (the article itself actually uses the word "survivors," which might imply that some cases existed wherein children were in fact killed). Compiled in part by psychotherapist Valerie Sinason, some of her observations included that the children were tortured by being held underwater or made to think they had witnessed the murder of infants. "Some children are born for the purpose of the abuse and are not registered on birth certificates," she added. This is congruent with similar findings in America—in Rutherford County, Tennessee, a man named John Lotts Jr. was arrested in February 2012 for abusing a small child after already having admitted to the practice of Satanism and to being responsible for the boy's injuries, which included burns to the hands, bruising, broken ribs, and a lacerated liver.[5] Lotts denied that the abuse was part of the rituals he performed but the prosecution intended on making that a focus of the case.

One could infer that these practices are not part of the organized, philosophically bent institution of LaVeyan Satanism (which, in a nutshell, is ultimately a humanist liberation movement that represents most of the "Satanist" culture), whose ninth mandate in the Eleven Satanic Rules of the Earth is: "Do not harm young children."[6] Though, if LaVeyan Satanists carry with them the same hypocrisy highlighted in chapter one of their fellow theists,[7] then they could very easily have been followers of this practice—or just as easily followed barbaric rituals of any other sect of an occult nature and labeled themselves "Satanists" out of ignorance or need for attention. The possibilities are open to debate—the injuries inflicted on young innocents for the purpose of a supernatural ideal are not.

Again, one needs to be reminded that scriptural abuse of children is not out of the realm of monotheistic precedent: that Judaism, Islam, and Christianity all revere and acknowledge the prophet Abraham, who was commanded by god to sacrifice his son (the only difference in mythology being whether or not the son was Ishmael or Isaac), and Abraham compliantly agreed, even binding him to an altar on a mountain in a highly ritualistic fashion (Genesis 22:9). It is also pertinent to note the slaying of the firstborn in Exodus; the death of the "suckling infants" in Samuel; Jephthah murdering his only daughter by burning her at the stake because the lord told him to in Judges; the killing of forty-two boys by bears after Elisha muttered a curse of god upon them in 2 Kings; the death of Job's children by the hand of god (for the contemptible motivation of winning a bet); and a handful of Proverbs (13:24, 19:18, 22:15, 23:13–14 & 29:15) where god demands the beating of children. Those who say that these verses aren't nearly inspirational enough to provoke violence against children in Western culture would do well to direct their complaints to Benjamin Edetanlen of Georgia, who beat his five-month-old child to death and as his defense referred to the Bible: "Spare the rod, spoil the child." Of course, one will now only be able to contend with him through plate glass until his eighteen-year sentence is complete.[8] That is all without even touching upon the numerous verses depicting abortion (sometimes in the very name of god) in graphic detail. (As though god is *really* 'pro-life'![9])

In Nigeria, a heart-breaking number of children have been accused of witchcraft by fervid Christian pastors and the enactment of Pentecostal anger has literally left the corpses of young ones lying in the streets. Child-abuse laws have since taken effect, primarily due to the exposure of the atrocity by the Emmy and BAFTA award-winning documentary *Dispatches: Return to Africa's Witch Children,* which left masses of its viewers (including myself) in tears and fury. Much of the superstition is founded on a tribal African belief that nothing happens naturally upon this world, so all bad outcomes are the result of witchery and evil spirits wreaking havoc in our lives. One Christian witch-hunter, Bishop Ulup-Aya, said without a hint of trepidation on camera that he has killed over 110 children he felt were possessed by demonic forces.[10]

A recent post by Irish Central on its website stated that members of the Association of Catholic Priests, who number somewhere around 800 and come from all over Ireland, have sworn they will not follow the newly imposed law that requires them to divulge the details of child sexual abuse that they are given in the confessional box. Despite the threats of ten-year sentences for not complying with this law, spokesman Fr Sean McDonagh told the paper: "I certainly wouldn't be willing to break the seal of confession for anyone—Alan Shatter [the Minister of Justice] particularly."[11] Given the high Protestant-Catholic conflict rate in the country of Ireland anyhow, this move only serves to stoke the fire against religious establishment-based thinking—under the deplorable guise that the confessional is answerable only to god and even talk of murder, rape, or anything else is for the ears of the almighty only. Here again do theists sacrifice the safety of their young for a paragon of illusion.

In America, some not only *hide* the abuse for the sake of god, but also *encourage* it. In an audio clip posted on the Internet in May 2012, Pastor Sean Harris of Berean Baptist Church in Fayettesville, North Carolina, spits inanities from his pulpit advocating for the beating of children based on their sexual mannerisms—not even for being gay or transgender, but if they *behave* antithetically to the prescribed male-female observations. "So your little son starts to act a little girlish when he is four years old and instead of squashing that like a cockroach and saying, 'Man up, son, get that dress off you and get outside and dig a ditch, because that is what boys do,' you get out the camera and you start taking pictures of Johnny acting like a female and then you upload it to YouTube and everybody laughs about it and the next thing you know, this dude, this kid is acting out childhood fantasies that should have been squashed."

To this horrifying chauvinism, no one protested or stood or even left silently. Instead, they cheered and heartened like the mob of the Roman Colosseum when first blood had hit the sand. He went on: "Dads, the second you see your son dropping the limp wrist, you walk over there and crack that wrist. Man up. Give him a good punch. OK? You are not going to act like that. You were made by God to be a male and you are going to be a male. And when your daughter starts acting too butch, you reign her in. And you say, 'Oh, no, sweetheart. You can play sports. Play them to the glory of God. But sometimes you are going to act like a girl and walk like a girl and talk like a girl and smell like a girl and that means you are going to be beautiful. You are going to be attractive. You are going to dress yourself up.' "[12]

I feel like no more needs to be said: the atrocity is evident. It is parallel to the bone-chilling scene in the cringe-inducing documentary *Jesus Camp,* where a vain and obese, unlettered Missouri woman berated an entire auditorium of children for transgressions—the imaginary acts of which she put into their heads—until many collapsed into frightful sobs for a preconceived guilt that she inflicted on them.[13] Apparently, it's not bullying if it's for Jesus.

The butchery of genitalia is predominantly religious in nature, most commonly in the invention of circumcision. While the origins of the method are unknown, a good estimate assumes that it began as a religious or ritualistic practice that became dogmatic convention. Nowadays, together with Islam, the faith most adherent to the subscription is, of course, Judaism, though whether or not the actual medical justification exists for circumcision, some truly unfortunate results have occurred from the religious justification— including an incident reported by ABC News on March 12, 2012, in New York City, where a baby boy died of a herpetic infection caused by the ritualistic circumcision performed by a rabbinical leader.[14] The practice known as *metzizah b'peh* is performed by removing the clipped foreskin of the child with the mohel's mouth, using suction to pull it away. The mohel in question was infected with the type 1 herpes virus, which was transferred to the baby during the bris, and ultimately led to his death, similar to two deaths of infants by a corresponding nature and the same practice in 2005. This horror has been utilized by Orthodox Jews for over 5,000 years, and while medical arguments may abound to the frequency of similar tragic events, it should at least birth the moral debate as to the appropriateness of an older man placing his mouth on the genitalia of an infant no matter the ritualistic justification. If we had heard about the actions out of context, we would be appalled. (Frankly, I am regardless—with great reason. And my revulsion extends to the apparent obsession with prepuces at all, considering—beyond the examples mentioned earlier and later in this work—that at the time of the Reformation, somewhere between ten and twenty churches claimed to hold the authentic foreskin of Jesus Christ. Indeed, Catherine of Siena was convinced that Christ had given her his foreskin to wear as a wedding ring. Let us not fail to mention as well that Moses was healed of an illness when Sarah wiped his feet with the bloody foreskin of their own son. David also provides Saul with a hundred Philistine foreskins to prove his affection for Saul's daughter.)

While such horrific imagery is already in your mind I would implore you not to forget the hellish savagery of female circumcision in African Muslim communities. Beginning in ancient Egypt, the modern practice involves the slicing away of the clitoris with a razor (whatever quality is available in the tribal developing world, predictably dull, rusty, and terribly unclean) and the infection, humiliation, and death that spreads from it. Let us also not forget the aforementioned marital right of husbands in Islamic cultures to force sex upon sometimes prepubescent wives, inflicting tearing, scarring, hemorrhaging, and sometimes death.

As with many other examples of facets of the argument of this book, I am constantly baffled by the inability to keep the inanity in one place or time. That is to say, if *only* the direct cause of concern for human health from spiritual practice was limited to hospitals with Christian Science patients and hidden cult abuse in the world!—alas, the examples abound even to the ridiculousness of *self*-torture. In a lighter sense known as penance, ancient monks and devout followers would punish themselves for sin or otherwise abhorrent actions in the eyes of god by fasting or engaging in extreme manual labor for unhealthy periods of time, being abstinent, remaining silent, and practicing self-flagellation. The ancient practice of castration called on certain devout men to have their testes ceremoniously removed before entering monastic life or office that required the social tact of an impotent man. Keep in mind that this barbarism was performed as early as the Sumerians, almost 2,000 years before Christ, when such a procedure was sure to be extraordinarily painful and potentially fatal. Many times, eunuchs also served as servants or slaves to powerful men, deigning to do the lowest and most humble jobs required—similar to the chores and baseness of monastic life— all willingly done in the name of humility, self-sanctioned, and sought after.

These practices morphed into something entirely more sadomasochistic and disturbing in the modern bloom of Opus Dei, made most commercially popular and known by the best-selling book *The Da Vinci Code*. Opus Dei is a strict, conservative Catholic sect instituted circa ninety years ago, whose most unsettling and publicly discussed applications are their extreme penances, known to them as "corporal mortification," designed to increase celibacy, promote psychological awareness, and give continuous reminders of the pain that Christ suffered, several methods of which were once practiced commonly by priests in the ancient Catholic Church. Now they are required regularly in order to be a member of this secretive and elite echelon of holy men. In it, a priest is required to wear a *cilice* (a gruesome, medieval-looking chain adorned with spikes) around the left thigh for two hours a day, penetrating the tender muscle with the steel, which digs deeper and causes intense pain when those particular thigh muscles become taught during arousal; utilize once a week a discipline, a whip-like device used to self-flagellate the back or soft buttock tissue, sometimes pulling the skin directly from the body or lacerating it, leaving long, harsh welts and open bleeding; partake in cold showers; abstain from seasoning or condiment in meals or drinks; and remain silent during the night.[15] Mandates of various levels of cruelty have always been a staple of the Catholic faith, but Opus Dei adopts its policies with such rigor that it often makes even other theists feel a chill run down their spines.

The lunacy of self-torture is surprisingly not reserved for men of the cloth—those who consider themselves especially devout will engage in whatever display they best think exemplifies their appreciation for Christ's pain, even to the level of direct imitation of it. During Good Friday in the Phillipines, ardent Christians *literally* crucify themselves, with masses (10,000 to be exact, all men and women whom I would been tempted to classify as "morbidly curious" at best or "sadistic" at worst) of community members watching in parade form. Several volunteers dress as Roman centurions (as badly depicted as how certain high school theaters might present their students as "Roman centurions") in the open air on a hill. Not just a few wildly religious fanatics—in any given year, as many as *seventeen* men and women of various ages have allowed themselves to be nailed through the hands and feet to crude crosses and hung there for extended periods of time. The ritual event dates back to the 1950s, and one of the men has even gone through it twenty-six times as of this writing, subjecting himself to the grisly torture out of love for the pain that Christ experienced for him.[16] That such an act is relished and lauded by a theistic community is ultimately unimaginable—I feel it would take a supreme lack of empathy not to look at a suffering human and wish to right the situation, no matter the objective. The idea of the historical Jesus perishing the way he had is a disheartening and gruesome story—and so beyond worshipping it ideally (which is macabre), why actually subscribe to and revive the same imagery everywhere?

In this instance, I reflect on a conservative Christian woman who I worked with in a hotel for a short time and a conversation we had about prime-time television. I was describing some of my favorite shows while she pursed her lips and glared. When I asked her if I had mentioned something offensive to her, she replied: "I would *never* allow my children to watch scenes of such violence. I'm a good Christian mother." Incidentally, the church which she and her family attended displayed in their front courtyard a massive wooden carving of Jesus on the cross, a piece so phenomenally detailed that one could count the number of exposed ribs torn into the light by the cruel talons of the scourges used to lacerate him, and the broken splinters of the thorns driven into his skull, complete with tears of blood and the messiah's mouth open in a heaven-directed scream of mercy. On further discussion of the matter, she intimated that they had gone as a family to see the Mel Gibson racial travesty called *The Passion of the Christ,* which apart from being farcically unashamed in its Shylock-ian depiction of the Jews as bloodthirsty and ravenous for the flesh of Jesus, was an exercise in gore that should have labeled it in cult-movie status on a level only Sam Raimi might have achieved. Upon this subject alone I wonder for many hours, trying to think of imageries that may be more violent, cruel, abominable, and inhuman than that of the Crucifixion—and mostly come up short. In fact, it would behoove one to remember that the very word to exemplify some of the greatest pain one mortal can experience—*excruciating*—comes from the derivatives of Western European philological influences describing the agony that Christ felt upon the cross. One looking to shield their children from brazen gore should hardly look to the Bible or the life of Jesus to find protection—and further contrary to the point instead demand that they eat his flesh and drink his blood. "Sinister," perhaps, falls short of description.

The Crucifixion presents an even more unfortunate premise with which I take great umbrage: that it was done for all living humans—myself included—as a benevolence from Christ and from god; that I need to take this sacrifice at full value because it was done with me in mind. This is a flagrant imposition on my liberty. I certainly did not *ask* for a man to be cruelly tortured in the Middle East in my name, and am completely allowed to feel insulted if one implies I should have. I refuse to be pleased that it happened, at any rate. I can, thankfully, take great consolation in that in never occurred at all.

Thus, I frequently cheer on the actions of the fictional character Frank Strang in the masterful piece by Peter Shaffer, *Equus,* who, apart from his motivation of being an atheist, tears down a picture of Christ in chains from his son's bedroom wall on account of the graphic and brutal nature of the rendition. The boy's subsequent behaviors emulate many fanatic religious actions, not limited to beating himself with a clothes hanger to identify with the pain his new horse-god felt as being whipped with a crop. Incidentally, *Equus* proves to be a disturbingly powerful comment on the potential dangers of veneration and the conflict that occurs when faith becomes obsession, both for those who have it and those who *want* it—and I am sure not many could deny that the act of annual self-crucifixion is hardly less satisfying than blinding six horses with a metal spike.[17]

Of course, the historical notions of people being tortured for the sake of theism run rampant, not only limited to actions of age or need or race, but even to mental illness. According to Beatriz Quintanilla of the Department of Psychology at the Universidad Panamericana in Mexico City, the bubonic plague was mostly to blame for the widespread paradigm that illness of most sorts was the cause of supernatural forces working malevolently against the people walking the waking earth, and were incurable by man's medicine.[18] The idea was that only the power of the devil on earth could cause such horrible travesties, and those responsible for channeling it must be severely punished (not quite unlike the blame the Religious Right set on AIDS as being divine retribution to the homosexual community in the 1980s). Thus was born the *Malleus Maleficarum* (The Witches' Hammer), a manual that specifically instructed on the identification, capture, and punishment of all those deemed witches both in the New and Old Worlds. This manual was also severely sexist, saying that women were inferior to men and therefore easier targets for the influence of the devil. Add to the notion that epilepsy was an established disease in the 1600s and those women who suffered from seizures were typed into the image of casting spells and were interrogated and killed by the Church for practicing the evil craft, and one gleans a general idea of how thorough and accurate the Church's style of witch-hunting actually was.

The number of how many of the mentally invalid were killed on this charge is unknown, but enough documented cases remain to know that those who did indeed suffer from mental illness were among the first to be suspected of witchcraft. The understanding of viral biology and germ theory might have saved thousands of lives if only mastered a few hundred years sooner—that and the fields of psychiatry and neurology. Alas, while each time a new forefront of our knowledge is reached, we must look back on the horrors that occurred without it and lament for the foolishness of those who came before, while mourning the fate of those heliocentric heretics and unabashed anatomists.

On the subject of neurology and seizure, a remarkable advance has been made in the neurological field to suggest we have some notion of where god exists *in* the brain. In this brave new field called neurotheology, scientists attempt to discover how neural processes affect our perception and belief of all spiritual activity, with some intriguing results. Similar to the studies that have shown the increase of dimethyltryptamine from the pineal gland leads to drastic increases in what are commonly and generically called "spiritual experiences," specific cases involving seizures in the temporal lobe of the brain have shown dramatic elevation in the same kind of experience, along with obsessions of religion, leading to questions of the susceptibility of people not typically adherent to belief in religion or other supernatural phenomena to change their minds if afflicted. Vilayanur Ramachandran (one of the leading neuroscientists in the world and a special name in my list of heroes) conducted a study in 1997 to test this very hypothesis.[19] His results, after showing patients various words connected with sexual arousal and religiosity and measuring their reactions using the galvanic skin response, showed that patients with temporal lobe epilepsy had heightened reactions to them—suggesting the correlation between this localized epilepsy and religious experience and belief. Naturally, more testing needs to be done in this area, though I would not be surprised if in the years to come we were to find the specific cognitive function, neuro-transmittal composition, and perhaps defined location of thought processes required for religiosity, much like the definition of other delusional patterns of cognition, like paranoia and schizophrenia.

Without a doubt, if Moses came down Mount Sinai today and said to the world that god had just spoken with him and that he was the prophet of the lord, his bed in any mental institution would be made before the hour was over—likewise in any other situation. Had I leaned into you over the water-cooler at work and intimated that I had a message for you from god, it is likely the word "insanity" would pop into your brain with far more conviction than "divine messenger." (In this, I am cheerfully reminded of the old joke, "If you talk to god, you're praying. If god talks back, you're crazy.") Let us not forget that when we first meet John the Baptist in chapter 3 of Matthew, he is wandering the wilderness dressed in camel skin around his loins, eating locusts and shouting prophecy—sound like any New York City street corner to you? It bears thinking on whether every religious experience one has ever had in the history of mankind is, in fact, a symptom of mental illness—a note of irony for those mentally handicapped killed in the name of the Church as witches and heretics—and, if it were true, I would be inclined to find poetic justice in the idea that most of the world's population unquestionably follow the words of ancient madmen. It goes without saying that if, during any time in my life after the publication of this book I become a believer and renounce all my former claims, let this be a plea in writing to first have my temporal lobe checked for seizure activity before people begin to take me seriously (if, as I would hope *not*, they do at all . . .).

**"You Sign Your Place and Calling, in Full Seeming,
With Meekness and Humility; But Your Heart Is Cramm'd
with Arrogancy, Spleen, and Pride"**
—Katherine, *Henry VIII* (II.IV.118–120)

Often, I am tempted to assert that the single greatest evil religion bestows upon a mass of people who frankly deserve better is the mandate of complete psychological slavery. There becomes a massively caging device about the central idealism of religion, in that it attempts to dissipate the desire (or, in many cases, forbids the inclination) to *ask questions*. "No further answer is needed—it's all in this book. This is how you live, how you learn, how you think—dissent and suffer the punishment on your own accord." In connection with the previous section, this scrutiny almost makes me feel a pang of pity in my heart for those deluded (seemingly on an insane level) enough to give themselves away to such moral and ethical tyranny. Still, it becomes much easier to understand the relative mind-frames of those willing to strap bombs to themselves and blow up abortion clinics or fly airplanes into skyscrapers—not only their hell-bent, stubborn need to see the pages and mandates and sermons they have been fed as an absolute affirmation of the meaning of life, but also their complete inability to register an opposing or different view or thought as potential for objective understanding—let alone truth. Robin Williams wittily surmised of fundamentalists: "Couldn't 'Let there be light!' have even been a *metaphor* for the Big Bang? . . . Nah, God jus' went 'click.'"[20] This type of deranged thinking lends itself to what I *yearn* to call psychological illness—though I somehow doubt the American Psychological Association will see my point and list "Religiosity" as a classified mental malady in the next edition of the Diagnostic and Statistical Manual of Mental Disorders.

Those who disagree that one can't be superreligious and open-minded simultaneously have only to remember the literal translation of the word "Islam" to mean "surrender" or "subservience" and the five-step repentance process of the Jewish *teshuvá*—or to look at the various printed examples by the former to see a violent exclusion of the latter, as per Cardinal Newman in his book *History of My Religious Opinions from 1833 to 1839:*

> *It would be a gain to the country were it vastly more superstitious, more bigoted, more gloomy, more fierce in its religion than at present it shows itself to be . . . From the age of fifteen, dogma has been the fundamental*

principle of my religion: I know of no other religion; I cannot enter into the idea of any other sort of religion.

The psychological and mental bent required to have faith may be just as unhealthy and problematic as the physical prostrations often displayed by theists. Most notably, I would like to remark upon an observation of pride that is, most commonly, attributed to atheists in the respect that "we know everything" and claim to hold the secrets of the origin of the universe in our nifty little chemistry books. This could not be more inaccurate, as even the greatest astrophysicists and studiers of quantum mechanics have quite blatantly stated we have only begun to scratch the surface of the origins of the universe (and potential multiverse) in which we live. Hitchens perhaps worded it most perfectly, in that we are quickly discovering how *little* we know, but that we "at least know less and less about more and more."[21] This is the opinion that most public atheists have, and despite the newest, most provocative, and indeed courageous claims about the actual ability to disprove the existence of god, much like Victor Stenger's work *God: The Failed Hypothesis*,[22] one can see the former train of thought being the standard.

That being the case, it becomes very obvious that the arrogance with which we are prescribed is unduly hypocritical, as theists *do* claim to know the origins of the universe and even the bent to which it is intended, not to mention the idea that life was only possible through divine creation and that despite the literal universe of chaos and destruction surrounding us for billions of light years, it is part of a design with us and only us in mind. Furthermore, that each of them has a speed-dial in their heads to this magnanimous being who listens to their thoughts ad nauseum and with infinite care, and will, in fact, intervene in the natural laws of reality specifically to aid them or hinder their enemies. This type of conceit breeds a world of consequence in psychological health that borders on asinine, such as the string of human sacrifices in Burma intended to sanctify a city, only to find the graves of two of those 56 sacrifices later empty; the remedy decided was to sacrifice 500 more innocent souls, about one-fifth of whom were successful before the British government intervened,[23] or the thousands of people in Aztec society who were killed every year in order to appease the gods and keep the sun rising, or the slaughter of crying children designed to summon rain. If one *believes unequivocally* that their answer rests in a god who sets divine commandments for them to do such things, any horrific outcome is possible. In the course of a moment, holy people become murderers, and deluded ones at that.

Another sickening cog in the machine of mental subservience is the mandate for not only the introduction of—but also the loving acceptance of!—fear. Apart from acknowledging that fear of a divine dictator is required for the perfect acquisition of a complete faith, holy texts even go so far as to insinuate all good things otherwise begin in a compelled terror of one's own god: Proverbs 9:10 works as a perfectly repugnant illustration of this— *"The fear of the Lord is the beginning of wisdom, and knowledge of the Holy One is understanding."* Maimonides was equal in this assumption, insisting that the 3rd and 4th of the Jewish Commandments, or *Mitzvot,* were to "love" god, then to "fear" him. Or the final sentiment of Job: "The fear of the Lord— that is wisdom." How terse and unenlightening this concept is, as the end of Ecclesiastes states: "Fear God, and keep his commandments, for this is the whole duty of man." So sadly unoriginal in romantic terrorism Machiavelli now seems—monotheism had ruled his panic-inducing paradigm long before the most famous topic of *The Prince* had ever invaded his sadistic head. The general unfortunate clamor of this device is entirely too visible—and brutally successful.

Young children are admonished that self-pleasure will cause eye issues, or feelings of sexual intimacy of one kind or another will lead to eternal torment, and are forced to watch bloody depictions of a man suffering a primeval torture. Girls are repressed from showing even so much as their skin, let alone their personalities, and are forbidden freedoms of choice in almost every life circumstance that most of us take for granted in the Western World. Harold Camping shouted from the airwaves that the Rapture was coming on May 21, 2011, and select families and religious groups went into hysterics, selling their possessions and bankrupting their futures, only for the Day of Reckoning to uneventfully arrive without the Four Horsemen of the Apocalypse and leave Camping with one massive Easter egg on his face.[24] Buddhist monks set themselves ablaze in fiery protest to the Roman Catholic influence of the administration of President Ngo Dinh Diem in South Vietnam.[25] Everywhere one looks, signs of irrationality pervade whenever the subject of god or his word or the word of his prophet pushes its way to the forefront, causing those who believe in it to act as expectantly as someone in asylum—hearing voices that do not exist, seeing things that are not there, and performing the very actions that those nonexistent voices persuade them to do.

As well, religiosity forces an otherwise healthy mind to see things where they are not *outside* of their own perception. Long gone are the centuries where priests around the world gleaned the knowledge of the eclipse and the flood and the wax and wane of the moon and cowed those only slightly more ignorant with their holy fervor—or are they? One would imagine falsely that these absurd showcases of religious masturbation do not occur today, but they do occur—in some cases, far more fraudulently. It is by this same delusion that we hear of the face of Jesus appearing in everyday objects from toast to sidewalk cracks, or feel the presence of the holy work in sanguinely weeping statues; the Virgin Mary birthed from water stains on weather-proof siding; ancient Samurai warriors in the backs of common crabs. Similarly, we also see the manifestation of the stigmata and other paranormal occurrences. Or in the case of extreme disasters, much like the aberration mentioned in regard to Falwell's blame on homosexuals and secularists for the September 11 attacks, attributing otherwise human or benign events to acts of god, in revelation or in retribution. The ability to see these things for what they are *not* is not a blessing of divine right nor is it a testament to the existence of the thing believed to be, but rather a warping of the perception of the witness—and when made unfalsifiable, bears more weight on an ignorant community than ever. On this trajectory, I could just as easily say that the travesty of September 11 was actually the wrath of god on America because we allow people like Jerry Falwell to make public orations, and I would in no way, form, or reason ever deign to believe that such a crude and improvable statement was correct—but I would be just as *not* wrong as he.

I remember with clarity the very moment I realized my own atheism—though I might wish to argue that I have never had a belief in god or the supernatural that extended beyond my days of magical fights against imaginary Balrogs or sitting in church for the pleasure of being close with my friends who came from devout families. This epiphany occurred when I was eleven years old, and I had just journeyed by Greyhound bus for two days from my home in Somers, Montana, to Palm Springs, California, to meet my father for the first time. I was accompanied by my mother, who had not spoken to my biological father since my birth, and the man himself had only been warned of my coming the night of our arrival. The reason for the delay of this father-son relationship bears drama worthy of a soap opera, so I shall do you the courtesy of skipping over it—however it requires mentioning that this was an unexpected and grave event for both of us, which had the potential of going several different ways emotionally. Thankfully, I was too young and naïve to understand the full impact of it or to be afraid, and therefore was mostly optimistic.

Let me just say, I hit the jackpot when it comes to impromptu families. My father and his branch of the brood accepted me with open arms, kisses, and hugs, and it didn't take me long to realize that they were people of a much firmer faith than I had ever been involved with (my mother's side of the family was secular only by social habitat, indulging in activities and lifestyles that might not have been readily admitted by conservative faiths); my grandmother had even written several large manuscripts on Bible study, which I have subsequently read and for which I must thank her profusely (saddened as she may be to see how the knowledge has ripened) for my education of biblical literature. My grandmother, the evening that I met her first, pulled me into her arms and gave me the warmest, longest hug I have since received in my life, and whispered the following words in my ear: "Jesus brought you to me. Thank God . . . Thank God that He brought you to me."

The initial impact of these words was severe and life-changing. I kept my reactions well hidden because my love for these new familial influences was instantaneous and I would never have bordered a response that would have upset or insulted these people who decided to love me unconditionally the moment I stepped in their door without second's notice (indeed, I kept that mindset as absolute and as stubbornly as possible, even only "coming out" to my father very recently, while in the beginning attempts at tinkering with this book). But, during the entire two-day trip by bus that we agonizingly endured to return home (my mother and I, that is), I found myself continuously thinking of my grandmother's first words to me, and—I'm ashamed to say if only in a semantic context—the unfairness of them. (Keep in mind that I was eleven, and had not yet gained an appropriate grasp of empathy—though many close people who love me today would argue that, at least in an artistic sense, I still haven't grasped it.)

Jesus had not brought me to them, nor vice versa. *I* did it—that fact was obstinately clear and repetitive in my mind. When the events leading up to going to California had manifested themselves, I was left as the sole judiciary party as to what would happen with this new knowledge of who my father was. What was I to do? Call him? Meet him? Ignore he existed and continue on with my life? After all, I had gone eleven years without him, and with a perfectly loving and supportive step-father. Was traveling so far to contact a complete stranger worth the effort it would demand? Even at a young age, my theatrical manner was evident, and I labored in a week of pacing and silent, pensive thought before making my decision: I wanted to meet him. I wanted to know him. And I wanted whatever consequences evolved from it. The decision was solely on me and me alone—and as an eleven-year-old boy only can I shouldered such responsibility with undue pride, but never once questioned the motivation until my darling grandmother whispered to me those spiritual sentiments. Was all that thought pre-ordained? Did I have control over none of it, or was I merely under the impression that I had been the entire time? What use was that effort, that deliberation, those worries, if all the time my deductive and sympathetic thought process was being controlled by the Invisible Sky Wizard? *I* made the decision, and I was proud of it. It was mine, and mine alone. These were incredibly heavy thoughts for a lad of my age and bright temperament to bear.

In that moment, I knew what it was to not believe in god, and for *none* of the justifications that would eventually come from seeing the world and its social movements in a mature manner—it was born from a moment of pure, unadulterated logic; some*thing* else had been given credit for a product I knew had been original to *me*. And while I would never suppose this argument as a reason for the lack of faith in god in a testimonial or religious debate, I hold onto the memory now as an anecdotal originator of what would become something much more solid and grounded; the initial spark that caused the inferno that burned away faith in my head, devoid of solipsism or even evidence, but from a very clear observation in an otherwise untainted young mind of what had *obviously* happened against what other people *thought* had happened. Much like the proverbial, brilliant musical performer once said: "When people tell me, 'God has blessed you with the gift of music', you're damn right I get offended. I did not practice hours a day for eighteen years to have my success attributed to a myth." I imagine that it is by this same, harmless process that young children commonly ask confounding and ultimately annoying questions about morality and god almost every day to parents and teachers who can provide no contextual answer, where contradiction is so transparent to someone who has no overlapping bias against it. *Tabula rasa* may certainly be the greatest gift we are given as children.

My grandmother had no more reason to believe that Jesus was responsible for our meeting than Michele Bachmann did to believe that he was just as responsible for Hurricane Irene, or the ancient Aztecs did to believe that blood sacrifices to their deities kept crops growing. They just *chose* to, expressly against the objective observations that might have yielded otherwise more solid results. And what would they—and indeed, every other believer in the manifestation of the divine in the natural world—have done if the contrary had been explained to them? If I mentioned that god wasn't responsible?

The Aztecs might have killed the person who uttered such blasphemy. Well publicized politicians would have made slanderous remarks about the same person, much like Bush, Sr. did when referring to atheists as unworthy of being called patriots, inviting them to don the mantles of social pariahs. My grandmother, who I love as much or more than any other living person on this earth, would have smiled and laughed and gently wiped away such a contrary remark, quickly forgetting it. But none of them—*none* of them—would have taken a fraction of a second to contemplate the fact that it might be *true*. None of them would have bothered. This is the psychological slavery which I so vehemently oppose and despise in the ideal of religion as a living entity on this earth. It ultimately confines while presenting the illusion of liberation, and the very people most afflicted by it are the ones least aware.

Such a deplorable train of thought is made more insidious still in reference to religion's need to thrust itself onto the promontory of public education. Though, thankfully, the American legislative system has (barely) been able to keep creationism and its pathetically uninventive clone "intelligent design" (giving the illusion that there is anything intelligent about it at all) out of most school rooms, fundamentalist parties clamor for the teaching of god's invention of the universe with more vigor for every defeat. While I may find the idea of human beings living alongside dinosaurs whimsical to a degree, I cannot hope to fathom that it ever occurred, nor that the earth—which has evidenced billions of years of cooling and changing—has been around for the mere thousands of years since the very *literal* creation of Adam and Eve in what some theological "experts" claim took place only 6,000 years ago. This pedestal of senselessness, often referred to by the highly oxymoronic study of "creation science," bears little objective evidence in basis of anthropology, geology, and biology, but radical morons like George McCready Price, a devout Seventh-day Adventist (another faith whose leader, much akin to the prophetic disgrace of Harold Camping, founded his infamy on cryptic "coding" of Bible dates which were supposed to lead to a grand, divine revolution that turned out to be hysterically anticlimactic), and Governor William Haslam of Tennessee have paved the way for it to be presented to children in an educational setting.

In early 2012, the Tennessee State Legislature signed into law a bill that allowed the "teaching" of ulterior methods from mainstream scientific discoveries as explanations for a variety of topics—most notably the creation of humankind and evolution—if they are brought up by a student.[26] Supporters of the bill hid behind the thin guise of wanting students to become skeptics and breeding objective thought, but this lie is apparent when considering that the only discussed alternative to evolution and Darwinism is divine creation, and in a hugely fundamentalist state it becomes very difficult to hide that boastful motivation. In what was perhaps the most concise explanation of the opposition, the National Association of Geoscience Teachers issued a statement: "Invoking non-naturalistic or supernatural events or beings are not scientific in character, do not conform to the scientific usage of the word 'theory,' and should not be part of valid science curricula."[27] This is the very crux of the objective, rational sentiment and bears nothing to the accusation of creationism being taught as *anything*—but as an *alternative* to proven or evidenced theory. Trying to teach theology as a science is exactly as futile as conducting a religious war to promote world peace—there is no place for it. Abandoning the study of religious ideals altogether would be nearly impossible in a country where the vast majority identifies with faith, but places for religious study exist outside of the taxpayers' classroom. Christian schools abound in the United States—parents who desire their children to know nothing of the natural world can just as easily send them there, destructive as that may be. Equally as incensed are those who could argue that the passing of this bill violates the First Amendment's promise of no law respecting the establishment of religion, but naturally that invokes a semantic debate of which there will likely be no end.

In states not accentuated by such legislature, the argument is equally as bizarre. In Louisiana, thousands of children are receiving *publicly funded grants* to attend private schools of their choice for a year where the Accelerated Christian Education curriculum has been instituted—the primary facet of which proselytizes young students to a fundamentalist mind-frame by teaching that Darwinism is false under the supposition that dinosaurs are still alive today, the obviously conclusive proof is that the Loch Ness Monster otherwise known as "Nessie" exists and "scientific proof" shows us she (because we also know the sex of the mythical beast) is a plesiosaur, a marine dinosaur that went extinct during the late Cretaceous Period claw-in-claw with the pterosaur and tyrannosaur. This is tied with similar claims that Japanese fishing boats have caught dinosaurs (I've yet to see a record of this outside of the Godzilla franchise) and that the terrible lizards were, in fact, fire-breathing dragons, making the curriculum similar to what researcher Bruce Wilson referred to as "medieval scholasticism." Not only are these programs funded by the public, but they also contain equally ridiculous propitiations of books that laud the Klu Klux Klan and the pseudo-scientific conclusion that homosexuality is a learned behavior. The notion that such painfully ill-bred harangues are not only tax-furnished but mandated by parents who have no worldly idea of evolutionary science or necessary education to children who have no idea of their human right to know better or to ask for objective edification is abominable. It is ultimately synonymous with child abuse.[28] Of course, these are students whom fundamentalist Christians do not withdraw out of the school system entirely and instead give them routine indoctrination, but consider that 75% of all home-schooled children in the United States are evangelical Christians. This huge concentration and purposeful isolation from secular thought parallels the Hasidic Jewish community in North London who send their children so exclusively through Jewish institutions that many grow up with accents completely unidentifiable to surrounding neighborhoods. (*"Get them while they're young, Evita! Get them while they're young."*) [29]

Suffice it to say that it is a foul world indeed that zealous idealism becomes permissible in a classroom where—no matter which side of the ideological spectrum the pendulum may have swung in this universe—objective thought should be the only mainstay. Again, I can only repeat the sentiment I have listed several times already: if sufficient evidence existed even to make the influence of god a rational theory, one would be happy to accept it as a nature of study, where now it only exists as supposed extrapolation. As it stands, it becomes a belief that deviates from the norm of natural observation and the scientific method, and therefore should exist privately only, not as a toxin to the already polluted world of public education. Instead, it is exalted in such infantile wastes of architecture and endorsement as the Creation Museum in Petersburg, Kentucky, which shows animatronic children with incredibly modern facial bone structures kneeling at ponds saddled next to baby tyrannosaurs, and offers guided tours of "biblical history" where one archeologist (most likely an actor) says that he believes a particular fossil to be only 4,300 years old—left there since the purging of Noah's flood. This poison of rational thought comes indeed from the same people who profess the existence of dinosaur bones as a test of our faith from god, and fall upon the insufferable argument of asking us to prove that it *isn't* so. Rather . . . prove I don't have superpowers. Or that the teapot isn't really in orbit. Or even (though I hate to debase myself to this argument even in analogy) prove that evolution *isn't* true. Thankfully, research is beginning to show us why this phenomenon exists. Evidence has surfaced suggesting that this inability to look at logical reason and this denial of empirical evidence to its face is actually an evolved trait used to defend oneself against the manipulations of motivational beings, i.e., if a rational person can use logic and empiricism to promote *any* message for his own means, one can implacably adopt a stance of *irrationality* and *believe* it in order to remain from being swayed. In a world where we no longer have to adapt to strength but to ideas, it is the fight response to those who would otherwise have the power to convince us of anything.[30] Apart from being another facet of a sadly unexposed psyche, this potential also proves to be a philosophical pain in the ass, simply because it *literally* can't be reasoned with, no matter what can be proven to be true or false—one operating under this supposition is cognitively compelled to deny all evidence, no matter how legitimate. This is also antithesis to the scientific method, which makes those whose brains labor under this parietal and nearly synesthesic delusion abhorrently unfit to teach such a method in public (or otherwise) education.

I don't imply that education necessarily posits itself *only* on what is objectively right and wrong—but we do know that faith is *not* correlated with a high IQ, and those attempting strong academic careers might equip themselves better without it. In fact, atheism *is* a much more involved intellectual practice. In another study also listed by Dawkins and presented at several of his lectures, Larson and Witham published in *Nature* that only 7% of National Academy of Sciences (NAS) members (the elite group of scientists and top minds in the United States) in 1998 believed in what we could refer to as a modern definition of god, with still a strong majority of 60% siding with godlessness out of those polled *not* within the NAS.[31] Professor Dawkins also mentions that in his search for believers among several hundred Nobel Prize–winning scientists, only *six* of them were claimed to have been believers, with doubt even for the proof of *that* many. These renowned men and women of their fields, contributors to the world and to the expansion of human knowledge, are certainly *not* the ones advocating for the study of creationism in schools, nor did they benefit from the pursuit of such rubbish. Not to paint a garishly totalitarian picture of who is smart and who is dumb and which side of the ideological spectrum they fall upon, but those scientists who have looked into it seem to have found the very same conclusion. However, I don't think it's exclusive; I don't think I am a genius for being an atheist any more than I think people are Neanderthals for being Christian—but operating under the assumption that snakes can't talk and people don't rise from the dead probably gives us an advantage.

Notes

1. Joseph R. Tybor, "Spiritual Healing on Trial in Christian Science Case," *Chicago Tribune*, November 20, 1988.

2. David Margolick, "In Child Deaths, a Test for Christian Science," *New York Times*, August 6, 1990.

3. H. Benson et al., "Study of the Therapeutic Effects of Intercessory Prayer (STEP) in Cardiac Bypass Patients," *American Heart Journal* 151, no. 4 (2006): 934–42.

4. Sophie Goodchild, "Satanic Abuse No Myth, Says Experts," *Independent*, April 30, 2000, http://www.independent.co.uk/news/uk/this-britain/satanic-abuse-no-myth-say-experts-721359.html.

5. "Admitted Satanist in Court for Child Abuse," NewsChannel5.com, February 16, 2012, http://www.newschannel5.com/story/16955373/admitted-satanist-in-court-for-child-abuse.

6. Anton LaVey, *The Satanic Bible* (Avon Books, 1969).

7. Ironically, though very clearly a "religious" sect, the LaVeyan Satanists have no belief in god or the devil as spiritual deities, making them almost atheistic by definition. This is one of the more tangled subject concerning the difference between faith and religion.

8. "Benjamin Edetanlen Sentenced to 18 Years, Defends Killing Son with Bible Passage," *Huffington Post*, October 12, 2012, http://www.huffingtonpost.com/2012/10/12/benjamin-edetanlen-sentence-bible_n_1961602.html.

9. God actually allows pregnant women to be ripped open in all kinds of grotesque manner in 2 Kings, Hosea, and Amos. He also approves and demands the killing of children in Numbers, Deuteronomy, Psalms, Isaiah, and Hosea.

10. "Nigerian 'Witch Doctor' Claims to Have Killed 110 Children 'Possessed by Evil Spirits,'" *Telegraph*, December 3, 2008.

11. Patrick Counihan, *Irish Central,* "Irish Priests Say They Will Disobey New Confession Box Laws on Child Abuse," April 26, 2012.

12. See Greg Hernandex, "Listen to a Pastor's Horrifying Advice: You're Your Son If He Acts Feminine, Make Your Daughter Feminine If She's Butch," GregInHollywood.com, May 1, 2012, http://greginhollywood.com/listen-to-a-pastors-horrifying-advice-beat-your-son-if-he-acts-feminine-your-daughter-if-shes-butch-67533?utm_source=feedburner&utm_medium=feed&utm_campaign=Feed%3A+greginhollywood+%28Greg+In+Hollywood%29.

13. *Jesus Camp*, SnagFilms, 2006

14. Susan Donaldson, "Baby Dies of Herpes in Ritual Circumcision Performed By Orthodox Jews," News Channel 12, ABC, March 12, 2012, http://www.wcti12.com/news/30658126/detail.html.

15. Opus Dei Awareness Network, May 13, 2002, http://www.odan.org/corporal_mortification.htm.

16. Rob Cooper, "Christians NAILED to Crosses in Gruesome Good Friday Re-enactment of Jesus's Death in the Phillipines," *Mail Online*, April 6, 2012, http://www.dailymail.co.uk/news/article-2126024/Christians-NAILED-crosses-gruesome-Good-Friday-enactment-Jesuss-death-Philippines.html.

17. I would highly recommend those curious to read or view a production of this show, as it portrays in a very unique sense and beautiful fashion the widespread pain that is originated by worship.

18. Beatriz Quintanilla, "Witchcraft or Mental Illness?" *Psychiatric Times*, June 21, 2010, http://www.psychiatrictimes.com/schizoaffective/content/article/10168/1596272.

19. V. S. Ramachandran and Sandra Blakeslee, *Phantoms in the Brain* (William Morrow, 1998).

20. Robin Williams, *Live on Broadway*, Cream Cheese Films, 2002

21. Christopher Hitchens, *God Is Not Great* (Twelve Books, 2007), p. 9.

22. Mr. Stenger's work, for what it is worth, does give the greatest assimilation of this argument that I think is possible—if there was a legitimate way to prove the nonexistence of god, he has accomplished it.

23. James A. Haught, "Holy Horrors," 1990.

24. Garence Burke, "Harold Camping Admits He Was Wrong about the End of the World Prediction," *Huffington Post*, March 9, 2012.

25. "On This Day: 1966—Vietnam Buddhist Burns to Death," BBC News, June 24, 2012, http://news.bbc.co.uk/onthisday/hi/dates/stories/may/31/newsid_2973000/2973209.stm.

26. Elizabeth Flock, "Law Allows Creationism to Be Taught in Tenn. Public Schools," *Washington Post*, April 11, 2012.

27. Simon Brown, "Tennessee Bill to Push Creationism in Schools," Opposingviews.com, March 20, 2012. http://www.opposingviews.com/i/religion/christianity/tennessee-bill-push-creationism-schools.

28.   Rachel Loxton, "How American Fundamentalist Schools Are using Nessie to Disprove Evolution," *Herald-Scotland*, June 24, 2012.

29.   Lyrics from *Evita*, by Andrew Lloyd Webber and Tim Rice.

30.   C. Cohen, "Reason Seen More as Weapon Than Path to Truth," *New York Times,* June 14, 2011.

31.   E. J. Larson and L. Witham, "Leading Scientists Still Reject God," *Nature* 394 (1998): 313.

5

Morality and Myth

———————◆♦◆———————

"There is nothing good or bad, but thinking makes it so."
—William Shake-speare, *Hamlet*

"You can never find a Christian who has acquired this valuable knowledge, this saving knowledge, by any process but the everlasting and all-sufficient "people say." In all my seventy-two years and a half I have never come across such another ass as this human race is."
—Mark Twain's Autobiography

Icarus stood on the cliff's edge, his glorious wings uplifted.

"Do not fly too close to the sun," he was told by his father, who had crafted the beautiful, feathery appendages. "For then your wings will melt, as they are made of wax."

But Icarus was filled with the passion of man's ambition—his heart yearned to soar, and with a daring leap, he swooped into the open air over the Mediterranean, gliding on thermals and slicing through clouds. Crete lay as a distant speck behind him. Then, bursting with the inspiration of standing with the gods, Icarus climbed into the air. Before long, the far-reaching rays of the hot, Apollo-driven sun touched grimly upon his lovely wings, and indeed the wax began to melt. Ere he could save himself, the wings fell apart in a dismal wreck, and Icarus, flailing, plummeted the thousands of feet over which he was mere moments before the master, and perished in the tossing, merciless waves of the sea.

The story of Icarus is a piece of mythology well known and often cited as an example of hubris or overreaching mortal ambition. Many such stories imitate the same theme, again in Greek culture with that of Phaethon and his father's sun-chariot; King Uzziah's curse of leprosy for thinking himself worthy to light the incense at the altar of god in 2 Chronicles; the tale of the pride of Babel in Genesis of the Pentateuch; even the tortoise and the hare.

But what do we learn? The purpose of any morality tale is, and always has been, to provide us with a definitive example of an anti-hero—to learn from his mistakes. ("Learn Your Lessons Well" from Stephen Schwartz's *Godspell* readily gets stuck in my head at the thought.) But morality tales have crucial flaws within them often overlooked by the casual listener, and provide excellent insight for those willing to dig a little bit: (1) they are constructed backward, devised to get specifically to their desired doctrine with clearly structured plots; (2) they serve as staples for cultural faiths and social paradigms that may or may not be expressive of the truth; and (3) they are all fictional, and therefore more easily subject to the bias of the teller. Yet, somehow, these myths have become infinitely more than mere folktale and entertainment from a time long before television and musicals and *Jersey Shore* (though I would happily take Icarus's fate over viewing a single episode of that monstrosity): they are the parables that make up some of the most notable holy books and lessons in monotheistic history.

Referring to Christian, Islamic, and Jewish literature as "mythology" as opposed to "history" still ruffles a lot of feathers—and I have never understood this apprehension, even from the truly devout. It serves as poignant a reason to tell someone of the wonder of Jesus' "love" whether or not he actually existed, or of the blind faith of Jonah while residing in the big fish (apparently, many theological scholars vehemently oppose the use of the word "whale"). One must take into account the singular definition of "history" against "mythology'" and since very little (in many cases, *no*) evidence exists to corroborate most of the actions and/or persons among monotheistic literatures, we must assume that they are not historical and refer to them exactly as they are, not as they aren't. This notion has been highly played up by other writers on atheism and anti-theism, often using the adage to believers: "You are, in fact, an atheist, too. You don't believe in Zeus or Krishna or Hecate, and nor do I. I just believe in one god less than you—for all the same reasons you don't believe in them." Much the same way a Christian or a Muslim will haughtily refer to Hermes or Mithra or Romulus as a piece of fiction lost in mythology, so we must look at Jehovah and Allah and Yahweh with identical scrutiny. Somehow, I doubt that most believers will sympathize with that line of logic, but it bears bringing up nonetheless.

With the supposition that *most* of the biblical teachings we are familiar with are fictional (I say "most" because some evidence does exist of various places and events, and much more historical testimony supporting Islam, with Muhammad being a definitely more recent prophet—and with more identifiable trace of his life on Earth than Jesus), we must approach them as morality plays and parables, with the intention of divining what it is they are designed to teach. This is far more insightful and tricky than not, on account of wayward interpretations and fearful misunderstandings. But let us start simply: what does a story like Icarus teach us? Is it a tale truly meant to ward off the vicissitudes of pride and human ambition? I fear so, but in what respect? Flight was a divine power, reserved for the gods—man was not to touch it. We know of man's obsession with the art of flight and his prescription of the power to their deities in the manifestations of flight during various spouts of apotheosis—the Ascension is a perfect example. Icarus reaped the reward for achieving his dream—destruction. While the telling may not be so vividly harsh, we must remember that Icarus embodied a normal, naturally occurring human trait that resides in all of us: ambition—the need to grow, to stretch beyond, to achieve something infinitely above the scope of our imaginations. One should identify with Icarus, and pity him and his human innocence. Beyond this, I admire hubris: it takes haughty ambition to achieve what was thought, previous to your successes, to be impossible.

The purpose of the myth, tragically, is to illustrate his punishment for expressing those very human and understandable yearnings. And with the recognition of this theme, we see it *everywhere*—those who seek to learn, to better themselves, to expand and grow wondrously in a theistic world are continuously cast down and punished by the divines in power. Eventually, we find a thick string of connection running from the ancient Talmudic writings all the way through the more modern advent of the Book of Mormon and Doctrine and Covenants: submission in the face of god(s) for no other crime than for being ourselves.

Before we expound upon that, it would well behoove me to head off the theist argument at the beginning and explain my own musings. After all, says the theist, without these stories and mandates and credos, without the *hadith* and the *Mitzvot* and the beatitudes (which are ultimately a long line of bribes and threats), where do we get morality? In America, our deist forefathers have stated that they are the gift of our Creator, which is, naturally, a vague and unsubstantiated origin for our inalienable rights ("unalienable" was the term used on the actual document—either are exchangeable although former

President George W. Bush's "uninalienable" still doesn't hold water.[1]). How do we know what is right and wrong? God must tell us, they say. And, of course, into this argument is lumped the hopeless supposition of the idea of free will and the definition of good and evil. I hope to touch upon all these themes in this chapter, and perhaps stumble into an explanation plausible enough to seem convincing.

In his decently pointed book, *Parallel Myths*, J. F. Bierlein says entirely too absolutely: "Myth, especially codified in religion, has always been the basis for the morality of a society."[2] This concrete tack is too often explored by people who have a slight bias toward the spiritual or existential development of man, who began to look at the thunder and the earthquake and the flood with a fearful eye and wonder what had the power to make such things occur and why. Such a proclamation is made infinitely more heavily (and in my opinion, obtusely) by Émile Durkheim, whom Bierlein quotes:

> *For centuries morals and religion have been intimately linked and completely fused. Even today, one is bound to recognize this close association in the majority of minds. It is apparent that moral life has not been, and will never be, able to shed all the characteristics that it holds in common with religion. When the two orders of fact have been so closely linked, when there have been between them so close a relationship for so long a time, it is impossible for them to be dissociated and become distinct. For this to happen they would have to undergo complete transformation. There must, then, be morality in religion and religion in morality.*

It is clear that Durkheim maintained a rather unconfident view of the human race—as though we couldn't possibly survive without slaughtering one another and raping children in the absence of divine law, or that we will *never* be able to develop sophistication to the point of losing the godly training wheels. He seems to say that such a dream is *impossible*. This is an overwhelmingly insulting premise. Beyond that, the rough hyperbole of the length of time we have relied upon religious morality in order to be properly human is revolting—to say "for so long a time" and "has not been" is a gross overestimation of the length of our chronology that religion has poisoned human existence. For example, if we were to take Hammurabi's code (incidentally, a man who referred to himself both as the Shepherd and the Father of his people) as a basic starting point for the evolution of future moralities found in monotheism, circa 1772 BCE, we can approximate about 3,700 years of what we could conservatively call "religious morality." Extrapolating from a popular scenario posed by Christopher Hitchens and quoted at the beginning of this book, Richard Dawkins estimates that the human species in a relative evolved form has been around for 250,000 years; lead scientist of the Human Genome Project and Christian Francis Collins has a much more conservative guess of 100,000—either way, what we can intone as "religious morality," dating back even before the Decalogue, etc., covers only a *minor* percentage of human existence—*literally* 3.7% of it if we go by Collins's estimation. If we are to subscribe to the brutally infirm theories of Bierlein and Durkheim, we would have to forget the *96%* of human history that we lived without this assumption. Rather than remembering that the need to apply a hominid fashion to the phenomena developed from something social in the first place, they run with the extrapolation that humans began with such a conviction and forget to acknowledge the some hundreds of thousands of years of interpersonal growth before that—from which all of our subsequent observations are based.

Furthermore, one must remember that, while religion has supplied no method of morality that wasn't already innate in us, or was invented without its help, as we will discuss in this chapter, it *has* donated a considerable amount of savagery that, *only* in the words of the faithful, might be called good or moral. On the British television talk show *Q & A*, in March 2010, Richard Dawkins was asked of an audience member: "Considering that atheism cannot possibly have any sense of absolute morality, would it not then be an irrational leap of faith . . . for an atheist to decide between right and wrong?" To which Dawkins aptly replied: "Absolute morality that a religious person might profess would include—what? Stoning people for adultery? Death for apostasy? Punishment for breaking the Sabbath? These are all things which are religiously based absolute moralities. I don't think I want an absolute morality."

In order to understand morality, one must realize that *Homo sapiens* is an extraordinarily social creature, evolved to be that way from a primate family whose best work was performed as an ensemble. The growth of social evolution is very apparent in the model of the triune brain, watching the cerebral development from reptilian brain to midbrain (limbic system) to cerebral cortex, or higher-level human functioning. This model was coined by neuroscientist Paul MacLean in his work *The Triune Brain in Evolution*, as a working progression of the central nervous system in vertebrates. The evolution of our social function is primarily noted in the prefrontal cortex, which, as the most recent part of the brain to evolve and the latter piece to myelinate in our lifespan, is surprisingly small and working over the next eon to grow. Yet pieces of our animalistic past still remain, such as our propensity for weak knees from when we used to walk on all fours, the loss of body hair that at one point protected us from the searing African sun, and our very overactive and sometimes controlling reptilian brain, especially with our huge adrenal glands and our demanding sex drive (for any of you doubting that our social proclivity is less evolved than our baser instincts, think merely of the time you had sex with someone you knew would result in social entropy—and did it anyway—to understand how weak our interconnected paradigms are. My single greatest disappointment in humanity is that it is a species that would serve each other infinitely better with more heart and less libido). Because our social mechanisms are so newly evolved, we will, for a grim portion of the future, be subject to our animal urges. This is a very gross generalization of the fact, and I am sure that any psychology major in his freshman year might have explained it better, but for now it serves my purpose.

For our human ancestors, survival meant social teamwork—much as we see gorillas, chimpanzees, and dolphins function today. In a world where our perception was limited to what we could eat, what we could reproduce with, and what constituted a danger for us, developing structure on which we based our world was happenstance, if it came at all. But anything that threatened those imperatives was reacted to with animal instinct, the need to survive kicking in with terrible ferocity. Anything that endangered the order of survival would have been dealt with squarely, and survival was mandated by staying within the tribe. Alone, a man would be picked up by a carnivore, be unable to take down large prey alone, or be killed by a wandering, rival tribe.

Ergo, social tensions develop. Rules are not made in stricture, but anything that disrupts the social harmony becomes taboo or punished. If a male attempts to mate with a larger, more dominant male's female, he is met with retribution, much as we see in the animal world today. This base possession can easily be seen as what would eventually, over thousands of years, become the type of thing that the invention of language might call "adultery." Just as likely, if a hominid in this tribe would attempt to kill another tribesman for whatever reason, he compromises the security of the group as a whole, and is therefore retaliated upon. Thus, killing is wrong. Swiping food from another hungry tribesperson leaves the latter open to starvation and death, weakening the group—survival of the fittest is only so much a part of our natural evolution. *Everything* was mandated upon the social order in an effort to survive and procreate. Animal possessiveness still remains abundant, but group ethic evolves out of safety for the whole. Generations upon generations of human animals learn to avoid actions that would cause them to be anathema to the group, leaving them on their own to die—and as communication develops we discover words can be eventually put to these actions. Killing. Stealing. Coveting another man's wife?

Morality came long before man did—it existed in the animal world in any creature highly evolved enough to develop something of a neocortical social machinery. Reptiles and fish rarely show empathy, or compassion, or obey social doctrine, because they lack most of the neural capacity to understand it. Social creatures, amazingly, have demonstrated group ethic in vast and touching examples—such is the base from which we climbed. Morality becomes so much easier to understand without the huge burden that the words "right" and "wrong" or "good" and "evil" try so desperately to lay on it. We've simply forgotten in the grand social miasma that the world has developed into that "right" and "wrong" only exist in human perception, and that something only ever feels this way because of the social consequences that would be enacted upon us—which in a time 10,000 years ago would certainly have meant death in regards to any of the actions listed above.

The example of primal social necessity is best exemplified by an experiment done by the psychologist Muzafer Sherif during summer camp with a number of boys split randomly into two groups while he carefully documented their self-made organizations, establishment of leaders, conflicts with the opposing group, and resolution of conflicts based on mutual interests. It also showed their inspired unity when facing a mutual threat (a key component to the idea of world peace, should such a thing ever hope to occur).[3] Such observations helped to make the theories of social judgment theory and realistic conflict theory into documentable fact.

We can see examples of this today quite clearly with any social taboo that causes scorn and contempt. We gossip and expose and alienate wrongdoers because we are subconsciously moved by the idea that ostracizing such people from society provides the greatest possible punishment—we remember it genetically, so to speak. We are moved to feelings of conscious morality and guilty immorality almost exclusively based on the damage we may or may not do to our fellow brother animals, how that damage may affect our survival in terms of social repercussions—and, most especially, our offspring (born from the continuous evolutionary drive to propagate the species, ergo why children are so special and we have a universal need to protect them). This is why pederasts and child abusers are ubiquitously looked upon with revulsion, even in prisons—we have evolved this sense of "immorality" or "wrongness" knowing that the actions of these people were detrimental to the tribe and the survival of our species, a threat to the social norm. It's how we know murder is "wrong" and theft is "wrong" and rape is "wrong"—it *feels* that way from our evolutionary biology even if we are objective enough to understand that the word "wrong" is meaningless when we try to attach it to a higher order or mandate.

Of course, we must remember that alpha-male dominance is and always has been a huge part of our animal history, and we can see the traits of it obviously from a time when, even though we had come a considerable way along the evolutionary chain, certain actions reflected the machismo of male superiority. Take the Decalogue as a perfect example, where the first three Commandments are inherently abject to anything not involving utter worship of the male leader, and the rest of his property. Killing, stealing, and wanting your neighbor's wife are thrown in practically as an afterthought—(wait a minute, that sounds awfully familiar!)—and were already an extension of laws that were commonly enforced at the time. Remembering that no evidence for Moses' extraordinary existence is available, we must assume that if the Decalogue had physical form at all before the several-hundred-year posthumous writing of the Pentateuch, apparently in the hand of the man about whom it was written, then we have an excellent indication of the man-made extent of the Ten Commandments, and flagrant signs of the evolution of the human animal and the "morality" that evolved with us—not that was mandated *to* us. Of course, if one *wants* to believe in the concept of god-given morality, one *must* also buy into the premise that god was foolish enough to supposedly create man with free will, be completely astounded when man didn't do as he wanted man to (so much for omniscience),[4] and then let man run around for a couple thousand years (by Christian reckoning) with complete ethical abandon before he thought to himself: "Well, damn—I guess I forgot to give them rules (minus the one they already broke in that garden with that stupid apple), so I should fix that. Presto, burning bush! Here, take this stone manual, read it aloud from the big hill, and you'll stop acting like a bunch of troglodytes."

Subsequently, one also needs to believe that those rules were exclusive, that the already supposed immoralities of rape, infanticide, sexism, and genocide (Moses and his followers waited less time to do in the Amalekites than a

Kardashian waits to get divorced) were too unimportant to mention in the Decalogue, and that god must not have cared terribly about them. This is without saying that we are still only in the Second Book of the Old Testament— we have *reams* of mythological immorality to get through before all is complete. Thus, since the Decalogue is essentially a morality tale without a decent plot, it brings me back to my original point: religion didn't invent morality—it hijacks morality based on a tyrannical will. David Hume wittily surmises: "The least part of . . . the Pentateuch consists in precepts of morality; and we may also be assured that that part was always the least observed and regarded."[5]

In another example of religious hegemony presented in mythology, there is the story of Prometheus. Prometheus was a Titan—in my opinion, the noblest fictional character who ever lived (or, rather, didn't live). His world under the kingdom of the Greek gods was dark with foul weather and human ignorance, and he sought to save mankind from the despair of both. When pondering on Prometheus, I am often reminded of the imperishable poetry of Lucretius (a contemporary of our old friend, Epicurus) in Book I of his work *De Rerum Natura*, or *The Nature of Things:*

> *When in full view on the earth man's life lay rotting and loathsome,*
> *Crushed 'neath the ponderous load of Religion's cruel burdensome*
> > *shackles,*
> *Who out of heaven displayed her forehead of withering aspect,*
> *Lowering over the heads of mortals with hideous menace,*
> *Upraising mortal eyes 'twas a Greek who first, daring, defied her;*
> *'Gainst man's relentless foes 'twas Man first framed to do battle.*
> *Him could nor tales of the gods nor heaven's fierce thunderbolts' crashes*
> *Curb; nay rather they inflamed his spirit's keen courage to covet.*[6]

The gods retained a beautiful and powerful gift known as fire (serving the purposes of this myth, fire is likely both a literal flame and the fire of knowledge—ironically akin to the first fire we attribute to the creation of tools with cavemen; perhaps the ancient Greeks knew more about their primal heritage than we thought). Braving the elements and the potential wrath of the gods, Prometheus ascended Olympus and stole this fire. On his way down the mighty mountain, he was caught by the gods, but not before delivering the gift to mankind, who used it to triumph with knowledge and prosperity. But Prometheus, for his everlasting punishment, was chained to a mighty cliff face perpetually blasted by storms, and made immortal by the god-king,

Zeus, who would send a ravenous eagle to rip Prometheus open every day and devour his liver. But, being immortal, he would heal overnight so the fearsome raptor could feast upon him again, and thus it would continue for all of eternity. This was the torture to which Prometheus was manacled to, for nothing more visionary, glorious, and selfless than expanding human thought and happiness. This, to me, explains the same theme for which Icarus was punished, but with a much more standard grisly circumstance—and this is the more common result: don't contradict the gods, no matter the good.

One should keep in mind that this story was orated from a time where people legitimately *believed* in Zeus, *believed* in Prometheus and immortality and giant eagles and the rest. (And this is ineffably scoured as pagan falsities by those who still believe in resurrections and transubstantiations and parthenogenesis.) To people of this mind-frame, for whom it was intended, it teaches only subservience, fear, and paralytic wonder at our lack of power.[7] There is no morality in this—no substantial secular lesson could ever helpfully be gleaned from it. But the parallels suddenly become entirely too poignant to miss for those who cling to the same hopeless fables of similar retributions. After all, does not Prometheus and his circumstance sound almost identical to another mythical but much more infamous character? Perhaps a character that ascended into the realm of the gods and tried to give humans something to increase their knowledge and potentiate the freedom of man and womankind?

If one can see Prometheus, his trial and his end, one should most readily and easily see Lucifer. The same petulant punishment of banishment was given to Adam and Eve by god after attesting to the identical visionary idealism. Tell the story of Prometheus to any modern theist (most laughably an American one) and see the apathy that occurs. But mention the devil, and (pardon the pun) all hell breaks loose. Do monotheists of today not see this hypocrisy?

The story of Prometheus is some hundreds of years older than Christianity and with the subsequent fall of Satan from Paradise, writers of Christian mythology learned from the mistake of the Greeks and likely discovered if you wanted people to fear their enemy, one needed to keep him in power. Making Satan imprisoned in hell and allowing him to perpetuate his influence on Earth is much more effective than condemning him to suffer the way that Prometheus (according to legend) still is.

Also, it is possible that one puts themselves in a rather delicate place by acknowledging the brilliance of Prometheus and alluding to Satan as a carbon copy—there is an awful lot of LaVeyan Satanism in that parallel of which I am very aware. At the risk of being called a Satanist myself, I can only say that I am very much a humanist, and that Satanism attributes the actions of the mythical Lucifer to that same ideal. The parallel may be coincidental. I don't consider myself a Satanist any more than I consider myself a Prometheusian. One can identify with a facet of an ideology without adopting the whole, so long as one doesn't wish to don the mantle of the whole half-heartedly. Much in this respect, no reasonable person could ever call me a Christian though I inherently adopt the Golden Rule, especially since the supposed "Christian virtue" of humility still tends to escape me regularly.

We are keenly aware of every major myth basing itself almost entirely upon earlier influences—such as the Koran being very much a mockup of the Bible and Pentateuch that came before it, even containing the same Ten Commandments (without forgetting the composition of the *hadith* made very slap-dash on the account of those who remembered the doings of Muhammad some time after his death, parallel to the composition of the Gospels). Christianity is no stranger to this itself, and one only needs to remember that Horus, Dionysus, Augustus, Krishna, Buddha, and Balder were all said to be products of divine conception, some of whom were born without mortal intercourse; Ba'al, Adonis, Osiris, Asclepius were all resurrected; Augustus, who was a leader at the time of Jesus' birth, referred to himself as the Son of the Divine and had the phrase emblazoned on the realm's coin; primitive headhunters of Borneo believed that man was made from earth; Pythagoras performed miracles; Muslims believed that the angel Gabriel delivered the word of god to Muhammad much in the same fashion as he delivered the birth of Jesus to Mary—some of these stories happening hundreds, and in some cases thousands of years before the Christ myths took place. And of course we all know of the use of Winter Solstice and Spring Equinox as two highly established pagan holidays at the time of the birth of Christianity as a new religion, the pagan reference of Sun Day (for worship of Apollo) for holy reverence and rest being converted into the Sabbath, and the convenience of transferring already very prominent themes and symbols such as use of evergreen boughs and rabbits into Christmas and Easter. (Not that, as an atheist, I have ever objected to getting presents, chocolate, and time off of work for any of these occasions.)

In tandem with these alluringly parallel influences of the stars and sun, some historical or mythological theories take into account the ages of the Zodiac. Biblical references to the passing of an age are more than abundant—but the significance of those ages (about 2,100 years) and their passing mean little without their zodiacal context. In astrological terms during the time of Moses, the sun was in the Age of Taurus, which was beginning its transition into the Age of Aries. It has been asserted that many of the parables suggest an allusion to these transitions: primarily, the anger of Moses at his people upon discovering their worship of a bull (Taurus) when he descended from Sinai. Moses' life is deeply symbolic of Aries the ram, with the vast majority of his people becoming shepherds and the Jewish tradition to, even in modern times, blow a ram's horn. Aries, in turn, gives way to the Age of Pisces, on the nearly exact year of Jesus' supposed birth—Jesus' symbol being the Icthys, his feeding of thousands of people with only two fish, his befriending of two fishermen, and his hinting in Matthew to the coming of a new age symbolized by a man dispensing water (Age of Aquarius), are all pieces of the zodiacal influence that preceded and inspired Christian myth. If any of these parallels were true, despite the fact that none of these events occurred and few, if any, of the protagonists actually walked the world, it seems to say that everything that *didn't* exist was mythical plagiarism at worst and uninspired at best.

Several kinds of people are entirely accepting of the use of myth as mandate even in the face of all its inanities and contradictions if only because it makes the ideal of the human condition easier to quantify—and, therefore, to understand. When one thinks of mythological apologists it is almost impossible to avoid the suggestion of the converted C. S. Lewis—the only creation of Tolkien's that I do not admire with love and nostalgia—who said that the Christ myth

> is simply a true myth: a myth working on us in the same way as the others, but with this tremendous difference that it really happened: and one must be content to accept it in the same way, remembering that it is God's myth where the others are men's myths: i.e. the Pagan stories are God expressing Himself through the minds of poets, using such images as He found there, while Christianity is God expressing Himself through what we call real things.[8]

To begin with, a thing is either a truth or it is myth—it literally cannot be both. Not to loiter on the etymological, but the word "myth" comes directly from the Greek *muthos* meaning "lie" or "fable." To say that the Christ story is a true lie is a paradox—but paradoxes are the norm for Christian apologetics.

Secondly, to further dissect the misuse of the word pseudo-semantically into the idea that *some* myths (i.e., only this one) are not myth at all and that the rest are fake is the ultimate claim of subjectivity. "All myths are myths except mine—because I said so"—this is the exact kind of thought that legitimates the response: "You're atheists, too. You're just missing that last god, there." Such is the water that a popular Christian view of myth holds, though a number of senior priests and clerics have freely admitted that the mythologies of the holy texts should be taken merely as that and nothing more, for the messages they teach us are still demonstrative of god's will.

Much of what we owe to the study of major monotheism as myth comes from the fact that there are no pieces of archeological evidence for the existence of Jesus, and the earliest writings *known* to have taken place regarding Jesus still occurred some decades after his supposed death around the time of Paul of Tarsus. Also, there is *absence* of mention in texts where he should be, such as in the writings of the biblical philosopher Philo of Alexandria (circa 20 BCE to 50 CE)—notably mentioned by John Remsburg in his book, *The Christ:*

> *Philo was born before the beginning of the Christian era, and lived until long after the reputed death of Christ. He wrote an account of the Jews covering the entire time that Christ is said to have existed on earth. He was living in or near Jerusalem when Christ's miraculous birth and the Herodian massacre occurred. He was there when Christ made his triumphal entry into Jerusalem. He was there when the crucifixion with its attendant earthquake, supernatural darkness and resurrection of the dead took place——when Christ himself rose from the dead and in the presence of many witnesses ascended into heaven. These marvelous events which must have filled the world with amazement, had they really occurred, were unknown to him. It was Philo who developed the doctrine of the Logos, or Word, and although this Word incarnate dwelt in that very land and in the presence of multitudes revealed himself and demonstrated his divine powers, Philo saw it not.*[9]

Incredibly, god's only son also escapes mention of his own accord. No writings attributed to the hand of Jesus now reside on church shelves—or anywhere, for that matter. In a time where writings of men before and after him merely by a span of a few years have survived (if drastically altered), nothing that we can legitimately claim to have been Christ's has been found. This is also true of the Koran, whose words were supposedly composed by god and merely presented to Muhammad, and the supplemental *hadith* chronicling the deeds and wonders of the prophet were compiled years later by those who supposedly knew him and witnessed his awesomeness. And let's not forget Moses—fictional *and* narcissistic, writing the first five books of the Old Testament in third-person about *himself.*

"Not Til God Make Men of Some Other Mettle Than Earth." —Beatrice, *Much Ado About Nothing* (II.I.59)

Let us look at ourselves for a moment—at our physical bodies: the wondrousness of our circulatory system, the intricacies of our nervous system, the sheer processing power of our cerebral cortex, the sublime beauty of our skin. Let us forget, for a moment, that no piece of our body implies perfect design—that the human eye has evolved backward to optimal efficiency and that our laryngeal nerve takes a roundabout and purposeless path to its destination; that our teeth are made to survive barely a quarter of a century unaided and that our propensity to store fat is directly adverse to a prosperous living; that hundreds of millions of sperm die with each ejaculation and that we have shed the hair that was once the protection we had against harmful UV rays; that we retain a prenatal tail. All of these beauties of the body are— to a theistic mind—to be attributed to the infallible, perfect design of an intelligent god, a willful creator who gifted us with the exorbitant prowess of being bipeds and command over surrounding nature—and they are sincerely offended at the idea that the grand result of the human form can be explained over large areas of time by tiny changes in selection and adaptation, which lead to an admittedly flawed but completely workable biological machine that we call the human species—oh no, that assumption is not nearly graceful enough for them, not hardly so elegant. We, they say, were made from dirt, and in the case of the fairer sex, a rib bone. Ah, yes—infinitely more wondrous.

Creation myths range across the world in various cultures with multiple similarities and contradictions, but almost all have the same invested interest that humans are the work of a process far more supernatural than can be witnessed today. In creation myths, we can see the reoccurring, egotistical structure that willingly shows that we are the epitome of the creations of the Creator of the Universe—of all things in a body with a radius of 14 billion parsecs (roughly 46 billion light-years), we are the single greatest craft project, and the materials from which we spawned are as numerous as they are preposterous.

Inversely, the atomic theory of the stuff that we are made on is equally fantastical—but has the unparalleled beauty of rationality. For example, every existing atom in the universe today—the pages in your hands, the fingers you turn them with, the oxygen you breathe—all came from the widespread phantasm of energy that filled the empty space of the universe after the Big Bang. They have existed since the beginning in various forms and substances, but all from the multitude of wandering, glorious stars that surround us. To paraphrase Lawrence Krauss, the atoms in your left hand could very well be very distant cousins of a neighboring star with the atoms on your right. When you die, those atoms will again change energies, forms, combinations, and the like—but they will continue to exist, much as they had before and after your consciousness. As such, we are all interconnected pieces of the universe that surrounds us, composed of the various furthest and closest particles of the known (and possibly unknown) universe that formulate the vision of humanity's understanding of the universe. The noted and idolized astrophysicist Carl Sagan famously pronounced: "The nitrogen in our DNA, the calcium in our teeth, the iron in our blood, the carbon in our apple pies were made in the interiors of collapsing stars. We are made of starstuff."[10] Of all possible explanations, I find this the most elegant—and even if I had not, it would not matter, as it garners the greatest amount of empirical support. Fundamentalists are still vainly searching for the evidence of our muddy origin and the breath of life that followed.

In the *Brahmanda Purana* of Hindu scriptures, the Creator Brahma quite literally farted demons into creation before his body became night, then after a rebirth, shining gods came from his mouth and he became day. In a similar move (one of many), he turned himself into energy created from his mind and sent it wandering about, which became humanity. In a rival myth of the same origin, the *Brihadaranyaka Upanishad,* circa 1,500 BCE, Brahma was lonely and split his own body into two, one half male and the other female, and humanity was conceived thusly. In Norse myth, Odin made men from ash trees and women from elms. In Greek legend, we spawned from a universal egg cracked open by the tail of the serpent-formed Ophion after making love with his bird-transformed wife. In West Africa, the chronicle goes that we were made of earth much like the Christian myth, as well as many Native American tribes and in Mayan culture. In Egypt, we sprang to life from the tears of Ra. From China, the world is spawned out of the decomposed body of the giant Pangu (including the indication that all the pearls on the globe are little drops of Pangu's semen). Polynesians believe that we are the incestuously born children of the god Kane and his clay-formed wife Hine-hau-ona, trapped here because of his taboo lovemaking. Islam claims we were created from a clot of blood. This is but a mere smattering of the conclusions to which primitive societies were drawn in order to explain the origins of human existence—and this indicates little more than the tendency of our species to fill the gaps in our knowledge with incredible narrative, drawn from our relative material understandings.

When I was in the third grade—*"And among the dreams of the days that were, I find my lost youth again"*[11]—I lived in a terrifyingly small ghost town (a rightful moniker) in the quite literally poisonous hills of Western Utah. Boasting a diameter of about two miles, Eureka was once renowned for its amazing wealth in silver and other precious metal mining at the turn of the century, but by the late 1990s, it had fallen into a dreary, redneck ruin; an incubator to drugs and high school dropouts *en masse*. I spent a good portion of my childhood climbing through long since silent mining tunnels and sifting through dusty remains of abandoned historic buildings. For myself and my band of young friends, it was all we knew and loved. It was our Anatevka. Such a town was so notable because despite its diminutive size, its desolation, and obvious lack of what could wrongly be called monotheistic morality, Eureka supported *three* running churches in a radius near enough to literally shout a conversation across—one Lutheran, one Methodist, and one, of course, Latter-day Saints.

The Mormon church being the largest, newest, and (being in Utah) most popular, I attended there in my youth sans family because my friends and their families were devout followers—at least, as devout as any of my nine-year-old comrades could believe themselves to be—and a few hours on Sundays were a bulky chunk of our valuable social time together, which was otherwise spent hitting one another with sticks and generally running amok. Because of this attachment, I was exposed at a juvenile age to the bizarre phenomenon of what would later be recognized by the word "communion"—though "cannibalism" might be a more appropriate adage.

In the Mormon church, communion was a quick, quiet affair and one that was never fully explained to me. With the rationalization so precious to adolescent boys, I grew bored with two-hour services and instead began attending the Methodist church a mere three-hundred yards away, where services were only forty minutes. As one can imagine, the definition and significance of communion were much more visceral in this form of Christianity than in LDS, and the revelation was at once horrifying and humorous. As a child, I was completely unable to grasp the importance of symbolism or metaphor, ergo the supposition that I was *literally* eating the flesh of Christ was unavoidable. This was a concept that, with the morbid humor of a boy but with the deep curiosity I have always innately harnessed, I found both hysterical and disturbing. I was *eating* someone. Drinking their blood! And so was everyone else in the room (being a Methodist church in back-hills Utah, "everyone" amounted to about ten other people on a good day), all with holy reverence. To me, it was just the childish equivalent of "gross," but why—*how*—could it be so *important* to them? One thing that further added to the simultaneous confusion/disillusionment was that after sermon every Sunday, my pastor (a Korean missionary, who, looking back, I have great wonder as to how he ever landed in a cesspool like Eureka) would very innocently and compassionately give myself and a friend of mine the rest of the communion loaf and juice to eat while sitting on the sunlit steps. As if the metaphor wasn't confusing enough in the beginning for my developing mind: now there was *leftover* Christ—pieces of the lord unfinished and handed out as snacks! Even to me, this was preposterous. All the reverence I had never understood anyway was absolutely obliterated by this kindly act of my pastor, bolstered immensely by the fact that the Blood of Christ came pre-bottled every week with a Welch's grape concentrate label. Paradox everywhere.

Shortly after, the Methodist church closed services, and while I missed my afternoon nibbling of the Messiah and the attention I received from being young in a small congregation, going back to the LDS church reintegrated me into my social sphere. I was only to stay a short time, as I was soon asked to leave because the poor condition of my clothing offended the more sensitive eyes and noses of the other church members. At the time, this never bothered me, because I retained the impervious rationalization of a nine-year-old which reminded me that I got my free time back on Sundays and that the flesh of Christ had been far more tasty at the other church, in any case. It wasn't until I was much older that I had realized the atrocity of all the events that had occurred—not even my being asked to leave from the Mormon church for something quite clearly no fault of my own, but the lewdness of convincing children that they were consuming the flesh and blood of another human being for the deplorable act of what Hitchens referred to as "vicarious redemption." My lack of understanding in the grisly ritual is far from uncommon among children of the same age, and it is coupled with other such heinous practices within this particular Christian faith alone as baptisms of the dead and adolescent polygamy—and plenty of other instances discussed in this book. In a world where parents howl in conservative agony over the violent influence of video games and graphic music, it's astonishing how easily they forget the subjective virtues of racism, discrimination, bigotry, torture, sexual abuse of children, slavery, and genocide that they often give to their children in the form of their faith. If we are to garner true meaning from myth or flesh, what are we to learn from human sacrifice, or from Lot condemning his daughters to the unmerciful erections of a bacchanal riot, or from Muhammad's rape of the nine-year-old Aisha?[12] The morality of any of these actions is nonexistent.

Imagine you are a primitive human, evolved enough to have the capacity to communicate and potentially to use rudimentary tools, but the world frightens you. There is pain and it is unexplained; great storms with no answers as to why; many, many kinds of beasts and massive light-giving orbs in the sky that move and burn and cool with equal tenacity. The only experience you have in life is sitting around you—the actions of those neighboring, and the nature to which you have been exposed. How do you answer these questions? One does what the pattern-seeking obsession of the human brain has done since its inception: it creates parallels. Each one of these creation myths has nothing more or less imaginative to it than what is directly in front of the eyes of the people observing: natural acts and animals, earth and air and water, sex and anger and death—all blended into painfully basic extrapolations on why things are the way they are. And we are guilty of the same kind of pattern forming in the face of the unknown today: in the science of psychology and neurobiology, the brain was constantly compared to complex contraptions that, at the time, seemed worthy of explaining the unexplained process of cognition—for a time we said the brain was like a switchboard, then like a computer, then like a system of servers, and now like something else entirely. There will hopefully come a time when we decide the brain is like nothing at all except for *itself*, much like the origination of the earth and the living species upon it. Affixing the wondrous event of human evolution with a child making figures in the sand or climbing from the decomposed flesh of a giant is beyond disturbing—it's insolent. Humans are as they are and behave as they do because we were intelligent enough to learn over a span of time what *didn't* work. If we hadn't been capable of such a thing—if our ancestors weren't clever enough to discover that slapping a grizzly bear with an open hand will likely result in your death, we wouldn't have the luxury of sitting today and laughing at the idea. *We* have learned and survived and grown and adapted as we have—*god* didn't do it any more than he did the hurricanes or the terrorist attacks or anything else we attribute to him, nor the morals we ascribe to his imaginary vestige. Did you kill anyone today? Sleep with another man's wife?

Play in traffic unheedingly? If not, congratulations—you've inherited the knowledge that those who came before you taught would lead to happiness and procreation. If you have—you've exercised free will. Consequences are possible and such is life. *We* deserve the credit—pat yourselves on the back. To steal a widely viral and unnamed quote: "You are the product of over four billion years of worldly evolution—now fucking act like it."

Notes

1. George W. Bush in Moscow, May 2002: "We hold dear what our Declaration of Independence says, that all have got uninalienable rights, endowed by a Creator." See *Weekly Compilation of Presidential Documents* 38, No. 21. (May 27, 2002), p. 905, www.gpo.gov.

2. J. F. Bierlein, *Parallel Myths* (Ballantine, 1994), p. 22.

3. Eliot Aronson, *The Social Animal*, 10th ed. (Worth Publishers, 2008), p. 327.

4. This was not the first nor the worst of the All-Seeing's foul-ups. In 2 Kings, god assured the prophet Elisha that the combined armies of Judah and Israel would defeat the Moabites. The armies of god were defeated instead. The Almighty was clearly either mistaken or a liar.

5. David Hume, *The Natural History of Religion*, ed. A. Wayne Colver and John Valdimir Price (Clarendon, 1976).

6. Incidentally, *De Rerum Natura* was a work undertaken by Lucretius to tell the world of the atomist theory: that the world was comprised of infinitesimally small units called "atoms"—a theory composed 200 years before Christ.

> . . . *as I tell of the primary atoms of matter*
> *Out of which Nature forms things: 'tis "things" she increases and fosters;*
> *Then back to atoms again she resolves them and makes them to vanish.*

Of course, *De Rerum Natura* and the atomist theory were considered heretical throughout the early CE years, and many copies were destroyed, burned, and defaced.

7. Such as Apollo killing his grandson because he had the audacity to challenge him to an archery contest. The same god was contested against Marsyas to a duel of music, and when Apollo ungraciously won, he tied Marsyas to a tree and flayed him. One can easily see the nauseous parallels between this story and that of Icarus and Prometheus.

8. Lewis, in a letter to Arthur Greeves

9. John E. Remsburg, *The Christ: A Critical Review and Analysis of the Evidences of His Existence* (Prometheus, 1994).

10.	Carl Sagan, *Cosmos* (Ballantine Books, 1985).

11.	Henry Wadsworth Longfellow, "My Lost Youth."

12.	According to *hadith* sources, Muhammad married Aisha when she was six and consummated the marriage with her when she was nine and he was in his fifties, an act that would by definition be considered statutory rape in any modern legal system that employs that or any like term. The majority of Muslims accept the authenticity of this particular account and, perhaps most troubling, some Muslims cite it as justification for child marriage in the present day. As mentioned elsewhere in this work, however, the veracity of *hadith* are often in question, even among Muslims, who consider some sources more reliable than others. Given the conflicting scripture, a minority opinion argues that Aisha was as old as nineteen when her marriage with Muhammad was consummated. See Myriam Francois-Cerrah, "The Truth about Muhammad and Aisha," *Guardian*, September 17, 2012, http://www.theguardian.com/commentisfree/belief/2012/sep/17/muhammad-aisha-truth.

6

The Artistic Plague

———◆ ◆———

". . . for anything so overdone is from the purpose of plays,
whose end both at the first and now was, and is,
to hold as 'twere the mirror up to nature."
—William Shake-speare, *Hamlet*

"Art is a collaboration between God and the artist,
and the less the artist does the better."
—Andre Gide

It is said there is a light in the Sistine Chapel unlike any other light in the world—a resplendent myriad of frescoes and scenes immortalized by the hands of masters whose inspirational worth is beyond measure. From a surprisingly tiny section in the very center of the vaulted edifice, the demure eyes of a serene Adam gaze lovingly upon his father; a poetic mixture of mythology and chiaroscuro that dominates the surrounding works, despite its minimal proportions. Flawless, awe-inspiring, complete, and timeless, *The Creation of Adam* hails both as the masterwork of the artist Michelangelo and the foundation of our visualization of the Genesis story. One is moved by the sublime elegance and humanity of the piece—if one can remain undistracted by Michelangelo's insertion of Adam's supremely unimposing genitalia (small even for the fashion of the Renaissance to portray the male figure in such a way so as not to distract from the nuance of the work with carnal exhilaration, combined possibly with the ancient Greek tradition that smaller and uncircumcised penises were aesthetically preferable to larger, circumcised members which they adorned on barbarians and monsters) and the blatant representation of cerebral anatomy hidden in the flying vehicle of the Omnipotent.

The Creation is a marvelous example of the power of religion to inspire what one could argue was the greatest artistic revolution in human history. Through the Renaissance, Rome and her counterparts birthed the since-eternalized works of Bernini, Michelangelo, Raphael, Da Vinci, Donatello, and many more manifested in the ways of sculpture, mural, fresco, painting, musical composition, philosophical essay, poetry, and architecture. In those short three centuries, classic art created names that even those unschooled and uninterested in the subject can identify with certainty: *Mona Lisa*, *The Annunciation*, the statue of *David*, the countless angelic decorations of the Castel San'Angelo—each more impressive and memorable than the last. A reported 18,000 pieces in artistic acquisitions of a primarily religious nature exist in the Vatican alone[1] (excluding St. Peter's Basilica), representing a remarkable amount of cultural, historical, and fiscal capital. Without a doubt, the Church may be responsible for the most important muse-like fervor in the history of art, a fact that many theists use to attack those dissenters with more Bohemian tastes. After all, where would the study of light on a figure be without Caravaggio, and where would Caravaggio be without the idea of god? Similarly, what greatness in poetry would we have lost without Dante or Milton or Donne; the craft of copper imprinting for the illustration of grand texts minus Gustave Doré; the subject of epic architecture sans Michelangelo's Basilica or the slightly pre-Renaissance influences of the multisupervised erection and restoration of Notre-Dame de Paris? What would any of these staples of artistic genius be without god—and where would art be without them? Unsurprisingly, the Church is responsible for the artistic rebirth and revolution between the fourteenth and seventeenth centuries—but not because the Holy Mother's organization's pure benevolence and almighty mandate proved to be an irresistible muse for all the great artists of the Western World. They garnered the response the same way they've received anything of benefit in their history—they bought it. This hard-knock philosophy is expressed by Ross King in his fantastic book, *Michelangelo and the Pope's Ceiling*.

> *The artist of Michelangelo's time therefore bore little resemblance to the romantic ideal of the solitary genius who would conjure original works of art from his own imagination, unfettered by the demands of the marketplace or the patron. Only in a later century could a painter like Salvator Rosa, born in 1615, haughtily refuse to follow the orders of his patrons, telling one of them, who had been too specific with his requests, to*

"go to a brick-maker, as they work to order." In 1508, the artist, like the brick-maker, worked to the demands of his patron.[2]

Even with the heightened intrigue and enigma that surrounds the Vatican Archives, what is known to exist are the receipts (some still reputedly inked by quill onto calf-skin parchment) for every artistic (or other) requisition made by the Church to adorn the Holy City. With so many pieces in sculpture, painting, and building paid for in gold by the Vatican since its inception, the list is extensive. Gianlorenzo Bernini alone has numerous works in Rome in busts, fountains, and sculptures, each one glorious and sublime, decorating St. Peter's Square, countless chapels, courts, and streets, and likely many confidential vaults. Bernini himself was treated well through most of his life by the Church, being knighted at twenty-three by Pope Gregory XV and being admonished of by Pope Urban VIII, "Your luck is great to see Cardinal Maffeo Barberini Pope, Cavaliere; but ours is much greater to have Cavalier Bernini alive in our pontificate."[3] Such a patronage surely affected the inspiration of Bernini while his hands could sculpt—though arguably his greater and far more worthy works arose out of a much more obvious pagan nature, such as *The Rape of Proserpina* and *Apollo and Daphne*.

Bernini, despite his well-paid contribution to the Vatican over the course of his life, was victim to the sexual repression that occurred in the minds of several popes over the sixteenth century, and in a zealous tirade they had ordered the visible penises of great works across Rome to be chipped off the statues, in an effort to curb lustful thoughts. Hundreds of gorgeous pieces of work were—to paraphrase a quote by fictional character Robert Langdon of Dan Brown's *Angels & Demons*—"vandalized." This is merely one of the numerous artistic purges and frothy-mouthed demands of the time—during the late 1400s, Girolamo Savonarola preached a famous sermon in which he suggested that the solution to ridding the world of sodomites was by burning them and "vanities," which included "chessboards, playing cards, mirrors, fancy clothing, and bottles of perfume . . . musical instruments, tapestries, paintings, and copies of books by Florence's three great writers: Dante, Petrarch, and Boccaccio."[4] Girolamo was a Dominican friar, of a sect so nicknamed the domini canes ("hounds of god") because of the ferociousness of their methods and stubbornness in their faith. Madame de Maintenon burned Leda and the Swan a century and a half after its completion, saying that Leonardo da Vinci's work was indecent. The Buddhas of Bamiyan, sixth century works of art loved around the world, were dynamited by the Taliban in 2001, who reported: "Muslims should be proud to destroy idols."[5] The religious are continuously happy to give themselves license to uncreate what the visionaries of our time and of times past have gifted us with.

But art can be destroyed in as many various ways as it can flourish. In 1577, preacher John Northbrooke of England became the first author of a published work to scorn the theater. In his foul manuscript, *A Treatise Against Dancing, Dicing, Plays and Interludes*, Northbrooke is posed of by a youth the question: "Do you speak against those places also, which are made up and built for such plays and interludes as the Theater and Curtain, and other such like places besides?" To which he responds: "Yea, truly, for I am persuaded that Satan has not a more speedy way and fitter school to work and teach his desire, to bring men and women into his snare of concupiscence and filthy lusts of wicked whoredom, than those places, and plays and theatres are: and therefore it is necessary that those places and players should be forbidden and dissolved and put down by authority, as the brothel houses and stews are."[6]

He goes on to say that young women and virgins especially should avoid these places, as the excitement to participate in the festivities will likely strip away their innocence. Beyond knowing such absurdity is erroneous from spending a life in the modern theater myself, one must realize the impact that this had on a world already driven unalterably by the fear of god and the advent of the printing press 120 years before, in a time where women were not allowed to be performers in any case, and—most fearsomely—the work of Shake-speare was just being birthed into the grander notice.[7]

And what a change this view was compared to the religious ideologies that not only lived harmoniously with the theater before, but that also permeated it. In ancient Greece, many plays could not have reached favorable endings without the arrival of a god at the end in the fashion of deus ex machina, and often began with invocations to whichever patron deity the play was intended. Japanese noh theatre, even today, frequently utilizes a type of stamping action on wooden stages designed to summon up the spirits to aid the actor in the truthful telling of a story. Indeed, even Shake-speare's *Henry V*, much akin to Milton's *Paradise Lost*, begins with a plea to the supernatural, compelling the powers above (or potentially below) to grace the theater with their presence. For the most part, it seemed Christian viewpoint had shied away from performance art—primarily because the tradition had included such a weighty adoration to pagan gods. This did not stop Christian troupes from performing passion plays that were popular somewhere around the thirteenth century, nor does it stop modern theists from lauding and producing shows with inherent godly circumstances, such as *Godspell, J.B.: A Play in Verse, Jesus Christ Superstar, Joseph and the Amazing Technicolor Dreamcoat*, and surprisingly, *The Book of Mormon*.

This simultaneous hatred and utilization of theater is well displayed in the fifteenth-century morality tale *The Somonyng of Everyman*, also tritely called *Everyman*, a play that was widely popular and depicted the struggle of a man making good or bad choices in his life, ultimately to be tallied like a game score by god in the end. Helped along by various virtues, who predictably give wisdom sprinkled with dogmatic flavor, the Everyman discovers the way to true happiness is in the goodness mandated to him by the divine, and his heavenly reward is the happy ending. We can readily imagine that Northbrooke would hardly have protested the following lines spoken on the stage:

> *Here begins a treatise how the high Father of Heaven sends Death to summon every creature to come and give account of their lives in this world, and is in the manner of a moral play.*

How condemning is the title as well, implying every breathing person on this planet to the same petulant judgment; to suggest that the protagonist could have been any of us. While art—and in this case, the theater—is more than accepting of any message that one wishes to throw into the medium, we once again see the vile hypocrisy of the Church, both Catholic and Protestant, to decry the theater for lewdness but exact it for its own tyrannical purposes.

We can thank whatever circumstance is available that Northbrooke seemed to have a substantially smaller audience than that of the Immortal Bard, Marlowe, Jonson, and Bacon. Indeed, when thinking of the influence that the Church might have wrought during the days when Elizabethan theater as we know it today was being born, fledgling and fragile, I cannot help but think of the incendiary words of Marlowe's Edward II:

> *Proud Rome, that hatchest such imperiall groomes,*
> *For these thy superstitious taperlights,*
> *Wherewith thy antichristian churches blaze,*
> *Lie fire thy erased buildings, and enforce*
> *The papall towers to kisse the lowlie ground.*
> *With slaughtered priests may Tibers channell swell,*
> *And bankes raisd higher with their sepulchers.*[8]

And, of course, we have Elizabeth to thank, who was both a Protestant and a lover of the theater and an ardent patron. Without this monarchial support, we might never have known most of the lines that introduce my chapters today and move the hearts of millions. Theater (thankfully) survived, though not without more opposition than came from Northbrooke. The London Corporation, backed by religious leaders of the time, condemned the playhouses for the sacrilegious art of putting men in women's clothing.[9] At this same time (just as The Man from Stratford was arriving in London) several catastrophic accidents involving the theater were occurring, including riots, the breaking of scaffolding on a set, the spread of plague, and an earthquake in 1580—all of which were burgeoning the opinion that god was angry with the theater and his punishment was forthcoming (a pre-Katrina-meets-9/11 sister-lunacy, if you will). Puritans and clerics bearing pamphlets wandered the muddy streets, shouting of god's will against entering a playhouse. Thanks to various methods used by Queen Elizabeth I to keep playhouses open, the zealots were outmaneuvered. After the death of Her Highness Elizabeth and the institution of royal protection on actors and other artists, the standard of stage-wrights became to justifiably mock those of the religious orders who had made their work so laborious during the latter half of the 1500s. The only downfall of the theater in true form came in the closing of the houses due to the protectorship of Oliver Cromwell, bolstered by plague and the strict laws against group gatherings, until they were reopened again with much joy during the Restoration in 1660, under the reign of the scientific and passionate Charles II.

Elizabeth's monarchial predecessor had his bouts of superstition versus art as well. In 1533, he ordered the murder of Elizabeth Barton, who was widely known as the Nun of Kent—a rather famed ventriloquist who used her thrown voices to insinuate that she was the medium through which higher powers communicated and who heatedly opposed the king's dalliance with Anne Boleyn. While her death was painfully ironic for a ventriloquist (her head was spitted atop of a pole) she was devoted hugely to Henry's politics and personal love life, and the wide conception that her voices were the dark counsels of demons when she took opinions contrary to Henry's desires thus reinforced her eventual charge of treason.[10]

The theater was lucky. Most work becomes the new corpses of religious carnage. I beg one not to misunderstand me in that I feel much the same way as Hitchens has frequently verbalized:

[R]eligion was the race's first (and worst) attempt to make sense of reality. It was the best the species could do at a time when we had no concept of physics, chemistry, biology or medicine. We did not know that we lived on a round planet, let alone that the said planet was in orbit in a minor and obscure solar system, which was also on the edge of an unimaginably vast cosmos that was exploding away from its original source of energy. We did not know that micro-organisms were so powerful and lived in our digestive systems in order to enable us to live, as well as mounting lethal attacks on us as parasites. We did not know of our close kinship with other animals. We believed that sprites, imps, demons, and djinns were hovering in the air about us. We imagined that thunder and lightning were portentous . . . Religion was our first attempt at philosophy, just as alchemy was our first attempt at chemistry and astrology our first attempt to make sense of the movements of the heavens.[11]

For these reasons, our historical knowledge of religion should always be preserved. I would no sooner advocate for the burning of a Bible than I would for the Koran or Zoroastrian scripture or the Kamasutra. These texts are both a window into the literary minds of a world before ours and a genuine try at what we would later find to be beyond our first inept attempts to quantify. When explaining this point, I frequently find myself in the same poetic vein as Maud Bodkin, who felt that the Bible was an epic poem and compared Christ to the tragic heroes of the Shakespearean and Greek canons.[12] In this sense, I unearth poetry in the Talmud, and epic storytelling in the Book of Revelation. I stumble on subliminal beauty in the imagination of the Book of Mormon, and vague stirrings of sentimentalism when musing over the *Summa Theologica*. These works should lie on a shelf for posterity as well as should *On the Origin of Species* or *Mein Kampf* or *The Communist Manifesto*. They are works that give us insight to theories of a time in which we were not privy to, and discussion for which we were not present.

Ergo, the practice of book burning in any sense has always been anathema to me, and I have found just as much evil in the act of Alexander the Great having burned the Avesta after defeating Darius III as I do for the Amazing Grace Church's Book Burning of 2009 where not only hundreds of copies of works by Rick Warren, Brian McLaren, and that dribbling, frocked gangster Agnes Gonxha Bojaxhiu, or Mother Teresa (again, regardless of my agreements with them or not) met a fiery death, but also various versions of the Bible, including the NIV, RSV, NKJV, TLB, NASB, ESV, NEV, NRSV,

ASV, The Evidence Bible, the Message Bible and others, were destroyed.[13] Book burning plays a supremely advantageous role in the war of thoughts created from a time where the only way to pass knowledge properly from one person to another was the written word, and even then when it was painfully copied. In our history, reading has been the single most predominant method of the communication of knowledge that we have mastered, despite its rapid decline since the advent of electronic communication, and the right to read is a uniquely human right that religion has never stopped thirsting to control.

At the Bebelplatz in Berlin, one can find a glass square set in a very divergent theme from the surrounding cobblestones. Inside, the walls are lined with garish, empty bookcases—the sight is rightly ominous and slightly dystopian. This is a memorial set in grim memory of the famous Nazi book burning conducted by Joseph Goebbels (who was the only Nazi formally excommunicated from the Catholic Church—for marrying a Protestant) wherein tens of thousands of books were destroyed, including works by Bertolt Brecht, Karl Marx, and Thomas Mann. Most strikingly, however, is a plaque set into the ground bearing the inscription: "*Das war ein Vorspiel nur, dort wo man Bücher verbrennt, verbrennt man am Ende auch Menschen.*"[14] This is a line by Heimlich Heine in his now near-canonical play *Almansor*, and refers specifically to actions committed by Christians during the Inquisition, but proved to be jarringly prophetic when considering the Final Solution. In his memoir *Joseph Anton*, Salman Rushdie ruminates on this as a large collection of his controversial novel *The Satanic Verses* was being piled in Bradford—indeed, the same Salman Rushdie who was in hiding for nearly ten years after the Ayatollah Khomeini issued a death sentence on him for the crime of writing a novel.

In Bradford a crowd was gathering outside the police station in the Tyrls, a square also overlooked by the Italianate city hall and the courthouse. There was a pool with a fountain and an area designated as a "speaker's corner" for people to sound off about whatever they liked. The Muslim demonstrators were uninterested in soapbox oratory, however. The Tyrls was a more modest location than Berlin's Opera Square had been on May 10, 1933, and in Bradford only one book was at issue, not twenty-five thousand or more; very few of the people gathered there would have known much about the events presided over more than fifty-five years earlier by Joseph Goebbels, who cried, "No to decadence and moral corruption! Yes to decency and morality and family and state! I consign to the flames the writings of Heinrich Mann, Ernst Gläser, Erich Kästner." . . . No, the demonstrators knew nothing of that bonfire, or the Nazis' desire to "purge" and "purify" German culture of "degenerate" ideas. Perhaps they were also unfamiliar with the term "auto-de-fe," or with the activities of the Catholic Inquisition, but even if they lacked a sense of history they were still part of it. They too had come to destroy a heretical text with fire.[15]

Salman himself knows a great deal about censorship at the hands of religion— after having written a chapter in *The Satanic Verses* in which a character clearly parallel to Muhammad is depicted, his life became a revolving door of death threats, new hiding places, and literary challenges. The *fatwa* on his head was renewed for years and the bounty rose into the millions. Rushdie, for the most part, fought for the freedom of expression against religious tyranny to the end. Arguably, contemporary literature is greater for his struggle.

Much in the same expansionist extremity that we have come to expect from religion, the faithful continued not only by destroying what literature they could but also by forbidding it wherever possible. A grand number of works we respect as foundations of incredible prose and poetry at one time has been held back from the objective public eye for the sake of spiritual bias—an effort to censor the right of humanity to view and think as they wanted to for the promotion of the same psychological slavery to which I alluded earlier. A perfect example of this celestial censorship is the case of *As I Lay Dying*, the moving classic by Faulkner, which had been banned officially by the Graves County School District in Mayfield, Kentucky, during 1986, because the book questioned the existence of god.[16] This monumental piece sits in the same fiercely important family of volumes that had been pathetically expelled for equally ignorant reasons, such as *The Diary of Anne Frank*, which apart from being forbidden multiple times in several countries, very recently was pulled again from school shelves during 2010 in Culpeper County public schools in Virginia after a parent complained that it contained homosexual themes;[17] *Fahrenheit 451* by Ray Bradbury—attacked in schools in the Conroe, Texas district because the novel took god's name in vain, contained scenes of Bible burning, and went against the "religious beliefs" of those who sniveled about it to the school district in 2006;[18] *The Handmaid's Tale* by Margaret Atwood utilizes some of the most elegant prose set to paper, and was attacked and prohibited in several areas, notably in Dripping Springs, Texas, when a group of parents howled—secondarily because of the adult content (which is understandable) but primarily because of the transparently anti-Christian narratives within it (which is laughable). *The Handmaid's Tale* is important to include in such a list simply because those fighting against its distribution can rarely hedge themselves in the objective argument that there is sexual content inappropriate for school reading ages, but it is ad infinitum coupled on the supposition that a trivial fairy tale earns mandatory reverence and the nonacceptance of that ideology is a crime.

Today, such demonstrations are vain and pitiable but terribly dangerous when they are successful—nothing retains the potential to hinder the progress of the modern mind more effectively than by abolishing the ability to read freely during youth. The capacity to examine literature is the nearest thing men have to magic—those who can, work wonders; those who can't, decry it and call it witchcraft. As for book burnings, they are mostly symbolic (and I might humorously even encourage book burning of this very work, if only to increase sales by a few thousand copies), as a group could never hope to wipe out a printed idea when it is commericially produced by trying to burn all the texts, and the internet and television medias can communicate a dangerous thought infinitely quicker and more permanently than the written word can. Splinter groups that have attacked websites for religiously inappropriate content have proven to be the new book burners of the age of the internet.[19] But take, for example, the Iconoclasm movements circa 730–787 CE and 813–843 CE, wherein a faction of the Byzantine Church advocated that a collection of portraits that depicted the Christ family and other biblical personages and events were not of Christian origin and should be subject to removal.[20] Many works that might have illuminated areas where our knowledge is lacking in the mythology of the early years of Christ and the periods surrounding him were lost under the barbarism of these groups, despite the efforts to label them as heretics by the Seventh Ecumenical Council.[21]

Even that which has to be argued to be classified as art is not safe from attack—and those who use religion as their canvas arguably (and sadly) wreak more havoc than they do inspiration or contemplation at their work. This is no doubt because of the painful self-perpetuation that is evidenced by the theist community and excellently summed by Douglas Adams: "Here's an idea or notion that you're not allowed to say anything bad about; you're just not. Why not?—because you're not!" Such words Theo van Gogh might have taken to heart before he was butchered like a sow in Amsterdam by a psychotic Muslim zealot after the release of his film depicting the mistreatment of women in Islam.[22] What would happen then, if a person for whatever rationalized reasons of their own made the prophet Muhammad into a cartoon for a Danish publication or immersed a crucifix in urine and took a photograph? I think we all know the answer.

In a surprisingly beautiful image known as "Piss Christ," New York artist Andres Serrano placed a plastic crucifix into a jar of his own urine, set the light accordingly, and took a photograph. The result was something ethereal and beautiful—and not something that could have ever been associated with human waste had he not titled it accordingly. The reaction from the public was predictable, and the piece was destroyed with hammers by "a campaign of French-Catholic fundamentalists"[23] during an antiblasphemy campaign. Serrano had maintained the piece was a commentary on the misuse of religion (ironically) but might have said anything regarding the justification of the piece and experienced the same result—the idea of a factory-produced, hardly sacred plastic image of the Messiah plunged in urine was simply too blasphemous to be tolerated for the locals. Regardless of the artistic power it shared with us, I daresay that had Andre placed a Poseidon action figure in the same saffron solution, his display might still exist.

Of course, we all know of the Muslim riots and rampage that occurred in 2006 when a Danish newspaper published twelve cartoons, most of which depicted the prophet Muhammad, making a statement on the Islamic virtue of self-censorship. In Islam, any depiction of the Prophet is blasphemous, and the Danish Muslim community took the cartoons to heart immediately, staging protests and lighting incendiary passion against the publications inside and outside of the country. This included adding a few images of Muhammad that were not printed in the *Jyllands-Posten* paper that were infinitely more insulting than the others had been.[24] The civilized protest of free speech vs. religious respect exploded when Muslims immolated Danish flags in Pakistan and Indonesia and several other Western countries (including the United States) that should have reprinted the cartoons as a gesture in the name of free speech but were too cowed to do so. Before long, the riots in the Middle East were unquenchable, and churches, embassies, and innocent tourists and citizens—the buildings with fire, the people with machetes—were brought down in Libya, Indonesia, and Pakistan. A one-million-dollar bounty was placed on the original artist of the cartoon even though there had been several, and protestors wielding terrifying signs demanding the butchery of all those who mocked Islam were photographed and displayed on global news. When Richard Dawkins wrote upon the same subject, he referenced Andrew

Mueller, a leading journalist in the United Kingdom, who has made a great many public statements on the global perception of Islam and remarked:

> [T]he values of Islam trump anyone else's—which is what any follower of Islam does assume, just as any follower of any religion believes that theirs is the sole way, truth and light. If people wish to love a 7th century preacher more than their own families, that's up to them, but nobody else is obliged to take it seriously.

How remarkably true every facet of that statement is. After all, it's just a cartoon—the response to it caused the death of over a hundred people in various grisly ways. And this event repeated itself so painfully in 2012 with the release of the film *Innocence of Muslims*. Rioters in Islamabad demanded the execution of the filmmaker. Businesses were burned in Karachi. How sorry is it that we have come, not only to accept, but also to expect this reaction without surprise or recompense?[25] How worrisome that we can take the death of a patriot at face value under the guise that a film has insulted Islam? This, again, forces the thinking world to realize that free speech doesn't exist on a planet where the religious feel justified to respond in this shameful manner.[26]

The image of Christ in America, on the other hand, seems hardly as sacred in juxtaposition to the graven form of Muhammad. If commercial Christians held the same vindication on depictions of Christ as French fundamentalists do, or as Muslims do with regard to Muhammad, the Christian world would have been torn asunder much sooner—but for the sake of free enterprise, reverence can be swayed. A day doesn't go by that I don't see a Buddy Jesus bobblehead; a new skit on television or a scene in a movie with a fresh sarcastic portrayal of the Christ, such as his characterizations in *South Park*, Will Farrell's performance in *Superstar*, and the toe-tapping musical renditions of the Messiah in *Reefer Madness: The Musical* ("Listen to Jesus, Jimmy!") and *Hamlet 2* ("Rock me, rock me, rock me, Sexy Jesus!"); or a bumper sticker, key chain, T-Shirt, or coffee mug with a slap-dash portrait of Jesus, in all manner of commercial accessibility. From all of this, one might even get the very mistaken impression that Jesus loves capitalism—or, at least, the very true impression that his churches do. But glib idolatry is perpetrated aplenty without monetary gain: in Montana, a large statue of Jesus stands on a promontory of the Big Mountain ski resort, placed there as a WWII memorial by the Knights of Columbus in the late 1940s, that skiers and snowboarders slap for "luck" on their way down the slopes.

As Ray Bradbury, through his profoundly sad character of Faber, said, "Christ is one of the 'family', now. I often wonder if God recognizes His own son the way we've dressed him up, or is it dressed him down? He's a regular peppermint-stick now, all sugar-crystal and saccharine when he isn't making veiled references to certain commercial products that every worshipper absolutely needs."[27]

What art else is destroyed—or is subject to religious mutilation? The cultural importance of the Stari Most bombed into nothingness during the conflicts in Croatia? The repeated sacking of Jerusalem during the Crusades with its constant revolving door of Christian and Muslim kings? The damage done to the Parthenon during the attack of Ottoman Turks by Christian Venice in 1687? The toppling of the English monasteries by Henry VIII when he created the Anglican Church and his liquidation of some of the most gorgeous architecture in Great Britain? The 128 churches and 618 mosques decimated in the Bosnia-Herzegovina conflict? What about the predicted destruction to occur—the joy of the Jews when their prophesied earthquake obliterates the Dome of the Rock so that they may once again reclaim the holy place shared by Islam and Christianity and Judaism and build their Third Temple, just so Christians can rejoice when Jesus makes the Second Coming and decimates that in his divine anger? Though I have never seen the Dome of the Rock in person, I know it to be beautiful in its own earthly way, as I can only imagine the Third Temple would be beautiful for similar reasons. Who couldn't recall the spinster naïveté and heart-felt words of Alma Winemiller when musing on Gothic cathedrals:

> How everything reaches up, how everything seems to be straining for something out of the reach of stone—or human—fingers? . . . The immense stained windows, the great arched doors that are five or six times the height of the tallest man—the vaulted ceiling and all the delicate spires— all reaching up to something beyond attainment! To me—well, that is the secret, the principle back of existence—the everlasting struggle and aspiration for more than our human limits have placed in our reach . . . Who was that said that—oh, so beautiful thing!—'All of us are in the gutter, but some of us are looking at the stars!'[28]

Winemiller herself was quoting Oscar Wilde, and though she had trouble remembering his name, she perhaps unwittingly stumbled into the very essence of his point. These buildings, whether they were built for god or not, were hardly inspired by his existence in tangible terms. They were rather erected in the hope of touching artistic greatness, subjective as that may be. And destruction of beauty is a crime in itself: it cannot be vindicated by anything short of necessity (except perhaps for the Mormon Temple in San Diego, which is just so garishly white that sunglasses are necessary within a mile radius of it). Not that I do not think that the world could do with a few less religious buildings, but I see the aesthetic of them to be a noble art of ancient practice, and cannot find the supposition that my imaginary friend is better than your imaginary friend reason enough to undo that.

On the first cover of this book, there were three religious symbols listed. I am willing to bet you can guess what they are without much thought. The Star of David, or hexagram; the Cross, or cruciform; and the Crescent of Islam—each are universally recognized as the symbols for the three great monotheisms, icons by which we recognize certain methodologies unerringly. Any building with a cross on the front we can easily identify as a church; any time we see a crescent and star emblazoned on something, we can distinguish its Islamic significance. The power of symbols proves to communicate authority and action with equal perseverance—but also emotion. Relating back to those same three symbols—how would you feel if you saw them splattered in blood?[29] Would it seem accurate to you? Offensive? Neither?

Circumstance steals symbols. In one context, they might serve as beacons of religious hope; in another, they might communicate the radical toxicity of religious influence. It's not difficult to do—and, in my case, acknowledgement of that influence is how my perceptions of those symbols are based for the rest of my life. And while it is true that creating and utilizing symbols is a form of art that has been evolving for millennia, one can almost always bet that a stolen good symbol will be utilized for an evil purpose much easier than an evil symbol for a good purpose. How well have practical historians been able to bring back the positive connotations of the swastika? How successful are modern pagans at showing the mystic nobility of the pentacle, or Catholics at undoing the Satanist connotations of the inverted Cross (which was adopted as a Catholic symbol long before Satanism, as St. Peter begged to be crucified upside down because he was not worthy to suffer identical punishment as Jesus)? Unfortunately, the philosophy of stealing and bastardizing symbols is very much a one-way street—and in the public view, religion is a master of it.

The swastika is a perfect example—at over 3,000 years old, the symbol boasts a shelf life longer than the Egyptian ankh. Its use was widespread through Troy and the Eastern Mediterrean on various pieces of art and ran through the Chinese world with gusto. For just over 2,900 years, the swastika was a symbol of good luck or virtue, the etymology stemming from the Sanskrit words literally meaning: "to be good."[30]

How quickly such a thing changed—almost irrevocably. How did the Third Reich butcher almost three millennia of a good standing symbol in as few decades? Arguably, there exists enough debate to support the notion that the Germans didn't actually use the swastika as their blazon but instead as a mistranslation of the same shape they called a hooked cross, the Hakenkreuz, which lends a further eerie connection to divine ordinance. But, excluding such a notion, the question of symbolic contamination stands. The answer, if we think about it, is simple: no amount of good makes up for a millisecond of atrocity. We firmly fixate the paradigm of evil upon a thing that has done evil, no matter how much good it may have stood for previously. And I'm not one to argue—ask an ex-lover, or a former employer, or a friend who has betrayed me. Holding a grudge is a human specialty for good reason: we are cerebrally hardwired to remember when bad things occur so as to avoid them in the future. It's nature's negative reinforcement. And how could we ever be expected to look at a flag bearing the sign of the swastika and not be heartbroken by the bloodshed over which it flew in Western Europe during the Second World War? How could we be expected to forget that? Frankly, we shouldn't—and I'm not arguing that we should.

But why do other such stolen symbols get a "Get Out of Jail Free" card?

The history of the cross is varied, but our most solid estimations claim the cross to be a symbolic descendant of the ankh of Egyptian narration, an icon of Sekhet and a symbol of life. The Copts later adapted it into what we know now as a typical Christian cruciform.[31] The *Encyclopedia Britannica* elaborates: "Various objects, dating from periods long anterior to the Christian era, have been found, marked with crosses of different designs, in almost every part of the old world. India, Syria, Persia, and Egypt have all yielded numberless examples . . . The use of the cross as a religious symbol in pre-Christian times and among non-Christian peoples may probably be regarded as almost universal, and in very many cases it was connected with some form of nature worship."[32]

In the beginning, Christians didn't even want to be associated with the symbol of the cross, since the very nature of the shape, being the most torturous tool of the time, conjured for them memories of their bloodied savior. For them, the cross was a hellish piece of barbaric sanguinities—oh, if only they could see the irony of that observation now! Truthfully, the horror of the image shouldn't have changed. In fact, some churches even banned the image of the cross to be used because of its pagan origins—particularly in the form of May Day, where druidic cultures carried crossed sticks in honor of their god Thau (so named after the Greek letter), though the day was later turned into St. Phillip's day in the holy calendar after his crucifixion on the same shape. It was abbreviated in early drafts of the New Testament by using a Greek monogram called a Staurogram, a combination of the Greek letters tau and rho used as a *nomina sacre* to avoid the pain of the actual image.[33] Thanks to some writers of the later second century, such as Octavius and Justin, we know that the Christian world by that time did finally claim the name of the cross for itself—and what had once been the Sign of Light of the Egyptian people had morphed into the torturous silhouette of Roman barbarism into the icon of Christ (in all sects until Jehovah's Witnesses, who think the sign is idolatrous—and the Mormons, who see Jesus as a living entity and the cross as a sign of the dying Jesus and therefore mark all their churches with the tell-tale white steeple). Sadly, the symbol went on to be the face of two millennia of bloodshed and discrimination, gory reenactment and vain justification. Swiss soldiers were mandated by holy authorities to use the sword as their most loved weapon because of the cross shape it made when displayed upside down during prayer, and the iconology of the two crossed swords used in the Cross of Independence and others were similar manifestations of the cross advertising conflict.[34] Much like the robbed symbol of the Icthys, Christianity adopted it so entirely that it is nearly impossible to disassociate the former recognition from the current one.

And one hardly needs me to point out that the history of the cross is at least as bloody as the history of the swastika (without even being reminded of the hugely Christian influence that even the Holocaust boasted)—chapter two was a breathy list of instances of religious bloodshed. Besides, the cross in the Roman sense began as an instrument of torture and death—at the time and location of Jesus, that was what it was known as, and arguably has not done much better in the ways of social improvement since then and so begs the question: how did the cross escape the same fate as the swastika when it drags a millennia fewer in years and millions more in deaths through its grisly history? How does the crescent of Islam escape scrutiny when it heralds tyrannical men like Saddam Hussein and Osama bin Laden, or the hexagram when it flies desperately on the flag of a nation whose primary focus is to reclaim a single piece of real estate from their Semitic brethren at the inhabitants' blood-soaked expense? Why does the multitude fear the sign of the Third Reich and not the symbol of the Klu Klux Klan, Al-Qaeda, the Phineas Priesthood, the waves of Puritans that wiped out nearly an entire coastline of Native Americans, the Christian Domestic Discipline, the Taliban, the Westboro Baptist Church, and the Rome-sacking military force of Constantine—to name a few? Why do the two interconnected male-male symbols inspire so much revolt and disgust when its literal meaning communicates nothing more than love, and its violently opposing symbology of the cross demands to be regarded as a staple of grace and peace?

Is it possible that the destructive intentions of a multitude can rewrite the meaning of the infinity symbol into something equally as horrendous? The heartagram? Pi? Delta? Or can these, too, be as easily manipulated into visions of horror, blazons of war, stern alarums and not merry meetings? What about the comparisons of the centuries of turmoil by flags bearing the eagle in Western Europe beginning with the Aquila of the Roman Empire that forcefully conquered nearly all of Europe with a bloody sword (the Hoheitszeichen Eagle of the Nazi Party not forgotten) and the glorious standard that the eagle of America is supposed to incite? I wish it sounded as ridiculous as it should—but when it comes to subverting symbols, the ridiculous is the norm and not the exception. Suffice it to say, the vision of Constantine when he hallucinated the cross shadowed over the sun and the words spoken to him—*In hoc signo vince*[35]— have dominated the definition of the symbol unequivocally.

Notes

1. Shawn Tully, "Cover Story: The Vatican's Finances," CNN, December 21, 1987, http://money.cnn.com/magazines/fortune/fortune_archive/1987/12/21/70001/index.htm.

2. Ross King, *Michelangelo and the Pope's Ceiling* (Penguin, 2003), p. 58.

3. Howard Hibbard, *Bernini* (Penguin, 1965), p. 68

4. Ross King, *Michelangelo and the Pope's Ceiling* (Penguin, 2003), p. 90.

5. Markos Moulitsas Zúniga, *American Taliban: How War, Sex, Sin, and Power Bind Jihadists and the Radical Right* (Polipoint Press. 2010).

6.   John Northbrooke, *A Treatise Against Dicing, Dancing, Plays, and Interludes*, ed. Jeremy Payne Collier (Shakespeare Society, 1843; reprinted, AMS Press, 1971), pp. 59–60.

7.   Everyone knows that the theaters in Elizabethan London did not employ women actors—men dressed as women instead played the roles that are now household names, such as Juliet and Desdemona. Fewer people, however, realize that this kind of theater was also branded as sin by holy men, as the book of Deuteronomy contains a passage that forbids cross-dressing.

8.   Christopher Marlowe, *The Troublesome Reign and Lamentable Death of Edward the Second, King of England: With the Tragical Fall of Proud Mortimer*, Stationer's Register, 1593.

9.   Martha Fletcher Bellinger, "Condemnation of the Elizabethan Theatre," and "Royal Protection," originally published in *A Short History of Drama* (Henry Holt & Company, 1927), pp 246–248.

10.   "Elizabeth Barton," *Catholic Encyclopedia* (Robert Appleton Company, 1913).

11.   Christopher Hitchens, *God Is Not Great* (Twelve Books, 2007), p. xvii.

12.   Maud Bodkin, *Archetypal Patterns in Poetry: Psychological Studies of Imagination* (Oxford University Press, H. Milford, 1934).

13.   http://www.amazinggracebaptistchurchkjv.com/Download99.html (retrieved May 4, 2012).

14.   "Where they burn books, they will in the end also burn people."

15.   Salman Rushie, *Joseph Anton: A Memoir* (Random House, 2012), pp. 127–128.

16.   "History of Intellectual Freedom Concerns in Kentucky," Kentucky Public Library Association, http://kpla.org/committees/intellectual-freedom-committee/ intellectual-freedom-awareness/history-of-intellectual-freedom-concerns-in-kentucky/.

17.   Michael Alison Chandler, "School System in Va. Won't Teach Version of Anne Frank Book," *Washington Post*, January 9, 2010.

18.   Deborah Wrigley, "Parent Files Complaint about Book Assigned as Student Reading," ABC 13/KTRK-TV, Houston, September 3, 2006.

19.   The new trend, it would seem, would be to destroy the writer and not the writing, as in the case of murdered atheist bloggers in Bangladesh and the punishment of Raif Badawi in Saudi Arabia.

20.   ISIS commits similar atrocities in our time. The Mosul Museum has been smashed, piece by piece with sledgehammers, and the archaeological site of Nimrud

has been literally bulldozed, due to ISIS claims that such sites are idolatrous and heretical.

21.   *St. Vladimir's Seminary Quarterly* 3, no. 3 (Fall 1959): pp. 18–34, http://www.schmemann.org/byhim/byzantiumiconoclasm.html.

22.   Emerson Vermaat, "Terror on Trial in the Netherlands," AINA, December 12, 2012, http://www.aina.org/news/20051212121618.htm.

23.   Angelique Chrisafis, "Attack on 'Blasphemous' Art Work Fires Debate on Role of Religion in France," *Huffington Post*, April 18, 2011.

24.   Richard Dawkins, *The God Delusion* (Mariner Books, 2008), pp. 46–48.

25.   Since the first edition of this book, the list of riots instigated by free speech criticism of Islam and Muhammad has only lengthened to include the obscene tragedy at Charlie Hebdo in Paris. More of my thoughts and arguments concerning that despicable crime can be found in my articles on *Patheos*.

26.   Michael Pearson, "Slain Ambassador Died 'Trying to Help Build a Better Libya,'" CNN News, September 15, 2012.

27.   Ray Bradbury, *Fahrenheit 451* (Del Rey Books, 1979), pp. 81.

28.   Tennessee Williams, *Smoke and Summer* (Signet Classics, 1976).

29.   That is how they appeared on the front cover of the first edition of this book. The artist's intent was to show the grisly consequences for which these three monotheisms are most commonly responsible.

30.   Jennifer Rosenberg, "The History of the Swastika," About.com, http://history1900s.about.com/cs/swastika/a/swastikahistory.htm.

31.   Orazio Marucchi, "Archæology of the Cross and Crucifix," *Catholic Encyclopedia*, Vol. 4 (Robert Appleton Company, 1908).

32.   *Encyclopaedia Britannica*, Vol. 6 (1946), p. 753.

33.   Larry Hutado, "The Staurogram in Early Christian Manuscripts: The Earliest Visual Reference to the Crucified Jesus?" in *New Testament Manuscripts*, ed. Thomas Kraus and Tobias Nicklas (Brill Academic Publishers, 2006).

34.   Daniel Rancour-Laferriere, *The Sign of the Cross: From Golgotha to Genocide.* (Transaction Publishers, 2010), p. 166.

35.   Latin: "In the name of this, conquer."

7

The End of the World
as We Know It

"As flies to wanton boys are we to th' gods,
They kill us for their sport."
—William Shake-speare, King Lear

"This is the way the world ends
Not with a bang, but with a whimper."
—T. S. Eliot

Somewhere in the middle of the first decade of the twenty-first century, the pop culture assemblage became obsessed with the Mayan calendar and its apparent foretelling of the end of the current world—whether in an apocalyptic sense that matches the proposed atrocities of the Zionist End of Days or the mere paradigm-transformational shift from one spiritual awareness to another is difficult to say. All seem to be a horrible practice of eschatology. What we do know is that the general masses jumped onto the hysteria in the same emotional tirade as they had when faced with avian flu or Y2K—irrationally and hilariously. It seems wondrous to me that anyone, when confronted with the idea that a finite, archaic calendar was finally running its course circa December 2012, would think such a circumstance signaled the *end of the world*—though the people who proclaim such a thing are likely to be clutching their copies of *The Prophecies of Nostradamus* and *The Pleiadian Agenda* as they do so. This is very much a "seek and ye shall find" mentality. That type of superstition is found even in the context in which it is taken, for one must realize that the Mayans were also a people of gross faiths and fallacies, as illustrated most vividly in an article by John Major Jenkins:

Maya ritual acts were dictated by the 260-day Sacred Round calendar, and all performances had symbolic meaning. Sexual abstinence was rigidly observed before and during such events, and self-mutilation was encouraged in order to furnish blood with which to anoint religious articles. The elite were obsessed with blood—both their own and that of their captives—and ritual bloodletting was a major part of any important calendar event.

For the Maya, blood sacrifice was necessary for the survival of both gods and people, sending human energy skyward and receiving divine power in return. A king used an obsidian knife or a stingray spine to cut his penis, allowing the blood to fall onto paper held in a bowl. Kings' wives also took part in this ritual by pulling a rope with thorns attached through their tongues. The blood-stained paper was burned, the rising smoke directly communicating with the Sky World.

Human sacrifice was perpetrated on prisoners, slaves, and particularly children, with orphans and illegitimate children specially purchased for the occasion. Before the Toltec era, however, animal sacrifice may have been far more common than human—turkeys, dogs, squirrels, quail and iguana being among the species considered suitable offerings to Maya gods.[1]

Ironically, the average, mundane theist would look at such acts as barbarous and futile, and they would be quite right about it, though it has spawned a large, commercial portion of the spiritual justification behind the End of Days phenomenon in monotheistic cultures (clinging to the ancient, blood-spattered advice of pagans!). Beyond the bounds of faith, no decent shred of humanity lies in such a practice—and it can be gathered that nothing of value was ever gleaned from it. Yet the tablet for which the culture is remembered so vividly is heralded as a mysterious work of potential mysticism, an eerie premise into the possibility of apocalypse. Why is that?

It only takes a bit of observation to see that a weighty part of theists today are infatuated with the end of the world. The drama, the epic theme, the involvement of such an episode occurring within the span of our lives mesmerizes us. It is the same thrilling motive that attracts us to stories like *The War of the Worlds*, *The Day After Tomorrow*, and even the zombie "apocalypse."

In a survey conducted by the Pew Forum on Religion and Public Life, 79% of U.S. Christians questioned believed in the Second Coming of Jesus Christ, and 20% of *those* believed that the event would occur in their lifetime. Obviously, it would beg the question: *why* do you think it's going to happen in your lifetime? And no compelling evidence exists. We can safely infer from this observation it is because they *want* it to. Keep in mind that the Second Coming is preceded by the war and torment that will occur (prophetically speaking) by the defeat of the Muslims by the Jews in order to take over the Dome of the Rock and rebuild their great Temple there, only to give Christ something to destroy in his fury when he returns. Naturally, there are moderate dissenters who take a more pacifist theory, claiming that the new Temple can exist simultaneously with the scintillating mosque—but as we have observed, there is little point in taking or arguing a pacifist view if the fanatical one bears more influence. As well, biblical prophecy heralds the encore of Jesus by global warfare and harsh travesty, including the Rapture—wishing for this event to occur is literally equivalent to praying for widespread destruction and suffering.

All this, of course, under the blatant egotistical notion that Jesus will be there for *you,* that the great creator of the universe has come to see you safely in his arms to heaven before making his world-based war on Satan. How important you must be, to receive such special escort. Muslims believe such a messianic victory can be overturned by the firm capture of the city of Jerusalem to make way for the arrival of the Mahdi, the Twelfth Imam, who will lead them on a glorious crusade to conquer the world for Islam. This fantastical affair even invades Islamic politics with no sensitivity, as the president of Iran said with no hint of facetiousness in his voice: "Our revolution's main mission is to pave the way for the reappearance of the Twelfth Imam, the Mahdi."[2] With the tension in the Middle East heating up in noticeable increments almost by the day, Christians engage all their support for a victory for the Jewish people, which they think will signal their own eventual conquest.

The Second Coming of Christ is prophetically partnered with the Rapture: the instantaneous liberation of all good souls from their bodies and their spiritual sojourn up to the Pearly Gates.[3] This removes pure souls from the world in order to protect them from the hellish scene to come. Then follows the Tribulation, a seven-year period in which all unbelieving and unclean souls (e.g., myself and other atheists, homosexuals, pagans, infidels, apostates—the ones who survived punishment on earth—those not baptized into the faith and those who had never been *exposed* to it, etc., etc.) will remain on the face of the barren planet and suffer the punishment that god drizzles down on us. (One who is familiar with the vomitous *Left Behind* series will recognize the setting.) This also signals the rise of the Antichrist and the building of the Third Temple. Then comes a long-winded list of imaginatively epic events (complete with several more Judgments of various titles) ending ultimately in a final war between Satan and Jesus, which will ravage the world anew and all us sordid soulless left here since the Rapture will be caught in the entropy. Jesus, of course, will defeat Satan, and set up a 1,000-year reign creating a new heaven on Earth. This is evidently an oversimplification and there are variations depending on which brand of lunacy one ascribes to, but I couldn't bear to give such morbid fantasy-fiction disguised as Christian eschatology any more ink than that.

People literally *hope* for this to happen—within the year.

With this coming conflict in mind, many American church groups tour to Jerusalem to see the Dome of the Rock and mark it in their hearts as the point of return for Jesus, and make great "charitable" contributions to Christian groups supporting Zionism and the nation of Israel, such as the International Christian Embassy Jerusalem. A grand portion of the funds that it raises goes to strengthen Jewish settlements in the West Bank, even though Israel's occupation there is in direct violation with international law, including Article 49 of the Fourth Geneva Convention, Article 1 of the United Nations Charter, and the International Covenant on Civil and Political Rights.[4] The International Fellowship of Christians and Jews *alone* has raised over $100 million for the Zionist resurgence.

This movement, known as Christian Zionism (notably headed at one point by Jerry Falwell and Pat Robertson), rally under the general proclivity of the Christian Right. Falwell is even alleged to have said in 1981, "To stand against Israel is to stand against God. We believe that history and scripture prove God deals with nations in relation to how they deal with Israel." How, then, can a good Christian object to the violent prescription of the coming End of Days but remain a fervid follower of god? Only subjectively—much like the morality of all religion, it varies by the follower. Zionism is ultimately a new state of ethnic cleansing perpetrated by the Jews to rid the nation of Palestine of all Arabs and Islamic influence and to set up an exclusively Jewish state—a rather despicable "eye for an eye" cause considering the intimate connection Judaism has with such events, both in mythology, with their slavery by the Egyptians and their Exodus, and in actual history, with their ghettos in Venice during the Renaissance and their ultimate nightmare of the Holocaust—mirroring similar influences in Palestine only propagates the same atrocities inflicted upon them in varying scales. But, as is true with all religious conflict, god gives the green light. Israel was god's gift to the Jews in return for self-lacerating their genitals—ergo, the division of a country by riots and radical warfare is completely validated, and the turmoil that occurs all along the Eastern Mediterranean from northern Egypt to Lebanon is merely a means to an end—the fulfillment of god's promise to Abraham.

Ultimately, the theology of the Rapture and the Second Coming is much debated, but an overwhelming amount of Christians believe in the literal letter of its happening, the events of which are predicted based on a couple of very loose interpretations of a few incendiary Bible verses and some bad mathematics. And it must beg one to divulge the motivations behind the *eagerness* for such a thing to occur—after all, the numbers ascending to heaven are select. Those who pray for the Second Coming to manifest soon—indeed, send money to Israeli foundations in order to help make it come about more quickly—must have predisposed ideas as to the purity of their souls. They must have an incredible faith in the righteousness with which they composed themselves to know that they will be spared the tortures of the Tribulation. In other words: they have judged themselves. Such ego is contemptuous and incongruous, knowing that the destruction of the world bursts forth only after *you* have been given the Jesus-Land Fast Pass and cut the line to the Paradise Ride.

But there is the corollary to consider: if one hopes for Rapture, one is by proxy hoping—*ardently* praying—for the continuous, unimaginable torture of one's fellow man. They are desperate for the destruction of nations, the leveling of the face of the planet, the raining of havoc onto humans related in blood and history, no matter their spiritual or sexual or philosophical backgrounds. It measures a cavalcade of pain beyond what can be aptly described and they *dream* of it—relish it! Without mincing words: this is sadism. This is psychotic masturbation. Above that, it's terrorism. To pray for the Rapture is to revel in psychopathy. It and its supporters should be slandered as those who perpetuated the Cambodian Genocide, the Holocaust, the Rape of Nanking, and the carnage of the 1947 Partition of India should be slandered.

The worst possible influence that the idea of the Rapture might exert upon the world is primarily identified in young people. Those who believe that the Rapture is imminent know that their time remaining upon the planet as mortals to enjoy the fruits of human existence is quickly ticking away—and many of them have been given specific timetables denoting all the things in life they will *not* get to cherish. In a chilling documentary called *Waiting for Armageddon,* a film crew interviews several evangelist families who are waiting with quiet savor for god to steal them away from Earth. One woman says to the film crew: "I know I will not get to hold a grand-child. I know [my child] will not get to graduate." Rather than saying this with dread, with pain and loss, it is communicated with a glassy vigor that is eerie to behold. The thought of sacrificing everything one has yet to live for is a price that is entirely unintimidating for these faithful souls, but the crime comes from allowing their uneducated youths to share in the delusion. One member of such a family, Kristen, says:

> *I just want to make it clear that I believe in the Rapture . . . I mean, I always wanted to be part of it but I wanted to be, like, eighty-five [years old]. It doesn't seem fair. I mean, you know, your grandparents have lived these wonderful, long lives, have all these stories to tell you, and they've kind of adjusted to the fact that, you know, they're not going to live terribly much longer. And so you grow up hearing all these stories and you want your own stories. And you want to live these experiences yourself, and if you're done at twenty-four there's only so many experiences you get to have.*

Her sister, Ashley, further intimates:

> *It scares me. Like Kristy feels—I kinda wish that I knew that I had time. I really want to get married and I really want to have kids and raise a family and work and do all that. I mean, I'd like to see the world, but . . .*[5]

To tell our young generation that their lives must be put on hold for the verification of someone else's spiritual justification is disgraceful. To be willing to communicate to a whole new world of people who have not yet loved or lost or triumphed or foundered that they will never get to do any of these things is the most hateful form of proselytizing I have known, and is perhaps the greatest evil behind the idea of the Rapture. To be at the midway or the end of one's own life, to rationalize your own experiences and hope for the end of the world to occur soon in accordance with your own ego—that private delusion is pitiful, but benign. But to convince a fledging batch of pristine minds that they will never have the opportunity to grow and achieve, to connect and transform—this is psychological abuse, and torturous to behold. It literally stops their creation and ambition, halts their future-bent visions for what they want for themselves because they are convinced, as soon as the thought occurs, that they will never have it. This is made more solid by taking these deluded young adults to Jerusalem to look upon the doomed Dome of the Rock and descant at its Islamic architecture and 24-karat gold roof, indulging in jokes about the inevitable destruction of the Jews in god's holy wrath, and relishing the idea of spiritual superiority. In all theology, the very perverse mythology of the End of Days leaves the worst taste in the mouths of freethinking peoples.

Naturally, this is not the first time that such apocalyptic fortune-telling has broached the public eye and, by extension, fallen short each and every time. There was a time when another group of people tried to decode secret messages of the Bible in order to pinpoint the Second Coming. William Miller, a preacher, used a verse from Daniel in order to predict the arrival of the Savior within a year—between 1843 and 1844, to be precise. As the story goes, Preacher Miller gathered together a decently large following and even wrote a book titled *Evidences from Scripture and the History of the Second Coming of Christ about the Year 1843*, published in 1836. When the proposed Day of Return came, Miller stood with his congregation—and the rest doesn't take a historian to guess. Jesus missed his cue, and Miller's group quickly rationalized as to why their calculations had been off, predicting a second future date several months later, which—to no one's surprise but their own—also failed. The group later became known as Seventh-day Adventists, who have since contented themselves with the idea that Jesus will surely return very soon, but haven't bothered to select another appointment.

Apart from this, history is littered with Christian mystics and pseudo-mathematicians prophesying the dire end of the earth—akin to what we might see nowadays as raving transients holding up cardboard signs in grease-written lettering: "REPENT! THE END IS NEAR!" Martin of Tours believed that the Antichrist had already arisen by the year 400 CE, and predicted the end of the world before the fifth century.[6] Pope Sylvester II held the widely maintained belief that the imminent perishing would arrive the first day of the year 1000 CE;[7] Isaac Newton (who also was a student of alchemy) assumed that the pope of his time was the Antichrist; even our old friend Pat Robertson threw in his pitiable two cents, intimating the date of April 29, 2007;[8] Ronald Weinland rolled the dice for September 29, 2011 by nuclear warfare and, like the antiprophetic Mr. Camping, having failed, reset the date, this time for May 27, 2012.[9] Islam is not free from this diatribe of sadistic obsession either, as the Islamic biochemist Rashad Khalifa prophesied a future date for the end of the world in the year 2280 CE, his basis made of a cipher he inferred from the Koran and popularized in his book *The Quran: Final Testament*, in which he explains his deciphering of the code.[10] As well, the theurgical, Britain-based cult known as the Hermetic Order of the Golden Dawn (descended from Masons, taking their hierarchy from Rosicrucian inspiration, and later fathering Wicca) hoped for the end of the world in 2010, in accordance with ritualistic prophecy.[11]

Of course, the wide scheme of apocalyptic thought is not limited only to theism or to the modern perspective. Ancient peoples did believe in predicted cataclysms to come, including the Roman conviction that the country would only last a finite time based on a number of eagles that appeared to Romulus in a dream.[12] Today, scientists tell us that the sun will (albeit in about four billion years) expand into a red giant and consume a grand portion of the solar system, effectively eliminating the possibility of all life on our tiny, climate-unstable planet by drying up oceans and incinerating carbon dioxide levels; and that the Andromeda galaxy (the nearest galactic neighbor to our own Milky Way) is on a direct crash course with ours, with some predicting that the effective collision will increase temperatures in our own solar system by trillions of degrees—also in about four billion years.[13]

On the other hand, a grand deal must be said for ascertaining evidence that may point to the empirically destructive end of our microscopic corner of the universe as we know it versus impatiently awaiting it and using it as an excuse to levy guilt on others before it arrives. There is nothing wrong with looking bravely into the end with a type of stoic certainty that it is in the natural order of all things—perhaps even our universe—to die. It is another piece of the grand cycle that is the miracle of our consciousness. It is, however, an act of incredible cruelty to witness this pattern and lay the blame for it on innocent people—to smear the ache of already painful destruction by pointing it out as the fault of an assembly of people whose spiritual beliefs are non-parallel to yours. As well, ascribing these natural events to a vindictive deity only further points out his capriciousness: it is a poorly made plan indeed for man to be the center of an ideological universe that is filled to the furthest parsec with unimaginable destruction—black holes and red giants and galaxies with an unusual penchant for bumper cars.

This shows no plan or design, or, at the very least, communicates an extraordinarily flawed one. And a wiping out of humanity merely on a global scale would confess the same ineptitude: to attribute our end to a god, whether by widespread, unstoppable virus or volatile asteroid or volcanic pyrotechnics, one must also recognize two crucial points about god—that god is incredibly cruel to create such events, or at least indescribably careless or weak to allow them to occur, and that god has a childish whimsy to "so love the world" one moment only then to cause or allow its destruction in the next. One cannot predict a godly end of the planet without trucking through pits of hypocrisy and contradiction, or at least, proving their god to be a callous and undisciplined child. Perhaps we should expect no less from an anthropomorphic deity who promised us so much in return for an old man and his descendents hacking the skin off their penises.

In preparation for the apocalyptic events, or inspired by the faiths that predict them, violence has been manifested.

In a kindergarten class in Gaza, a graduating group of children taught by jihadists enacted a scene in which they played soldiers condemning Israeli prisoners for fighting against Allah and the nation of Palestine. As well, they performed scenes depicting Palestinian soldiers brutally mistreated by Israeli officers—children hid crying behind plastic cages while handcuffed and others pretended to be Zionist soldiers walked around in army uniforms bearing toy guns. Toy coffins were draped with flags and presented in the fashion of martyrdom. The purpose of the exercise, the teachers claimed, was to remind the children of their love for Jerusalem, Palestine, and their resistance to Israeli invasion. Al Arabiya News, which did an article covering the story that might now seem perfunctory in the Middle East, quoted one child: "I'll fight the Zionist enemy and fire missiles at it until I die as a *shaheed* [martyr] and join my father in heaven . . . I want to blow myself up on Zionists and kill them on a bus in a suicide bombing."[14]

The hostilities occur on both sides, exacerbated by those desperate for the occupation of Jerusalem in anticipation of divine destruction. So much so, in fact, that one could argue the theatrical antics of the jihadist school were not far off from truth. In mid-2009, the BBC shared the story of an Israeli commander who divulged the details of the treatment of Palestinian children while in custody.

You take the kid, you blindfold him, you handcuff him, he's really shaking . . . Sometimes you cuff his legs too. Sometimes it cuts off the circulation.

He doesn't understand a word of what's going on around him. He doesn't know what you're going to do with him. He just knows we are soldiers with guns. That we kill people. Maybe they think we're going to kill him.

A lot of the time they're peeing their pants, just sit there peeing their pants, crying. But usually they're very quiet.[15]

These are the words of Eran Efrati, who was stationed for a decent part of his career in West Bank. Children were typically arrested for throwing stones at Israeli soldiers, sometimes with the use of a sling, wearing scarves to hide their faces. In one instance, a single Palestinian child was taken by an entire group of Israeli soldiers—they put iron weights on his back and beat him so viciously that he could not get up for a week. According to the same article, the "human rights organisation Defence for Children International (DCI) has written a report accusing Israel's military of what it describes as the systematic and institutionalised ill-treatment and torture of Palestinian children by the Israeli authorities." Mohammad Khawaja, a child of thirteen, described his capture by Israeli soldiers:

They dragged me from my home by the scruff of the neck. The more I cried the more they choked me . . .

My mum was screaming. They pulled me along on my stomach. My knees were bleeding. They beat me with their guns and kicked me all the way to the jeep. They cuffed my hands and legs, blind-folded me and left me there for 24 hours. I thought I was going to die.

Later interrogators wanted me to tell on other people. I wouldn't. They beat me with plastic chairs. They told me to sign a paper written in Hebrew. I don't read or speak it. Because I signed it they put me in jail.

To say that these—and thousands of other accounts within this conflict alone—are the casualties of war would not be an incorrect statement. To further say that not all war is religiously motivated or that secular bodies are equally capable of war are equally true statements. But that is no distraction from the fact that this one *is* the subject of religious fanaticism and all the more barbaric for it. As one walks through the Middle East, one is beset with the vainly shrouded enmity between two peoples who are convinced that god made this place especially for them—and to know that a grand number of the civilized West supports and encourages this divergence is despicable. If god does indeed desire this feud to fester all around the Eastern Mediterranean and turn it from what could be thought of as a splendorous realm of ancient culture into a pious abattoir, then monotheism has successfully made it so—and should be all the more ashamed for such fascism. And, as we must note, into this scrabble has been introduced the potential threat of mass destruction by the Israeli government's acquisition of thermo-nuclear material and the common knowledge that they possess the weaponry as well.[16] With the threat of Iran attaining the same devastating equipment, the parties of god grow closer to a kind of horrendous fallout every year.

In his book, *Walking the Bible*, Bruce Feiler paints a gritty, realistic portrayal of the barbed-wired and concrete-walled separation of theism currently in the Middle East. The author, who traveled to all of the known places listed in the Bible in order to walk in the footsteps of everyone from the Patriarchs to Jesus, visiting tels and tombs alike, describes in vivid verbal portraiture the enmity that springs from conflicting ideologies, notably when he pays observation to the town of Hebron, where the tomb of Abraham is located:

> *A police van stood waiting to escort the bus, which had bullet-proof glass on the windshield. Inside, every seat was taken, mostly by ultra-Orthodox Jews . . . As we neared Hebron the tension mounted. We stopped to pick up hitch-hiking soldiers, who stood in the aisles with their machine guns . . . Hebron has been a flashpoint for nearly a century. One of the few spots to have an almost continuous Jewish presence since 1540, Hebron enjoyed largely peaceful relations until 1929, when local Arabs rioted, killed sixty Jews, and wounded fifty more . . . In 1980, a local Jewish high school student was murdered in Hebron, and eight more were shot from a building. Jewish settlers swarmed the neighborhood, seeking retaliation. That began a cycle of murder that only worsened after the 1993 Oslo Peace Accords, which gave the Palestinians control of the city . . . Tension flared dramatically in 1994 when Baruch Goldstein, an American Jewish settler, entered on the last day of the Muslim holy month of Ramadan and gunned down twenty-nine Palestinians, before being beaten to death. Thirty more Palestinians died in the riots that followed.[17]*

Feiler went on to describe his experience in Hebron with its extraordinary security measures, passing through metal detectors, being constantly asked whether or not he was Jewish, and seeing signs lavished in marketplaces that said: THIS MARKET IS BUILT ON LAND STOLEN FROM THE JEWS. This reflects several other places of note also mentioned in the book, such as Bethel with its thick entrance gate, isolating the Jewish town from the

166 • OH, *YOUR* god!

surrounding Palestinian influence—and his conversations with locals, who seemed to give him thick inspection as to his religious affiliations before answering questions or giving him tours. In places of particular religious significance, guards checked visitors even for compact mirrors. "Crack a mirror," one had said to him, "and it becomes a weapon." Cars required special stickers designating them either as Palestinian or Israeli to have permission to use certain highways and enter city gates. No copy of the Bible is allowed on Temple Mount, where Muslim security personnel check every incoming visitor for the holy text. The great divide between Israel and Palestine was abundant everywhere, and Feiler was able to capture the violent dichotomy in a way few journalists could. Perhaps not for his theological yearnings, but for this excellent picture of the true nature of the entropy in the Middle East, Feiler's book is worth perusing.

Anyone who stubbornly refuses to believe that the Jewish invasion of the state of Palestine is not primarily inherited from a spiritual validation but rather a political or secular claim on the same land for historical reasons merely needs to peruse the Israeli Declaration of Establishment. In it and in Zionism, one can glean the same sense of "God, gold, and glory!" that was evoked by Americans in their rush West, slaughtering pagan natives and claiming everything they found as they went:

The Land of Israel was the birthplace of the Jewish people. Here their spiritual, religious and political identity was shaped. Here they first attained to statehood, created cultural values of national and universal significance and gave to the world the eternal Book of Books.[18]

"What's Yet in This, That Bears the Name of Life? Yet in This Life Lie Hid More Thousand Deaths: Yet Death We Fear, That Makes These Odds All Even" —Vincentio, *Measure for Measure* (III.I.38–41)

As mentioned earlier, the greatest possible incentive for the fixation behind apocalypse comes from ego—the unmitigated disregard for the foundering of the surrounding world if the chaos is a sign of your ascension during life. And for a heaven so splendid, who would *want* to wait for their seventy-two virgins or their chance to catch the autograph of the Invisible Sky Wizard? But is there more behind the morbidity? Do theists have a fascination with death that gives them cerebral license to yearn for Armageddon, the zombie apocalypse, the Rapture, alien invasions, and the like? I contemplate my own mortality practically on a daily basis—but to contemplate the mortality of *others* and divine their ultimate spiritual destination is an act that I have not had the audacity to attempt.

Death, meanwhile, seems to be the most subjective topic of all. The supposition that I know what happens after death and you do not—and mine is a glorious heaven of which you will not get to take part because you worshipped the wrong god or ate meat on the wrong day or slept with the wrong sex—is this what gives people the motivation to make a career condemning others or blowing up buses with home-wrought explosives strapped beneath their jackets? Why the obsession with death? Isn't life beautiful enough to cherish while it lasts, and death unknown enough to inspire the timidity to cross that bridge only when it arrives?

An excellent and tragic example of religion's mania with death took place in Uganda, where a group known as the Movement for the Restoration of the Ten Commandants of God (ultimately a Catholic splinter cult) formed in the 1980s after receiving visions from the Virgin Mary admonishing them to live in strict adherence to the Decalogue. They, too, had a date predicted for apocalypse, but when it failed, followers were filled with doubt. Leaders of the cult designated a second date, March 17, 2000, when all one thousand cultists were invited in celebration for their redemption. The scene turned into one of the worst group suicides (or supposed mass murders) in history— 924 bodies were found after a fire destroyed the building where the festivities were occurring, a reported 78 of them being children, and poisons were discovered in a large portion of the served beverages.[19] All five of the principal leaders are thought to have perished or disappeared in the blaze. What would possibly prompt the sadism of the leaders to conduct—or the delusion of the followers to indulge—in such ludicrousness? For most, it is an impatience to meet their maker. For some, it is a means of escape.

Psychologists have begun to make great strides in finding connections between what prompts suicide or morbid thoughts in healthy people. According to one online article by author and commentator on religion Arthur Fredrick Ide, many times the principle of bullying is involved— despair created from an authoritative figure that exudes control over one's life can only be escaped by suicide, as is commonly found in the oppression of religious factions, mandates, or even gods themselves. The article elaborates:

Until recently, few have looked at the bully and what motivates bullying. The bully is anyone: a parent, classmate, religious figure, sibling, etc. Because bullies are found in every walk of life, every vocation, every religion and social outlet, it is critical to understand the psychology of a bully if we are to better understand the psychology of the person committing suicide.

A bully is any individual struggling for attention, authority, and sadistically revels in causing emotional, psychological, and/or physical pain. The bully can be a narcissistic bully, imitative bully, impulsive bully, accidental bully. What they have in common is low self-esteem and the desire to control—which is the reason for such bully organizations as Opus Dei (international, but originally started in Spain) and the Tea Party in the USA. This is especially true among religions seeking absolute control over the individual as occurred in the Roman Catholic Spanish Inquisition that led to the death of millions and thrives to this day in such nefarious groups as Opus Dei, Councils of Bishops or Elders, one-dimensional religious groups such as the Wisconsin Evangelical Lutheran Church (WELS), Pentecostalism, Mormons and evangelical communities such as within the New Apostolic Reformation of the twenty-first century. It is found from Poland to Peru, the USA to UK, Canada to Chad, and throughout the world. [20]

Ide has made a series of writings on this very subject, culminating in one of his most provocative works, *Evangelical Terrorism,* in which he explains:

[S]uicides and violence are especially prevalent among fundamentalists groups and those that preach hatred is peace and tolerance is weakness, as found in Islam, Pentecostalism, The Family, and Latter-day Saints and is increased among evangelical fundamentalists to the point that they form a psychological dictatorship that destroys hope and personal self-esteem. Religion, while many psychologists have not commented on it because they have not studied it and its effect on others, is one of the greatest tools for subordination of people and the illusion(s) it fosters can weigh heavily leading many into reprehensible acts or violence, as with the jihad movement in Islam and Christian terrorists in India, Norway, and elsewhere. [21]

Ide's point is made doubly and devastatingly clear when one looks at various mass suicides over history, such as the eighty people of a Seventh-day

Adventist sect led by David Koresh in Waco, Texas, who died during an FBI standoff when the building was allegedly razed from within in 1994; the thirty-eight members of the Heaven's Gate cult and their infamous leader Marshall Applewhite, who killed themselves in order to shed their carbon-based life-bags and ascend to the heavens to board the spaceship traveling in the wake of Halley's Comet in 1997, escaping the peril that was going to inflict the world shortly after their departure; the Buddhist monks who ritually immolated themselves in protest of the Vietnam War; the 960 Jews who committed suicide in an act of resistance while being besieged by Emperor Lucius Flavius Silvius in King Herod's fortress in 72 CE; the forty-eight adults and children of the Order of the Solar Temple, a cult thriving on the belief of the continued existence of the Knights Templar, who killed themselves in October 1994 in their compound in Canada, believed to be in anticipation of the Second Coming of Jesus—and many other gruesome theatrics besides.[22] This is, of course, without mention of the heinous amount of suicide bombings flooding out of the Middle East in the last few decades, or without noting once again on that ever-present theme of hypocrisy that suicide is forbidden in monotheistic faith: "Do not kill yourselves, surely God is most Merciful to you."[23] Evangelicals and fundamentalists even label suicide as a murder of the self, and therefore against the Commandment: "Thou shalt not do murder." So, equally as palpable as the bloodshed that the religious are so fond of inflicting upon everyone else, they should be as much perturbed about turning the tool of death upon themselves—but have, once again, ignored this poetic and civil law and instead glorified their actions into something only a god who revels in gouts of gore could be proud of. As the Reverend John Hale from Arthur Miller's *The Crucible* cries: "Life, woman! Life is God's most precious gift, and no principle however glorious may justify the taking of it!"[24]

The undiscovered country has long been the province of theism—almost every spiritual practice imaginable has had some claim to the world after death and has tried to impose their knowledge of it for various mortal purposes. The obvious and most sinister portent, of course, is hell. For millennia, Christians have used the fear of hell to essentially scare any living person into whatever doctrine they deemed applicable. Even in reference to transgressions where no specific spiritual punishment is listed in the Bible (such as their favorite, homosexuality), followers of Christ in too many denominations have copied and pasted "hell" as an eternal reprimand in order to give the law the little jolt of terror that it needs in order to be a successful mandate—even though hell never made an appearance in the Bible until the arrival of Jesus.

Thankfully hell has been weakened as a tool of negative reinforcement, because—much as portrayed in chapter one—theists are extraordinarily good at rationalizing anything since belief is purely subjective. Those who fear hell or don't want to believe in the existence of such a sulfurous time-out merely ignore the idea, or say it doesn't exist. (They finally get one right!) This unlikely little tool has been utilized to strip most churches of their power almost definitively since the Protestant movement, the invention of the printing press, and the translation of the Bible into German, English, and other languages, allowing the masses to read it themselves and draw their own conclusions separately from the priests who sought dominion over them—Catholics and fundamentalists are still pinned by an incredible amount of dogma and guilt. For them, what exists is what their doctrine says.

In this fantastical series comes the grossly appalling, assumedly drug-inspired cosmic lobby that was purgatory, where venial sins are purged in absence of baptism during life.[25] What essentially turns out to be a very uncomfortable waiting room between the fires of hell and the assuredly doleful company of heaven, purgatory has long been feared by parents of the Catholic faith as the undeniable destination of all their children who had perished before their baptisms—condemned to wait out the trials of their mortal and venial sins in the meantime, with nothing to be done but hold on for the celestial punch-card to time out. Imagine, briefly, the torture and culpability Catholic parents must have felt for *millennia,* the fear that they had been responsible for the soul of their child hanging in painful limbo because they had not thrown on the holy water quickly enough. This excruciating shame the Church let continue for the better part of twenty centuries, and it is still listed, as recently as 2005, as the legitimate place for impure souls to linger in *The Compendium of the Catechism of the Catholic Church.* Everyone from Aquinas to Alighieri has written on the subject of purgatory, some even with cruel indifference—but it remains to be seen definitively no where in the Bible. As well, the idea of purgatory completely negates the hope that the sacrifice of Jesus was enough to purge *hoi polloi* of the world of their sin anyhow. Thus, it remains nothing more than a torturous phantasm that further corrupts consistencies regarding ideas of the afterlife.

But, of course, there are disparities. Ancient Greeks believed in the underworld of Hades, ruled by the god of the same name, that one was led to over a ghostly river warded by a grim ferryman; Native Americans all had different versions of their own Underworld, some dark and mysterious; Norse pagans spoke of Valhalla; Romans had Elysium—all of which were mandated by a set of stock rules judged over by a divine. Heaven and hell, in whatever culture they manifest, are undoubtedly the largest bribes in the history of mankind—follow the rules, and get an eternal reward; break them, and suffer eternal punishment. It is entirely too easy to sort out the dominance of this kind of radical fear, because it gives inherent and ultimate power to the people who *make the rules*—the clerics. For an enormous space of history, the general, hell-fearing population couldn't read (modern people simply refuse to); they therefore *had* to listen to what the mighty robed figures told them to do in order to avoid a crispy afterlife. The prospect was still so horrendous that even when holy texts became available for the common man, religious figures were still at liberty to use the convolutions and inanities of the content to keep those less familiar with the literature on the edge of subservience for fear of divine punishment. One would *wish* that an enlightened society such as ours would have the intelligent decency not to take the word of such charlatans at face value—but one would be sadly disappointed.

There is a need within us to go on, to live beyond ourselves—and I would be the first to agree that the idea of nothingness after our final breath is not an openly welcoming prospect. However, one must remember that our fears of the unknown give absolutely no justification to a whimsical substitution. The want to be immortal does not magically create the capacity for it—the reality of heaven is less in question than the *desire* for it. People *choose* to believe in it because it feels better to think that such a marvelous thing could happen, that we would be reunited with loved ones in a safe and happy place for all remaining universal time. This poses two drastically important questions, the first being: does this cloudy playroom justify everything sacrificed in order to pay the cover charge? Does the idea of heaven alone vindicate not only every travesty I have described thus far in this work, but likely millions of unmentioned examples of equal or more throbbing gruesomeness besides? Unequivocally, and without hesitation, I can say no—the unimaginable ache of billions of people before me in the name of such a place is more than I am willing to accept for my own happiness—even eternally. What seas of blood bought the admission ticket to heaven! Accepting entrance to heaven under the precepts that religion has provided at *least* in the history of monotheism is to sign tolerance onto every tragic act that such a place watched over with indifference. I could not condone such a horrific, selfish philosophy any more than I could engage in it myself. Of all people, those who trouble deaf heaven with their bootless cries and look upon themselves and curse their fates are the people who prove such a place is unworthy of our adoration and prediction.

Secondly, what does an idea of heaven ask for that shouldn't already be prescribed into human action? In the basest, most generic point, eternal reward lies with being a good person—and what a sticky, vulgar bribe it is. So many centuries after Plato, the Euthyphro Paradox comes out to haunt the theist—is what is good mandated by god because it is good, or is it good because it is from god? The reasonable world is forever indebted to Plato for throwing the idea of heaven that marvelous Chinese finger-trap. In this sense, I am endlessly reminded of the character of Monsieur Geborand, from what I can say without blush is the greatest work of literature ever written in prose, *Les Miserables* by Victor Hugo. Geborand had accumulated millions as a merchant of various goods, and one day listened to a priest in mass—who was a very vivid speaker—describe the bowels of hell that awaited all those who do not have charity in their hearts. From that service on, a sou came from his pocket every Sunday into the grimy hands of a beggar-woman who pleaded alms in the courtyard outside of the cathedral. Once, the bishop watched Geborand perform this rather compulsory act and, turning to his sister, said: "There is M. Geborand purchasing paradise for a sou."

One can very likely see my point—compelled goodness is no goodness at all, it is pseudo-altruism disguised as humility. The idea of heaven in the first place is entirely destroyed if entrance must be bought—the goodness of the world itself should be perfunctory regardless of reward. As such, any loving person should know that worth of a kind act lives in the act itself, and any other motivation destroys the purity of it. Sadly, there are many who believe that people are not capable of such goodness without the hope of a divinely stamped gold star, or couldn't help themselves from performing atrocities without the fear of eternal punishment—that basic humanity is impossible without obligatory retributions. For this, I can only say that people who take such stances have an extraordinary lack of trust in the human species, that they are cowards who do not understand the social necessity it took for us to become evolved primates in the first place.

As well, one who sees goodness merely as a way to get into god's good graces may actually be operating without knowledge under the dire tomfoolery of Pascal's Wager—a simple logical standpoint that states: the only way to be sure of a happy afterlife is to follow the rules whether you believe in them or not—that way, if you're wrong, there's nothing lost. Being a good person for the sake of getting into heaven seems to exhibit an incredible lack of faith in the omniscience of one's god, who would surely be clever enough to see through such a pathetic ruse. Thus, by practical application, the only merit of a good deed is the good deed itself, making the need for an eternal reward completely devoid of point. Heaven suddenly becomes as banal as hell is irrational—one has simply substituted the candies and closet monsters of youth for the infinitely less sensible motivators of adulthood.

Naturally, I take great solace in knowing that no such places exist, and unexpected comfort knowing my death—and the eventual death of the world, perhaps the universe—is in the accepted order of life, and bribing the heavenly makes no ultimate difference. If there is nothingness, I would prefer it—my immortality lies in the work I did while I was alive. I will spend my years investing in *that* rather than in the false hope of redemption for me and hellfire for my enemies. And if the world should come to a designed destruction, whether by Rapture or Cthulu, there are numerous adorations to be said about one who refuses to sacrifice their humanity in exchange for subservience to a vengeful and crass force. It is this resolve that I imagine gave Darwin the temperance and courage to look into the place from whose bourn no traveler returns and boldly say into the darkness: "I am not the least afraid to die." [26]

Notes

1. "Maya Civilization," Canadian Museum of Civilization, June 7, 1995.

2. Address by Mahmoud Ahmadinejad, president of the Islamic Republic of Iran, before the UN General Assembly, Sixtieth Session, September 7, 2005.

3. St. Peter standing at the Pearly Gates is actually another torpid conjuration of theologians that has no basis in the Bible. This and many other imaginative thoughts, such as the affair of Solomon and Sheba; Jesus carrying lambs; Christians being killed in the Colosseum; selling one's soul to the Devil; hatred of abortion; and the terms "venial" or "mortal" sins are all made up by religious scholars and not to be found in Scripture. Ken Smith, *Ken's Guide to the Bible* (Blast Books, 1995), pp. 15–16.

4. *Independent Law Report Commissioned by the BBC Board of Governors,* BBC Governors' Archive, February 2006, pp. 48–50.

5. *Waiting for Armageddon,* Eureka Film Productions, 2009.

6. Richard Abanes, *End-Time Visions* (Four Walls Eight Windows, 1998), p. 119.

7. Jason Boyett, *Pocket Guide to the Apocalypse: The Official Field Manual for the End of the World* (Relevant Books, 2005), p. 32.

8. Pat Robertson, *The New Millenium: 10 Trends That Will Impact You and Your Family by the Year 2000* (Word, 1991).

9. Ronald Weinland, "Moving Forward Rapidly, February 7, 2008," http://web.archive.org/web/20080509064159/http://www.ronaldweinland.com/

10. Rashad Khalifa, *Quran: The Final Testament: Authorized English Version, with the Arabic Text* (Universal Unity, 2001).

11. Eva Shaw, *Eve of Destruction* (Lowell House, 1995), p. 223.

12. Damian Thompson, *The End of Time* (University Press of New England, 1996), p. 19.

13. Fraser Cain, "When Our Galaxy Smashes into Andromeda, What Happens to the Sun?" *Universe Today*, May 17, 2007.

14. Abeer Tayel, "Children at Gaza 'Jihad' Kindergartens Trained to Fight Zionists: Report" *Al Arabiya News*, June 13, 2012.

15. "Israeli Troops 'Ill-treat' Kids," BBC News, August 9, 2009.

16. Luke Harding, "Calls for Olmert to Resign after Nuclear Gaffe," *Guardian*, December 12, 2006, http://www.guardian.co.uk/world/2006/dec/12/germany.israel.

17. Bruce S. Feiler, *Walking the Bible: A Journey by Land through the Five Books of Moses* (Morrow, 2001).

18. *Declaration of the Establishment of the State of Israel*, May 14, 1948.

19. Ian Fisher, "Uganda Survivor Tells of Questions When World Didn't End," *New York Times*, April 3, 2000.

20. Arthur Frederick Ide, "Psychology of Suicide and Bullying—and How Religion, School/Classmates and Family Affect Both," Arthur Fredrick Ide's Blog, November 23, 2011, http://arthuride.wordpress.com/2011/11/23/psychology-of-suicide-and-bullying-and-how-religion-schoolclassmates-and-family-affect-both/.

21. Arthur Frederick Ide, *Evangelical Terrorism: censorship, Falwell, Robertson, & the Seamy side of Christian Fundamentalism* (Scholars Books, 1986).

22. "10 Most Notorious Suicide Cults in History," *Brainz, Learn Something*, http://brainz.org/10-most-notorious-suicide-cults-history/ (retrieved August 1, 2012).

23. Koran, Sura 4 (An-Nisa), ayat 29.

24.   Arthur Miller, *The Crucible* (Penguin, 1996).

25.   At least we have made progress of a kind—the first baptism was performed by Moses with ox-blood.

26.   The Complete Work of Charles Darwin Online, ed. John van Wyhe, http://darwin-online.org.uk/content/frameset?keywords=to%20afraid%20die%20least&pageseq=9&itemID=CUL-DAR262.23.2&viewtype=text.

8

Good Sans God

———————◆◆◆———————

"Wisdom and goodness to the vile seem vile."
—William Shake-speare, *King Lear*

*"If you pretend to be good, the world takes you very seriously.
If you pretend to be bad, it doesn't.
Such is the astounding stupidity of optimism."*
—Oscar Wilde

It has never been the aim or message of atheism or anti-theism to say that without religion the world would be unimaginably utopian, or that all the problems of our distracted globe would be resolved. Truly, should any proponent on my side of the debate claim such a thing, I would be ashamed to be in philosophical tandem with them. Lacking religion, our species would still encounter the epic and potentially insurmountable obstacles of famine and disease, political feuds, climate and resource challenges, and other economic, ecological, and social troubles besides. A secular global society, in the absence of religion, would have much to answer for—could it be done? In a world without religion—or, to say the least, where religion was unable to taint objective decision making and violate civil liberty—could the *answers* that we desire (e.g., the order of the universe, the meaning of life, the remedy to despair, the essence of hope, etc.) be discovered and implemented?

One may be surprised to learn that the objectives of secular society and its tools, science and philosophy, have been struggling to accomplish those very Herculean tasks for centuries. The quest for reasonable truth is by its very nature deplete of solipsism, and is meant to be entirely altruistic—defining principles of the universe by which our entire species benefits. Though this entire book has been one long exercise of finger-pointing, almost every hurdle that has been thrown in the way of any secular body's progress on resolving these issues has, in fact, been dealt by the hand of religion for its own fantastical reasons. One must wonder how much more innovative we might be today without the hobbling nature that arrant faith has provided. Indeed, Richard Carrier, historian and author, goes so far as to give us an estimate: "Had Christianity not interrupted the intellectual advance of mankind and put the progress of science on hold for a thousand years, the Scientific Revolution might have occurred a thousand years ago, and our technology today would be a thousand years more advanced."[1]

The unfortunate pull of secular advancement that seems to give ammunition to its enemies is the observation that logic and science suck the humanity out of our existence—that understanding how particles behave and how neurotransmitters create our plethora of virulent feelings like sorrow, ecstasy, and rage, nullifies the wonderful mystery of the spirit. Well, one is welcome to have such an opinion—but one would communicate one's patent ignorance through it. After all, how does knowing how something works ruin the majesty of a truly incredible process? What unimaginable brilliance is there in the space and time-bending logic of a black hole or the indescribable mystery of the space between subatomic particles, and the potentially smaller building blocks that could, possibly, make up strings? What intriguing imagery could a rabble of frogs and a few Egyptian locusts offer when placed side by side to the relativity of traveling at the speed of light, or cybertronic limbs for disabled patients?

As well, there is the untarnished ring of empirical truth to all of these observations. I find no loss of poetry at knowing that my human experience is ultimately the result of chemical cocktails always churning in my skull—indeed, I find utter inspiration at being privy to such knowledge. This is not depressing—it's liberating. And again, *none* of these recognitions require anything of my person or my constitution in return: no sacrifice is needed for access to their benefits—a claim that religion, sadly, is expressly unable to boast. No matter how supposedly drab or unfeeling the truth may be, is it not better to live in grey truth than rainbow lie—especially considering there is no reason to consider the truth to be grey at all?

Steven Weinberg, physicist and Nobel laureate, articulates similar sentiments:

At the other end of the spectrum are the opponents of reductionism, who are appalled by what they feel to be the bleakness of modern science.

To whatever extent they and their world can be reduced to a matter of particles or fields and their interactions, they feel diminished by that knowledge . . . I would not try to answer these critics with a pep talk about the beauties of modern science. The reductionist world view is chilling and impersonal. It has to be accepted as it is. Not because we like it, but because that's the way the world works.[2]

With the pursuits of physics, tangible answers to the meaning and origin of the universe are quickly being provided—each one stronger and more graceful than the last. For thirty years, Einstein mentally plodded uphill attempting to find his unified field theory that would explain the grand physical divide between general relativity and quantum mechanics. In the 1980s superstring theory was born—a vast step in understanding the collective ways in which the universe communicates through its various forms of matter and anti-matter, and with so many unsolved pieces of the puzzle remaining in limbo for us to reach toward, there is so much room left to play. The possibilities are almost literally endless.

In August 2012, the Mars lander "Curiosity" made its official touchdown on the surface of our neighboring planet and sent back photographs within seconds. Coupled with its extraordinary goals to find potential traces of previous or current life, we have the incredible opportunity to look at the sheer innovation of Curiosity's journey—the lengths we have come in *all* sciences that were required to propel a computer to the surface of Mars, and the struggles that we are obliged to acknowledge: what it took to make such a thing possible. The unmistakable good of this struggle and the worldly benefits it bestows was captured superbly in an article covering the event:

The news these days is filled with polarization, with hate, with fear, with ignorance. But while these feelings are a part of us, and always will be, they neither dominate nor define us. Not if we don't let them. When we reach, when we explore, when we're curious—that's when we're at our best. We can learn about the world around us, the Universe around us. It doesn't divide us, or separate us, or create artificial and wholly made-up barriers between us. As we saw on Twitter, at New York Times Square where hundreds of people watched the landing live, and all over the world: science and exploration bind us together. Science makes the world a better place, and it makes us better people.[3]

These are the events that objective truth manifests, and the subsequent emotions that it instills. No other endeavor known to man has had the same underlying goal—unifying the world through truth as opposed to persecution of those who differ. This is why mathematics is a universal language—two plus two equals four no matter what country from which one originates, from which college one matriculated, or in which god one believes. One might consider these and other scientific milestones to be rather blasé accomplishments in the face of a god who created a universe in seven days, but considering the other side offered us the grand astronomical conclusion that the rings of Saturn were the celestial depository for Jesus' foreskin upon his ascension, I think we've made better progress without them.[4] As Victor Stenger so notably said: "Science flies us to the moon. Religion flies us into buildings."[5]

In his book *The Elegant Universe*, Brian Greene gives a magnificently adept layman explanation of the reasons to suspect string theory as the great, unifying scientific discovery of our age. He also approaches the topic with incredible humility, acknowledging—as is admirable of all scientists—the necessity of continuous study and growth, that no knowledge is ultimate in and of itself.

> *What is largely beyond question and is of primary importance to the journey described in this book is that even if one accepts the debatable reasoning of the staunch reductionist, principle is one thing and practice quite another. Almost everyone agrees that finding the [Theory of Everything] would in no way mean that psychology, biology, geology and chemistry, or even physics had been solved or, in some sense, subsumed. The universe is such a wonderfully rich and complex place that the discovery of the final theory, in the sense we are describing here, would not spell the end of science. Quite the contrary: the discovery of the T.O.E., the ultimate explanation of the universe at its most microscopic level, a theory that does not rely on any deeper explanation, would provide the firmest foundation in which to build our understanding of the world. Its discovery would mark a beginning, not an end. The ultimate theory would provide an unshakeable pillar of coherence forever, assuring us that the universe is a comprehensible place.*[6]

A comprehensible place, indeed—the continued work in which we have endeavored since Newton first put his Laws to paper, and long before. There are many who look at the gaps in science with disgruntlement and say that the hypothesis provides inept answers because, truly, it does not yet have *all* the answers. Scientists of all fields have been continuously plowing both into the future and into the past, looking steadfastly into what would be the possible origins of life, of the cosmos; what would be the edge of the universe and the reason behind every interaction of matter known to us—and, of course, the work is incomplete. It likely will never be complete. That being said, we are lucky enough to be gaining on it—in his conversation with Lawrence Krauss at Arizona State University mentioned at the beginning of chapter one, Richard Dawkins said that the gaps were quickly narrowing, and that the chemical reaction that spawned the first life is within our grasp to discover. Physicists working on the Big Bang theory temper it every year with more quantifiable evidence. Even when the destination is complete, with empirical knowledge, the work is never finished.

These methodologies, even containing gaps, are impressive for a number of reasons. Primarily, because the solid foundations of science have come close enough to mathematical certainty as can reasonably be expected, and the flawless art of proof has supported them time and time again. No longer do we need to question whether or not the earth is flat, or why things fall to the ground. We know the human body is not kept in health by the balance of humors, nor that disease is the work of evil spirits. The grand leaps that science has brought us in just a couple of short millennia compared to the multimillennia before is simply astounding—our knowledge and innovation, quite clearly, grow exponentially. On this track, who knows how quickly the extraordinary genius of man will find those remaining gaps in our knowledge, however large or numerous, and put them to a timely end?

This process is important to recognize because there is only one other opposing hypothesis that exists in the wide scale of human acceptance— to look upon the vast unknown of the universe, to sit with wonder at the coming tides or the falling stars and with an air of timidity and fear say: "god did it." That's it—don't bother to explore, to discover. Much like the fear of retributions cast upon Icarus and Prometheus, too many millions stare slack-jawed without inspiration at an entire cosmos of mystery and are content to leave it, quite literally, to the imagination.

While this type of cerebral laziness is sad, it somehow has attempted to stem the flow of the former, an indomitably more productive style, for too many hundreds of years. It claimed that the earth is a flat disc in the center of its own, compliant universe; it negates of the use and study of stem cells that could, eventually, be used to cure Parkinson's, diabetes, and Alzheimer's, among hundreds of other diseases and ailments; it assumes the time when the "soul" enters the fetus, thereby making the act of abortion into murder; and it credits the various outcomes of any logical circumstance to the cause of divine intervention. In these cases, theology is impractical in its conclusions, but all science can do is provide continuous, unbiased support for the sake of objectivity, and hope that sense wins out. One would be reminded of Laplace, the astronomer and mathematician who, during the time of Napoleon, was invited to share his work on universal systems with the emperor. After reading it and glancing at Laplace's orrery, Napoleon asked why there was no inclusion of god in his work, to which Laplace replied that there was no need for such an assumption to make it complete.

It is reasonably easier to comprehend mythology over science—the gaps are complete, and the work is perhaps more entertaining. To understand the Big Bang theory, one must know something of physics, chemistry, and relativity, and be able to imagine indescribable speeds over phenomenal periods of time. To understand the world via creation—read Genesis, or insert any other creation myth here. Some deity clicked his fingers and there it was. The law of parsimony fails us at this point—one god and six days may be simpler than billions of years and untold numbers of elements, but it does not lead us toward a stable hypothesis. However, one can see the lure behind such reasoning—the minimalism lacks intimidation as much as content. Science, unfortunately, seems to be only one benevolent tool of atheism that is the subject of scrutiny.

Dialectic thought was nearly lost in Western society by the overwhelming popularity of Plato's philosophy and his argument from design. It was the Arab cultures, which had already had an appreciation of observation and which were introduced to Socratic and Aristotelian philosophy by the expansion of the Hellenic empire that kept the knowledge flourishing during the Dark Ages. With the Arab conquering of Spain in 711 CE, and the academic capital of Córdoba giving welcome to Christian and Jewish scholars of Western Europe, the basis for methods of experimentation and observation were once again integrated into Western culture. This wonderful piece of luck is somewhat sadly eclipsed by the deluge of theistic intervention in the advancement of science in the ancient world, such as: the trial and guilt of Anaxagoras in Athens after his proposal that the sun and moon were not gods; the conviction of Galileo; the University of Paris's rejection of Aristotelian philosophy in 1210 CE on the grounds of calling it "pantheism"; or the 219 forbidden concepts listed by the Bishop of Paris in 1277, including "the eternity of the world, denial of personal immortality, and denial of free will."[7]

This is a typical, capricious change of pace for religion, which throughout the ages had referred to science as Aquinas patronizingly stated and Stenger quotes, "the handmaiden of religion." For years, the first two laws of thermodynamics were even used as proof of the existence of a divine creator. Waffling back and forth, religious leaders spanning the centuries seem to have a very difficult time toeing the line of science between where it serves as a useful tool and asset to humanity versus and where it exposes the religious myth at the seams. For a time, science appeared to be the wild animal that religion tried so desperately to cage, and failing this, to put down. This extends not merely to science as a practice, but also to secularism as a whole in every philosophy or method in which it manifests itself.

"Strong Reasons Make Strong Actions"
—Louis, *King John* (III.IV.186)

Through April and May 1940, a tragedy was occurring.

In the Katyn Forest in Russia, 22,000 Polish prisoners captured in the Soviet invasion of Poland and in other events were being methodically massacred by the hands of Soviet Secret Police and the approval of Joseph Stalin. Stalin, as is widely known, was a militant atheist—this, much like the inaccurate ruse of Hitler's atheism, is why many theists think he was capable of such barbaric and deathly acts during his time as premier, which totaled numerous millions of victims. One typically forgets that Stalin reopened the churches in Russia during WWII despite his political misgivings, and that his cruel actions that bordered on a mass genocide were causes of his politics, not his anti-theism. Indeed, while his government tried to negate religious influence in his country to an almost unrecognizable level, the horrific deeds in which Stalin indulged were not tied to his religious beliefs at all, but from the Lenin-inspired idealism that the only adept Communist government that could exist was one without churches.[8] The nature of history has been to combine these two arguments rather than to separate them—but one must always remember that being an atheist has never come with the predilection to burn churches. That, sadly, is the reflection of a corrupt governmental power or innate psychopathy, which is not to be empathized with more than any motivation that can be thought of to justify mass persecution.

The same can be said of Pol Pot, another favorite and mislabeled target of preconceived atheist brutality. Pol Pot operated under a type of political maxim that included the warning that Communist governments operated most fluidly without the impracticality of religion. Pol Pot was also an extreme advocate for violence, which is likely what gave him a temperament to conduct the Cambodian Genocide and banner the affirmation of statesman Mao Tse-tung: "Political power grows out of the barrel of a gun." Both Stalin and Pol Pot (and the other men ruling in tandem with Pol Pot during the Khmer Rouge period) were willing fighters for the sake of Communist dictate, with their own revisions on the political process as needed. This ideology, while condemning use of the church in a political sense, is *not* secular and cannot be called that, nor can it be attributed to the mandates of anti-theism—because there *aren't* any.

In referencing the Holocaust and other supposedly god-lacking political movements, Pope Benedict XVI said: "As we reflect on the sobering lessons of the atheist extremism of the 20th century, let us never forget how the exclusion of God, religion and virtue from public life leads ultimately to a truncated vision of man and of society and thus to a 'reductive vision of the person and his destiny.'"[9] Beyond our examination of some of the historical evidence of the religious motivation of the Third Reich to begin with—Benedict might have done well to remember that some of the greatest victories Hitler achieved in Germany during his rise to power was due to the signing of the Reichskonkordat, a 1933 treaty between Germany and the Holy See under Pope Pius XI (whose successor Pius XII wrote a grossly indulgent and gaudy letter to the Fürher offering his support), which fundamentally allowed Catholicism to be practiced and taught in Germany under the rule of the Third Reich if the Vatican essentially kept its mouth shut about Nazi affairs.[10] This treacherous act, beyond being cowardly in itself, was rather inspired in similar terms by the demagogue Mussolini in the Lateran Pacts of 1929, from which the Vatican received its sovereignty and money for silence.[11]

These procedures of the Church, at least during the timeframe of the Second World War, proved substantially more supportive to the actions of fascist and Nazi atrocities than nonfaith ever could have. Nor, do we note, an air of objection whatsoever from the Vatican during the reopening of the churches by Stalin in Russia. Indeed, the Russian Orthodox Church stayed staunchly in Stalin's corner until the very end and supported his regime. Whatever untrue philosophical underpinnings may be vainly attributed to Stalin's massacres, Mussolini's rape of Northern Africa, and Hitler's concentration camps are diminutive when compared to the silence—and benevolence—of the Church in regard to the same events. One hopes Ratzinger chokes on his own hypocrisy.

What Communism expressly does in these political examples is negate the secular demand of the individual and instead relegate control to single leaders in an almost deified sense. While it may not be overtly religious in nature, the overall picture cannot be claimed as secular when Stalin exploited a very ingrained Russian belief that the czar is the mortal intermediate between heaven and earth, and conflicting spiritualities undermine that power if enough people believe in it. He yielded results in his government that were heralded—despite their scientific origins and medically devastating effects—as miracles, such as advancements in agricultural science. He and other Communist tyrants deified themselves by presenting their images as true leaders of country, magnanimous and imperturbable. This is akin in more than a passing glance to the tyranny of North Korea, which indulges a Great and a Dear Leader (and now with Kim Jong-un has finally created its own Trinity) of the same family, and upon the birth of the Great Leader the birds sang in Korean. We would also be neglectful in forgetting to mention Emperor Hirohito—an often overlooked contributor to the Axis powers by those of faith, whose bodily form on earth was literally heralded as god. Such a radically spiritual claim seemed not to ruffle the feathers of his partners in fascism, devout as they were. All these governments have done, contrary to the theory that they exist without god, is traded a divine deity with a mortal one. Their leaders may or may not have been atheists, but their actions and governments do not hold a trace of secularism nor fair philosophy about them—nor can anti-theism be the primary motivator for their policies when political power was the incredibly prominent reward.

For a person to say: "He killed one million people because he is an atheist" is an absolute non sequitur. It is as much to say that I ate an orange because it's cloudy outside. There is no prescription to the ideology of atheism. There is no written rule or authorization or stipulation. When one is an atheist, all that can be said about them is that they do not believe in god—and nothing else can be inferred. If one is an atheist and commits mass genocide, they do it because they are told to by an insane ideology, or compelled by some equally empty reason, and not because their non-god told them to do it. It's an absolutely irreconcilable accusation by theists to connect the actions of Communist dictators to their lack of faith as I could as easily attribute it to their probable dislike of skateboarding. Being an atheist does not mean one is automatically a nihilist—nor did Dostoyevsky ever say that this was the case, as is often claimed, save through the ruminations of a fictional character.

Subsequently, one cannot argue that the ill-doings of religion are due to the same kind of evil people acting independently of their creed. Too many times has the argument crept into debate that perhaps the bloodshed and chaos that religion has caused are actually the afflictions of bad people in power. I wish, if only for the sake of a more united and wholesome humanity, that this were so, but the theology simply doesn't corroborate. When a holy text commands—or, in the case of the odd schizophrenic, god himself tells— one to commit genocide (as we have seen too often), *religion* is the motivator. When one reads Leviticus 18:22 and marches against civil rights, *religion* is the divine cheerleader. In all aspects of the anti-theist argument, we see travesties that, unlike the works of Stalin and Pol Pot which were in fact inspirations of Communism, the deductive trail leads only back to the justifications of one's faith. And let us for a moment contend with the possibility that someone— specifically in the name of atheism—committed genocide, wouldn't it be just as wrong? And how many *billions* of bodies would need to crowd the loam before "atheism" could begin to match the mortality rate that religion has had in its short time on this planet? One should be thankful that there are no precepts of atheism that compel us to try—or, in the case that there were, we would be loving and intelligent enough to forsake such requisites and maintain the social connectivity that gave us such liberated existences in the first place.

Atheists, thankfully, are beginning to educate both themselves and those surrounding. While I do not think that congregation is necessary for the validation of anti-theism, I cannot deny that the combining of thoughts, ideas, and a widely visual proof of the acceptance of this philosophy is beneficial to those who may not be strong enough to withstand the bluntness of religious opposition by themselves. For this reason, events such as Reason Rally and social network groups like Global Secular Humanist Movement have taken great strides in uniting nonbelievers and compounding arguments.

It is through communication like this that we shed the negative veil that has been unjustly thrown on freethinkers. As every new statement is made, book written, and lecture presented, we drive back theistic bias. With the soul of wit that is brevity and a touch of his own original brilliance, Dr. Peter Boghossian, assistant professor of philosophy at Portland State University, was asked the following question in an online interview: "Recent studies suggest that atheists are among society's most distrusted groups, comparable even to rapists in some circumstances. Why do you think being an atheist has such a negative stigma attached to it?" His response: "Ignorance."[12]

Such conversations and engagements are vastly important to opening the public eye to the needs and goals of secular society—otherwise the blood of Katyn and Auschwitz will forever wrongly be blamed on us, for nothing more than saying that human morality is the only kind that exists. And by that morality, Christians should not be fed to the lions. Muslims should not be incinerated. Jews should not be fenced. Pagans should not be drowned. And no decent secular person could think so without committing the very vile acts that religion is responsible for making so infamous. Perhaps that is the grand unifying theory of everything in a social sense—that *people* matter. Many atheists would agree that this is the definition of secular society: respect for life, not for idealism.

Thankfully a type of cabalism is not necessary for the truth of these observations to be perceptible. A fallible idea should be ridiculed and slandered when it evokes division and hatred, even if the lives of its people deserve a kind of civil respect. In this sense, I cannot be compared to Greg Epstein, Humanist Chaplain of Harvard University, who writes an entire chapter on the hope to live harmoniously with religion in his book *Good Without God*,[13] if only for my observations that religion could not allow it socially and the advance of science cannot allow it ideologically.

Despite this, some people staunchly strive for symbiosis. Quoted in the dedication of Epstein's book, a verse of Sherwin Wine's *Song of Humanistic Judaism* is written:

> *Where is my light?*
> *My light is in me.*
> *Where is my hope?*
> *My hope is in me.*
> *Where is my strength?*
> *My strength is in me . . . and in you.*

Wine's stanza calls for unity among all peoples—a type of heavenly synchronization that will remedy the trials caused by all ideological schisms. Unhappily, the war of ideas is too great a challenge to ignore or to dismiss— someone must win. I will no sooner give up my thirst for rational truth than a theist will give up their hope of heaven or their vindications of discrimination. For this conflict, there is a multitude of weapons. Atheism, it seems, favors study and observation, objectivity and education. Religion wallows in violence and in corruption—and, despite my equal desire for peace in the world, I would stand against *any* ideology that uses such pains for its devices, or seeks to dismantle my civil rights and the rights of others. To combat this, discord is acceptable. While Epstein is insightful and wonderful in his observations of the goodness atheism provides to the world, his softness betrays those who have suffered under the oppressive thumb of faith for millennia—those who are still suffering. For them, no peace is possible while religion exerts the toxin that it does.

Since 1946, UNICEF has been working diligently in its humanitarian endeavor toward aiding mothers and children abroad. Beginning in World War II, it began immediately supplying food to nations in Western Europe that had been ravaged by warfare and hasn't stopped, turning it into one of the largest charities on the planet, dispersing 2.6 billion vaccines to eighty countries in 2008. By and large, UNICEF care has gone toward a variety of maladies, including HIV/AIDS in Africa, (and *not* by telling those afflicted to avoid condoms, I might add) and measles in Lebanon and Pakistan, and toward basic education combined with gender equality in a number of developing nations, with headquarters in over 191 countries.[14] Having raised nearly $200 million in North America alone, UNICEF is but one of the leading charitable organizations making a difference in the world, in tandem with Amnesty International, Doctor's Without Borders, S.H.A.R.E., and Goodwill Industries.

Each and every one of these charities has something intrinsically common in their character—they are all secular. Charitable donation as a whole has been a forefront for the defense of theistic integrity: time and again, religious leaders use the vanguard of their humanitarian endeavors to give a good façade to the church that they represent. This is as it should be—the very nature of the few benevolences religion has had the good form to attempt are of charitable themes.[15] While these actions do not have the ability to rectify the various crimes that theism has previously committed, it has also been the foul nature of too many religious activists to infer that those without religion do not have the capacity for this generosity—that true charity is only capable through god. These insulting premises are less hinted at than painfully displayed through pseudo-surveys, but secular organizations have the unparalleled freedom of knowing that no matter how much money is raised (and it is, at least, a considerable amount), not a penny of it came from moral guilt, celestial bribery, or priestly coercion.

Perhaps that is the strangest and the most compassionate point of secular society and of godless philosophies—they are not mandated to do good as much as they are not mandated to wreak harm. Because there are no compelling sacrifices that must be made in a secular mind-frame, all those that *are* made are done for the benefit of the cause. I will always give money to a homeless person if I can—*knowing* that I won't go to heaven for it. The typical medical worker at UNICEF likely does not think they will be getting a complementary seat in Paradise for every polio vaccine they administer. Nothing is bought. It is merely given.

In a brief discussion I had with Ken Ham via radio on August 11, 2014, the founder of the Creation Museum and the driving force behind Answers in Genesis and the Ark Encounter told me that atheists have no basis for a system of morality. When I asked him whether or not Noah cursing his grandson for a crime he did not commit was a moral action, Ham replied:

Well, actually, um, when it says "cursed be Canaan"—yes, it was, you know—when, when you say "cursed," it was, because you have to understand what the Hebrew word there means. But it meant that there was to be a judgment on Canaan, because, obviously, he did something that was wrong, and he did something, uh, that was a problem. And the interesting thing is, uh, we can see the consequences of that, because when you look at the descendents of Canaan, they became the people of Sodom and Gomorrah, the Canaanites, some of the most wicked people that ever lived on Earth. Uh, wicked for their morality. Of course, as an atheist, you have no basis anyway for morality, and so why would it worry you what Noah did? Because, as an atheist, you can't say that anything ultimately is right or wrong, you have no basis for saying anything is just or unjust, so it's only within a Christian system of having an absolute God who is an absolute authority that you can even decide if something is right or wrong, that something is just or unjust. So that's important for you to understand from the start. So, I don't even know why you asked the question, as an atheist.

While I've responded to Mr. Ham's contemptible assertion directly via Twitter and blog posts, I feel that the new edition of this book provides a strong answer as to whether atheism or theism is a more stable platform for morality.

In many ways, secularism has yet to have been given the chance to show the bounty with which it is capable of blessing the world—it has been subject to too much opposition in the course of human history. Spinoza tried his best to make the contrast apparent in *Theological-Political Treatise*, explaining:

> But if, in despotic statecraft, the supreme and essential mystery be to hoodwink the subjects, and to mask the fear, which keeps them down, with the specious garb of religion, so that men may fight bravely for slavery as for safety, and count it not shame but highest honour to risk their blood and their lives for the vainglory of a tyrant; yet in a free state no more mischievous expedient could be planned or attempted. Wholly repugnant to the general freedom are such devices as enthralling men's minds with prejudices, forcing their judgment, or employing any of the weapons of quasi-religious sedition; indeed, such seditions only spring up, when law encounters the domain of speculative thoughts, and opinions are put on trial and condemned on the same footing as crimes, while those who defend and follow them are sacrificed, not to public safety, but to their opponents' hatred and cruelty.

If ever came a day when the true test arose, the end result of a country based entirely and fluidly on secularism (like the United States tried to begin with, but is quickly sinking under the weight of a Christian populace), I am confident that an objective civilization would yield indescribably positive results. It is a faint hope, however, that in such a religiously dominated globe—a world that has sunk to such a wearisome level that some United Nations leaders can seek to ban blasphemy in an effort to placate religious fanatics[16]—a nation in this vein will ever get the chance to be conceived.

Notes

1.   Richard Carrier, "Christianity Was Not Responsible for Modern Science," in *The Christian Delusion: Why Faith Fails*, ed. John W. Loftus (Prometheus Books, 2010), p. 414.

2.   Steven Weinberg, *Dreams of a Final Theory* (Pantheon Books, 1992), p. 52.

3.   "Mars Orbiter Catches Pic of Curiosity on Its Way Down!" *Discover Magazine*, Bad Astronomy, blog, August 6, 2012, http://blogs.discovermagazine.com/badastronomy/2012/08/06/mars-orbiter-catches-pic-of-curiosity-on-its-way-down/?utm_source=feedburner&utm_medium=feed&utm_campaign=Feed%3A+BadAstronomyBlog+%28Bad+Astronomy%29.

4. Leo Allatius, *De Praeputio Domini Nostri Jesu Christi Diatriba.*

5. Victor Stenger, *God and the Folly of Faith* (Prometheus Books, 2012).

6. Brian Greene, *The Elegant Universe: Superstrings, Hidden Dimensions, and the Quest for the Ultimate Theory* (W. W. Norton, 1999), p. 17.

7. Victor Stenger, *God and the Folly of Faith* (Prometheus Books, 2012), p. 75.

8. Dimitry V. Pospielovsky, *A History of Soviet Atheism in Theory and Practice and the Believer, Vol 2: Soviet Anti-Religious Campaigns and Persecutions* (St. Martin's Press, 1988), p. 89.

9. Pope Benedict XVI, in his meeting with state authorities on the grounds of the Palace of Holyroodhouse, United Kingdom, September 16, 2010, http://www.catholicnewsagency.com/unitedkingdom10/resource.php?res_id=1438.

10. Reichskonkordat, Article 32.

11. Lateran Treaty, Articles 2–5, 24.

12. Jason Korbus, "Losing Faith: An Interview with Peter Boghossian and Matt Thorton," May 18, 2012, http://thebentspoonmag.com/2012/05/18/losin-faith-an-interview-with-peter-boghossian-and-matt-thornton/.

13. Greg Epstein, *Good Without God* (HarperCollins Publishing, 2009). See especially chapter 5 "Pluralism: Can You Be Good With God?" pp. 151–168.

14. UNICEF, *Annual Report*, 2008, http://www.unicef.org/publications/index_49924.html.

15. My thoughts on religious charity have been more thoroughly explored in my article on *Patheos:* "The Theist's Claim to Ultimate Charity Needs to Stop," June 29, 2015, http://www.patheos.com/blogs/danthropology/2015/06/the-theists-claim-to-ultimate-charity-needs-to-stop/.

16. Bradley Klapper, "Arabs Seek Blasphemy Ban; US, Russia Spar on Syria," *Boston.com*, September 26, 2012, http://www.boston.com/news/world/middle-east/2012/09/26/arabs-seek-blasphemy-ban-russia-spar-syria/qYTHalaGM1uoxedsF1FeKM/story.html.

9

Questions from the Audience

————————◆◀◆————————

"I am not bound to please thee with my answers."
—William Shake-speare, The Merchant of Venice

"I am bound to furnish my antagonists with arguments,
but not with comprehension."
—Lord Byron

I love to argue. Admittedly, not always in the most civilized fashion.[1]

But I hate arguing the same thing *over and over* again. Part of it is my inherent laziness. Part of it is my distaste for simple repetition. But mostly it comes from wondrous annoyance at having to explain what I find to be so obvious—not that it *is*, or *should* be to anyone. A lot of the inspiration from writing this book came from having the same conversations continuously with different peoples (some more amiable, some much less so—a lamp may or may not have been thrown during one of them)—as in a defiant gesture of saying: "I am tired of saying it again—here, *read* it." I realize how petulant that might sound, since it would imply that I think writing this book would serve as an escape from endeavoring in future arguments on the same subject. That, unfortunately, is a goal much beyond my means and the means of this work. But, perhaps, a *percentage* of people might be referred to this instead of me having to explain it all over again verbally.

Even so, I realized as I was drafting an outline that there are pieces of arguments, finer details, unembraced ideas that I hadn't noticed—untapped, unmentioned. (A note of thanks to Thomas Hardy for my apparent obsession with compound adjectives in the absent sense today.) There were perhaps *millions* of points that a theist might argue, or an atheist might supplement for this book that I never thought of, and while I realize that one can only

193

contain so much in a book and keep it at a readable pace, I felt that these must *somehow* be acknowledged.

So I opened it up. I gave others the chance to argue one final time.

Over the course of several days as I was writing this chapter, I made requests for questions, comments, arguments, and concerns from people of every walk of spirituality from atheism to monotheism and back again through Facebook and social circles, and, in one case, even from a stranger in a park. I put forth the position that religion plays a negative role in the world as we know and knew it and asked them to provide feedback—if a question or position of special merit was made that wasn't previously addressed in earlier chapters, I decided to put it in here. After all, I never would want to be accused of ducking an issue, and that challenge cannot be met if I don't give the issue a chance to come to me.

What follows are the thoughts of people who may or may not have studied backgrounds in religion. Some of them I don't know personally. All are listed here anonymously. My hope was that facets of the great anti-theism argument that I had never considered would arise from minds with processes and experiences infinitely different from my own—I wasn't disappointed. Here is the collection of ones I felt most individual and alien from themes I had previously written on in an attempt to cover as much of the debate as possible.

Why is atheism and anti-theism so prevalent now?

One will notice that the numerous examples of immoral and wicked behavior listed—not only in my work but also in the works of many others—are from the recent past. This is not done merely as a marketing ploy to get the reader involved on a personal level with pieces of history for which they were a part. Rather, it is also because the scale of religious influence in the last century has grown to such a palpable and miserable point that even laymen in the subject can easily recognize it as the primary progenitor of too much evil. Only so many times can skyscrapers in New York be demolished before thinking people will respond: "Well, that's about enough of that." The same can be said for the murders of diplomats and the torching of embassies.

I also usually detect an air of conservative intrigue to this question, as if to imply that the asker actually knows the answer, and it has nothing to do with the merits of atheism and anti-theism, but rather with the notion that the human race has spiraled so irretrievably downward that it should come as no surprise that a growing group of people are proclaiming distance from god.

To this assumption, it can only be remarked that the true test of secularism has not yet been conducted—if we are indeed moving away from god as a society, it is impossible to tell how successful our futures will be (though it can be reasonably bet upon). If, on the other hand, we were to go backward, both in time and in supposed morality, it is *absolutely certain* what it is we shall come across—namely, two thousand years of racial and sexual contempt and compulsory wish-thinking, in which the majority of the world's population were kicked and beaten and raped into submission before they went on to corrupt organized civilization and invade both our bedrooms and our borders.

Forward, ho!

Is there no good in religion that is worth fighting to keep?

Most simply: no. There is no original good that only religion can provide or can ultimately provide better than any nonreligious force can. Any charity can be matched by a secular organization. The psychological benefits of faith in terms of community, hope, love, and morality are intrinsically human and therefore religion is not required to achieve them, as is true with all other quantifiable qualities of faith. A favorite challenge of mine posted by Hitchens was to name a single moral statement said or action done by a person of faith that could not be done by a person without it—the challenge, to the best of my knowledge, stands undefeated. Conversely, a myriad of immoral statements and behaviors can be made *only* with the existence of religion that would be impossible otherwise without it. In essence, all the religiously incited deplorable acts listed in the wide scope of this book would not be possible if religion had never existed.

This is not to say, per example, that *war* would not exist without religion, but *religious* war would not. This can be applied to every other spiritual justification ad nauseum, and to say that since war would exist anyhow there is no point in criticizing religion for the sake of criticizing religious war is ultimately in tandem to saying a patient is dying of cancer anyway so let's not bother with pain medication. One despicable facet of the whole is always, *always* worth combating.

So, what good things do you think are worth keeping?

A theist that had once been a good friend of mine, who promptly terminated our friendship after reading some public remarks I had made about Christianity, once said to me: "Everyone worships something." I had neither the heart nor the patience to fight him on this theme, as once again my old enemy, semantics, had crept up into the fray. Obviously, he was incorrect that everyone "worships" something—but short of that, had he made a valid point? Were there things worth living for with as much vigor, spirit, stubbornness, and tenacity as theists do for their faith? If so, then why? That, companions, is a question worth answering.

As mentioned above, there are a multitude of things that religion does not exclusively provide that are entirely worth fighting—even dying—for. The virtues of love, of unity, of companionship, of hope, of truth are all excellent examples. These wonderful things, nonetheless, are philosophies not limited to spiritual entities and do not require of their followers anything that could remotely be considered "worship" in the adult sense. Truly, they behoove themselves to dedication and honor and trust and, sometimes, even necessity—but they are not facets of a larger existence that demand subservience or even acknowledgement in order for their benefits to be experienced.

On this same note, where is my proverbial church? Where does my heart sing, and my—for lack of an adequate analogy—spirit glow? Obviously, one could respond: the theater. Art moves me. Literature astounds me. Music inspires me. Philosophy intrigues me. Science amazes me. Civil rights compel me. There are likely many others. These movements would be, I suppose, comparable in reaction to how a theist might feel in presence of their work—a transcendence, if you will, of humanity into something beyond our singular persons and into the realm of something greater, something more wholesome, more beautiful, and infinitely more wondrous. Are these, then, things that I "worship"? Are these my god?

And I'll even play devil's advocate for the sake of fairness—let's say yes. Let us pretend that these glorious pieces of human invention are, in fact, what I "worship," ergo we can call them my "god." What evil does my god do? Where has been the grossness of music? The genocide in theater? The discrimination of science? Find me one person stoned to death by literature, or one civil right revoked by art. Above and beyond these, my god is silent, and asks nothing of me—he only gives inspiration and enjoyment to *everyone* who experiences it. He doesn't discriminate, he doesn't mandate. He is a wholesale fountain of joy, available to all without telling one who to have sex with, how to think, or who to kill.

Nor will my god ever attack yours. My god lives only to manifest in himself, not in obliteration of contradictory ideas. Even science, which can easily be argued is the single greatest combatant in the war of ideas against religion, has no innate mission to destroy contrary ideologies—it simply seeks objective truth; it allies itself to evidence. It goes where the evidence goes. If evidence went toward god, science would follow. Everything that it passes it does not destroy, it merely ignores. If religion is one of the many constructs that the evidence shies aside from and turns the eye of objective truth away, it is no more malicious than a river bending around a mountain—water simply doesn't flow up cliffs.

Given how painful that analogy was even to write, I hope one will take it to heart. Thankfully, these precepts are *not* gods, or else everything I have just alluded to would be turned false—they would strike into action the very crimes and evils of which I have attested they are absent. Do I think that these things are good, are worth fighting for in most senses?

Wholeheartedly yes—because they are equal and whole and completely objective. They are free to all. They give to all. They amaze and inspire without prejudice and without sacrifice. These are the great and fantastic inventions of the human condition, completely opposite from the retribution, indulgence, and impetuosity of religion. Without a doubt, all arts are the supreme accomplishment that the progress of human evolution has produced, and worth the worship that they do not necessitate.

Are there facets of religion that are worse than others?

If religion was ever brought into a courtroom and prosecuted, what would be the charges filed against it? What crimes would a stuffy voiced juror read in accusation to the 2,000-year-old perpetrator? And which of them would be the most severe—the *actus reus* of them all? Would it be the racism? The misogyny? The genocide?

To look at the wide list of misdeeds that religion has enacted upon the world and to decipher which one is the bearer of the worst offense is subjective at best—impossible, more likely. It would take a far more prudent judge than I to decide that burning heretics is better or worse in nature than forced genital laceration—for me, it is all circumstantial and of an equal level of depravity. However, there are pieces of religion that *I* revile more than others, while they all continue to rankle at me in some way.

Already noted in chapter four was my hatred for the psychological dependency religion inflicts on its followers—the succubus-like quality of cerebral rape, most especially on children who do not yet have the maturity to think objectively: asking no questions, subservience to unempirical ideas and unworthy men, incapability of accepting alternate or conflicting credos. Of all the cesspools that religion has dug and fills in our lives, this might be my greatest, loathsome enemy. Also, there is the easily made observation that women are treated (quite literally) in a biblically historic sense as livestock, and downtrodden for no other purpose than for having a vagina, used and abused violently for such a wonderful transgression. In several classic artworks, including those by Raphael and Michelangelo, the serpent—Satan—in the Garden of Eden is quite blatantly and literally female. But, for the sake of this question, there is a close second.

The dispensation against sex that religion has always kept is of ultimate anathema to me.[2] Not just to the action, which holds no more or less moral relativity than anything else, but the devices and circumstances by how it is enacted. Physically, the discrimination begins at birth with the popular practice of male circumcision and the tribal (but still entirely too prevalent) deed of female circumcision; it is then followed in adolescence by continuous verbal and physical admonitions against sexual acts or education[3]—that masturbation is immoral, that condoms are a pathway to hell, that sexual attraction toward a member of your same gender is recompensed with eternal suffering. All through critical development, children in religious fundamentalist families are constantly imprinting negativity to the idea of sex and everything involving it—years before they even get the chance to attempt it for themselves (unless it's forced upon them by older members of religious authority).

In a fundamental principle of religion, sex is confined to the marriage bed—and divorce is spiritual treachery. This means a fledgling adult has *one* chance at a compatible sexual partner if they are to remain pure in the eyes of god—*one* person, with whom no previous practice is permitted before the exchange of vows, to gamble physical satisfaction with. And if, for whatever reason, this compatibility doesn't exist: one is bound to this person for eternity, unable to escape the spiritual and pseudo-romantic prison that has been set up for them. Keep in mind that the freedom to indulge in this matrimonious civil sentence is infinitely more obtainable for women than it was in times past, for which marriages were predetermined and enforced violently—indeed, for many poor girls in the Middle East, such a custom is still thriving. And one who breaks these supposedly holy bonds will answer to god much quicker than expected, as the punishment doled out by the angry hands of surrounding men is usually death in one grotesque fashion or another, such as the man who beat his pregnant wife quite literally to death in Egypt after learning she had not voted for the Muslim Brotherhood presidential candidate in June 2012.[4]

Further than decrying sex, limiting its availability, punishing its variety, and butchering its manifestation, religion also supremely monopolizes sex as a spiritual and transcendent act, revoking all other connotations of recreation or human enjoyment. Pagan societies used ritual sex for an act of fertility, blessing, or conception and monotheisms put upon it the terrible stress of the necessity of procreation. To steal a wonderfully human and basic machination and add significance to it is perfectly acceptable—and we've done it with every process that our species has been intelligent enough to pursue. But to eliminate entire pieces of the purpose, for love or even for pure fun simply because it doesn't fall within the exceedingly subjective bounds of one person's spirituality, is an infiltration of liberty. In every vast stage of the sexual process in humanity, religion has tainted, maimed, or warped it into something taboo, unwelcome, and feared.

Finally, the faithful intrude dearly upon the *results* of sexuality, as though their hand in the limitation of the action of it wasn't quite offensive enough. Every biological occurrence that has been the result of sex, for good or ill, now has some religious label upon it in order to justify inept dogma: AIDS was the curse of god upon homosexuals, or a fetus is a soul-given organism which god says cannot be aborted, no matter the circumstance—and then all children that *do* have the luck to be born after this multitude of restrictions and margins must immediately be circumcised, christened, baptized—and the process begins again. Nor can we turn away from the sordid horrors of sex being using as *punishment*, such as the horrifying reports in France of literal *gang rape* of Muslim girls for the perceived "crime" of not being a virgin, or of not wearing a headscarf.[5]

Sex in its many varied forms may be a mysterious subject for some, and the unknown can be daunting and met with retaliation. But it is also unique to the biological process, and noticeably precedes the first religious thought or action that ever occurred on this planet. The plethora of sexual explorations of our species is unique to us, another one of the brilliant varieties that we have had the genius to create. I find that no matter the consensual carnal form, it is integral to the human condition and therefore should not be hated any more than having blonde hair or lacking gills—it is a piece of what it is to be human. Religion, with its continuous and all-sacrificing reach for the divine, has therefore rejected it with utmost fervor, ultimately to the detriment of all who follow it.

The words you use in your writing are extreme and sharp, in some cases much like the religious leaders you speak out against. Is there a note of hypocrisy in the way you structure your argument since it uses the same incendiary devices as your opponents?

I would not be tempted to answer this question save for the fact that I truly hear it a great deal. The short answer is no—for two reasons.

I never have and never will deplore those who disagree with my statements or have opposing statements of their own for their use of passionate, provocative words. The skill of persuasive writing and speaking is a powerful device that can be used for any purpose—no one person is incapable of using it to their own ends. As such, it would be remiss of me to attack my opponents for their utilization of it. Hand in hand with this is my very personal and fervid principle that to be moderate in anything is an ore deposit for general disappointment. I have infinitely more respect for any person who makes a declaration with emphasis than one who lowers their head for avoidance of a conflict of any kind and becomes a professional fence-sitter. By all means, if an opinion must be said, it must be *said*, and not whispered—while, of course, realizing that the most emphatic shouts are just as subject to the scrutiny of truth as anyone else, perhaps more so. I can appreciate candor and fire and gusto, even if I heartily diverge with its context.

As well, the civil liberty of free speech is, without question, a philosophy that is nearest to my heart and most intimate to my work—its principle is one that I follow with utmost devotion. No sooner would I cultivate a statement that advocated for the removal of this right (or any civil right, for that matter) from another individual, no matter their spiritual or philosophical persuasion, than I would sever my own hand. Indeed, I can say without a hint of drama in my meaning that I would, in fact, perform the latter in preference to the former. For this, and in review of all my printed statements, I cannot be accused of trying to hinder this right or this device from those who speak from a platform of faith. In this way, I could not blame a theist for using powerful language and resist the tool myself any more than I could stop driving a car because theists do, or quit breathing oxygen. There's no hypocrisy in it.

Still, there are things that are anathema to both of these principles that are inherent in the words that countless religious orators and proponents have used frequently. I have no patience for the spread of religious propaganda in secular establishments—akin to recent productions of *Godspell* or *J.B.: A Play in Verse* in public schools such as Flathead High in Kalispell, Montana, and likely many others, paid for with tax dollars and perpetuating Christian morality in an environment where such matters should be sterile and objective and unabashedly flout the Establishment Clause of the First Amendment. I have no empathy for U.S. senators passing bills limiting the powers of choice for abortion with motives that are clearly based on their own spiritual standards. While things like these undoubtedly fall within the boundaries of "free speech," they are practices that subvert the principle to a subjective bias in places where free speech is made to provide an even platform for all listeners, not captive audiences.

"Free speech" misses the point when it bleeds over from the realm of expression of thought into bending of policy. It might also be of special note that I have never once used the frightful and frankly fascist imagery that many religious leaders have—one will never hear me call for the need to throw all Christians behind an electric fence in the unlettered hypothesis that they will all die out, such as the bovine Charles Worley demanded to be done to all gays from his pulpit in North Carolina in 2012, in grim mirroring of the memory of concentration camps.[6] No one will ever hear me give the gross validation through powerful language that fuels *fatwa*s and horrifying religious crusades. Not one word of my writing emulates Curtis Knapp, a pastor in Kansas, who implored the U.S. government to literally eradicate his spiritual enemies in the name of god:

> *They should be put to death. That's what happened in Israel. That's why homosexuality wouldn't have grown in Israel. It tends to limit conversions. It tends to limit people coming out of the closet.—"Oh, so you're saying we should go out and start killing them, no?"—I'm saying the government should. They won't but they should. [You say], "Oh, I can't believe you. You're horrible. You're a backwards Neanderthal of a person." Is that what you're calling scripture? Is God a Neanderthal, backwards in his morality? Is it his word or not? If it's his word, he commanded it. It's his idea, not mine. And I'm not ashamed of it.[7]*

Of course, I would be beyond remiss if I did not regretfully call to memory the outstanding tactlessness (at the very least) and cruelty (more aptly) of Bryan Fischer, who appeared on television mere *hours* after the elementary school shooting in Newton, Connecticut, in December 2012, putting the blame for this terrible tragedy on the fact that god was no longer allowed in public schools through prayer and the posting of the Decalogue. Before the blood of innocent kindergarten children had even been cleared from the carpets, this indescribable demagogue poisoned the airwaves with such contemptible phrases as:

> *The question is going to come up, where was God? I thought God cared about the little children. God protects the little children. Where was God when all this went down? Here's the bottom line, God is not going to go where he is not wanted.* [8]

I will leave it to you, gentle reader: does one think there were no prayers uttered in the classroom that day? I would contend there were more than we could imagine: in voices so tiny and helpless that they would be better left unheard by us who could do nothing to help them. I submit that, even so, the despicable character it would take to make such a statement while the corpses are yet warm requires callousness beyond what I could ever conceive of myself. I hope you share my conviction in this.

In instances like these, I hold no candle in terms of extremism and have no heartburn at being insulted at the comparison—those who insipidly try to compare anything I have said to this sort of barbarism must be deluded as well as illiterate. To express an opinion is the civil right of every freethinking person—but woe betide the day one reads me advocating for the removal of any rights—let alone the lives!—of my neighbors who have done nothing to merit such punishments. Beyond lacking the capacity even to tolerate such things, I have an incredible drive within me to fight them, with every fiber I have available, with the admittedly faint but driven hope that someday my actions may have contributed to the illustrious Second Enlightenment that would have overturned such pieces of religious parasitism.

If, when you die, you see god and realize you were wrong about everything, how will you react?

If, when I die, my soul leaves my body and I am brought before god as he sits in judgment over all the doings of my life, my reaction will be highly premeditated. At one point in my much younger, less outspoken existence, I would have been comforted in the deluded rationalization that god would understand precisely why I think the things I do, he would forgive me on account of the very real and evil doings of his followers, and my lack of faith—nay, my hell-bent fight against it—would be empathized with. He would open his loving arms to me, seeing the goodness of my struggle.

That is what I used to think, but frankly, this is a poisonous kind of capitulation. It implies *I* was the one at fault, and *I* was the one who needed to be forgiven. If god is there, the god who allowed all this to happen in the first place, who idolized himself and performed his capricious masturbation of a divine rule over the world in a helter-skelter riot of laws, disaster, war, and gross mandate, I would remember the millions of deaths, slaves, beatings, tortures, and brutalities. I would think of Eric Borges and Matthew Shepard and of David Kato and the children at Wedgwood Baptist Church; of the babies who died from their herpetic mohels and of corpses in hospitals at the stubborn behest of Christian Scientists; of abused children whose cries would never escape the confines of the confessional and of countless dying of AIDS for which his preachers ultimately blamed the "debauchery" of innocents—and I would have one response for him, one simple gesture of contempt, defiance, and well-deserved criticism.

Notes

1. "Civility is overrated."—Christopher Hitchens

2. This is, of course, excluding the Song of Songs in the Old Testament—which reads very much like romantic erotic poetry. Biblical porn, if there ever was such a thing.

3. One of the many commandments listed in Exodus is that no altar to god should have any steps, lest in climbing, ones genitals may be exposed. The general Christian tradition in art was to never depict nude forms unless they were suffering in hell—this made Michelangelo's Sistine vault very taboo; a replica of his statue *David* was refused by the city of Jerusalem in 1995 until it was made to wear undergarments—to name a few.

4. Yasmin Helal, "Egyptian Beats Pregnant Wife to Death for Not Voting for Mursi," *Al Arabiya News*, June 24, 2012, http://english.alarabiya.net/articles/2012/06/24/222413.html.

5. Lara Marlowe, "Immigrant Girls Who Live in Terror of the Ghetto Rape Gangs," *Irish Times*, March 5, 2003.

6. Matthew Picht, "Baptist Pastor Calls for Concentration Camps for Gay People," *Newsy Multi-Source News*, May 23, 2012.

7. Michael Hayne, "Kansas Pastor Wants Government to Kill All the Gays," Addicting Info Online, May 29, 2012.

8. Meredith Bennet-Smith, *Huffington Post,* "Bryan Fischer: God Did Not Protect Connecticut Shooting Victims Because Prayer Banned in Schools," December 15, 2012, http://www.huffingtonpost.com/2012/12/15/bryan-fischer-god-did-not-protect-connecticut-shooting-victims-prayer-banned_n_2303903.html.

Afterword

In the few months that it took me to write *Oh, Your god!*, I was suffering privately a great deal. Like some gross parallel of a classic tragedy, I had lost most of everything that had defined me—the person I loved, a home with a surrogate family I admired, a job I adored, a community I cherished. I found myself in the middle of an unknown city, with very few I could call friends, some whom I could conceivably call enemies, and no money. While things continued to improve, as they invariably do over time, the *loss* was a constant presence, like my own shadow.

This caused an uncomfortable series of questions in my head that—I am ashamed to say—bordered irrationality. For the briefest of moments, it made *sense* to me that, if a god existed, this would undoubtedly be his chosen course of punishment, to strip away most everything I had cared for and leave me, in a melodramatic but veritable method, alone. This realization gravely made me ponder the efficacy of this work, the timing of it. Would writing an anti-theist movement during a spiritual crisis when I had already hit bottom be the wisest of choices? For a time much longer than should have been necessary, I sat staring at a blank page on my computer screen, with a slow blinking cursor mocking me. From the reasoned portion of my brain, I heard the continuous shouts of my rationality calling: "To be, or not to be . . . ?"

Thankfully, the only piece of myself that I dearly prize—my unwavering aeipathy—kicked in. I nudged myself along having found the obvious motivation—I *wanted* to do it. What the hell else mattered? And if I was suffering inwardly at the behest of god for my philosophies, actions, and reasons, then this only proved my point and further begged the work to be done. It only took a couple of days of flowing argument for the caliginous fear that had so desperately gripped me to be left behind, forgotten and unrequited. How, then, does one proceed following the footsteps of greats like my atheist mentors? How does one strike out on a path that *needs* traveling even when others have done it so brilliantly before you?

And here is my point—it doesn't matter. No hindrance or burden or fear should ever be measured or respected. Much like the case of theology: anything that takes away the drive to create or accomplish or succeed in whatever form of happiness one can fathom is not worthy of the grace of one's consideration. I found myself confronted with new fears with every chapter—not only by the retribution of religious influence but by the scorn of my own people. Would atheists think I had done a poor job of presenting the argument? Would anti-theists hear too much of previous writers in my voice? Would Richard Dawkins, in some editorial review, feel compelled to write: "An understandable effort by a young atheist, but devoid of effect"? One by one, as such nightmares crept into my thinking, they were swept aside by the fires of my labors. Because the grand truth is so simple—*no one* should control you. No one should mandate your happiness, least of all the imaginative whimsy of god or your own fright. The conjuration of the inane to cow you into submission is something the rest of the world is more than happy to do for you—don't meet them half way.

So, beyond the very purposeful message my book sought to convey about religion, it also demonstrated a very private but equally important context that should be emblazoned on the heart of every person with the capacity to want—to *yearn,* much like Icarus. The answer to the question that rattled on in my head during those hours of lonely misery and quiet fortitude, staring away at a blank page—the answer to everything:

"To be!"

Acknowledgments

The act of beginning this book was an effort in self-reflection—deciding whether it was a frivolous rant or a work that needed doing for my sake and the sake of those reading was a question answered only by those who gave me so much encouragement. For every nudge, hug, thought, and severely needed drink, I cannot ever express gratitude enough. Beyond this, it is not easy to stand my company for any lengthy period of time: all those below should be honored, if for nothing else, for accomplishing that indescribable feat.

For the Pitchstone edition of this book, I would like to thank a few people specifically, and then happily reprint the many people who helped make the original work possible. As it was said in the closing credits in many films of the '20s and '30s, a good cast is worth repeating.

First, to Kurt Volkan and the good people at Pitchstone Publishing, who were willing and enthusiastic to take this work and make it better and more available to the public at a moment's notice. I cannot thank them enough for their effort and patience.

To Markay Kern, who graciously offered to help me with edits and diligently followed through.

To Dan Arel, Matthew O'Neil, and J. D. Brucker—colleagues, friends, and dearest brothers-in-arms. Our work together has been of utmost importance to me, and I love you dearly.

To Sydoney Blackmore, who I do not deserve and will never stop loving. And to Thain Bertin and Andrew Sisk: may the debates never end.

To Dustin Mennie, for support and for obliging me with his photography.

To Dr. Jay Ball—one of the most supportive, brilliant, and effective professors I have ever had. I cannot tell you how much better of a person and a scholar I have become due to your efforts.

To my father, Kevin, and grandmother, Ruth, who supported this when they had more reason than anyone else not to—if all religious people were like they are, there would have been no reason to write this book. And to all the rest of my family, for showing me true love and fidelity.

To Scott Logsdon, who has remained one of the closest friends and supporters of my life. I do not have nearly enough thanks for the incredible goodness that his mere friendship has lent me, let alone his many kindnesses beyond that. He is unparalleled as a mentor and an example of success and humanity.

To Joe and Julie Legate—for reasons beyond words, but I hope they know them anyhow, and mostly for loving me. Their ability to show a person "family" is unparalleled and has been my refuge more times than they could ever be aware of. And to Rich Haptonstall, for being my faux-dad—an aeonian task that he performed with infinite love; what few good qualities I barely retain I owe to his guidance and friendship.

To the Hyde family, my first and most adamant surrogate kin, and most especially Vicky, without whom I would be not only less of a person but also still struggling vainly through high school; and to Morgan, who soldiers on with a grace unmatched by anyone I've ever known.

To Ryan Syme, who taught me how to love reading, thereby giving me my most loved and utilized tool.

To Carrie Hanenberger, who quite literally supported and fed me during the extraordinarily rough final weeks of this book's completion.

To Richard and Alissa Ruth, who seem to have supportiveness within their very blood, for endless discussions on the topic, thoughts, and laughs, and for giving me their couch. And to Michael McBurney, for loving me without question or footnote, who is the only person on the earth in whom I not only place trust, but also something that could reasonably be argued as faith.

To my own A-Team: Tara Roth, Colleen Unterreiner, Sally Johnson, Sue Evans, Matt Springer, Matthew Zak, Nancy Clawson, and Katie White for enduring my endless bouts of procrastination, ranting, frothing at the mouth, and personal demands. With the patience of butlers and the enthusiasm of a pep squad, they have knit themselves closer to my heart than they know.

I expressly need to thank the many people who read earlier drafts of this book and offered their thoughts, opinions, and good-natured arguments, most of whom I consider my closest and dear friends, including Morgan Hyde, Karissa Brown, Carrie Hanenberger, Shane Smith, Eric Jeffords, Ben Walker,

Ashley Trautwein, Linnea Springer, Rick Owens, Ben Robertson, Kirk Garner, Brandon Simpson, Andréa Cheroske, Michael McBurney, Richard and Alissa Ruth, Mighet Matanane, Victoria Miller, Aaron Morris, Chris Aguilar, Rebecca Harvey, David Boyd, Luke Rainey, Karen Kolar, my dearest, missed friend Shylo Kestle and family, and countless others, together with all my friends who didn't have the text but offered support and love and thoughts otherwise. Having an objective backboard off which to bounce ideas is the single greatest help I could ever ask for.

To Dawkins, Dennett, Harris, Stenger, Darwin, Krauss, among *innumerable* others—most notably Christopher Hitchens—for opening the door.

Finally, to Ashley Trautwein—for walks in the rain, endless hours of discussion, and for being my biggest fan; for never allowing me to feel less than superior; for giving us the marvelous gift of Umbi; for sitting in the front row and cheering (and crying) the loudest; for your reams of pages whose words embodied passion and love and daring; for a constant smile that, even now, is etched so in my memory it is a challenge to recall you wearing any other feature; for calling me every five minutes when I was nothing but a puddle of tears and drink in a dark corner; for your poetry; for your kindness; for your courage in the face of our mutual enemies—cupidity, moderation, superstition, and ignorance. For the truly incredible rarity of another human—that somehow, I still manage to learn from you. Thank you, infinitely.

Select Bibliography

---◆◆◆---

Recommended Reading

Abanes, Richard. *End-time Visions: The Road to Armageddon?* New York: Four Walls Eight Windows, 1998.

Allatius, Leo. *De Praeputio Domini Nostri Jesu Christi Diatriba.*

Angebert, Jean-Michael. *The Occult and the Third Reich: The Mystical Origins of Nazism and the Search For the Holy Grail.* Macmillan, 1974.

Angeles, Peter A. *Critiques of God: Making the Case Against Belief in God.* Prometheus Books, 1997.

Applebaum, Anne. *Gulag: A History.* New York: First Anchor Books. 2003.

Armstrong, Karen. *A History of God: The 4000-year Quest of Judaism, Christianity, and Islam.* New York: A.A. Knopf, 1993.

Aronson, Elliot. *The Social Animal.* San Francisco: W.H. Freeman, 1972.

Ballantine, Jeanne H., and Keith A. Roberts. *Our Social World: Condensed Version.* Los Angeles, CA: SAGE/Pine Forge, 2010.

Bellinger, Martha Idell Fletcher. *A Short History of the Drama,.* New York: H. Holt and, 1927.

Benedict. *Jesus of Nazareth: From the Baptism in the Jordan to the Transfiguration.* New York: Doubleday, 2007.

Benedict. *Jesus of Nazareth. from the Entrance into Jerusalem to the Resurrection.* San Francisco, CA: Ignatius, 2011.

Benedict. *Jesus of Nazareth.* San Francisco: Ignatius, 2011.

Bierlein, J. F. *Parallel Myths.* New York: Ballantine, 1994.

Bloom, Paul. *How Pleasure Works: The New Science of Why We Like What We Like.* New York: W. W. Norton, 2010.

Bodkin, Maud. *Archetypal Patterns in Poetry; Psychological Studies of Imagination,*. London: Oxford UP, H. Milford, 1934.

Boyett, Jason. *Pocket Guide to the Apocalypse: The Official Field Manual for the End of the World.* Orlando, FL: Relevant, 2005.

Breivik, Anders Behring. *2083: A European Declaration of Independence.* [S.l.]: [s.n.], 2011.

Carroll, James. *Constantine's Sword: The Church and the Jews: A History.* Boston: Houghton Mifflin, 2001.

Compendium, Catechism of the Catholic Church. Washington, D.C.: United States Conference of Catholic Bishops, 2006.

Csikszentmihalyi, Mihaly. *Flow: The Psychology of Optimal Experience.* New York: Harper & Row, 1990.

Darwin, Charles. *The Origin of the Species.* Ware [England: Wordsworth Editions, 1998.

Dawkins, Richard. *The Blind Watchmaker.* New York: Norton, 1986.

Dawkins, Richard. *The God Delusion.* Boston: Houghton Mifflin, 2006.

Dawkins, Richard. *The Greatest Show on Earth: The Evidence for Evolution.* New York: Free, 2009.

Dawkins, Richard. *Unweaving the Rainbow: Science, Delusion, and the Appetite for Wonder.* Boston: Houghton Mifflin, 1998.

Dawood, N. J. *The Koran.* London, England: Penguin, 1990.

Dennett, Daniel Clement. *Breaking the Spell: Religion as a Natural Phenomenon.* New York: Viking, 2006.

Eliot, Alexander, Joseph Campbell, and Mircea Eliade. *The Universal Myths: Heroes, Gods, Tricksters, and Others.* New York: New American Library, 1990.

Epstein, Greg M. *Good without God: What a Billion Nonreligious People Do Believe.* New York: William Morrow, 2009.

Ehrman, Bart D. *Misquoting Jesus,* HarperCollins. NY, 2005.

Feiler, Bruce S. *Walking the Bible: A Journey by Land through the Five Books of Moses.* New York: Morrow, 2001.

Fisher, G. Richard., M. Kurt. Goedelman, W. E. Nunnally, Stephen F. Cannon, and Paul R. Blizard. *The Confusing World of Benny Hinn.* St. Louis, MO: Personal Freedom Outreach, 1996.

Grady, J. Lee. *The Holy Spirit Is Not for Sale: Rekindling the Power of God in an Age of Compromise.* Grand Rapids, MI: Chosen, 2010.

Greene, B. *The Elegant Universe: Superstrings, Hidden Dimensions, and the Quest for the Ultimate Theory.* New York: W.W. Norton, 1999.

Grossman, Dave. *On Killing: The Psychological Cost of Learning to Kill in War and Society.* Boston: Little, Brown, 1995.

Haidt, Jonathan. *The Righteous Mind: Why Good People Are Divided By Politics and Religion.* New York: Vintage Books. 2012.

Harris, Sam. *Free Will.* New York: Free Press, 2012.

Harris, Sam. *Letter to a Christian Nation.* New York: Vintage, 2006.

Harris, Sam. *The End of Faith: Religion, Terror, and the Future of Reason.* New York: W.W. Norton &, 2004.

Hibbard, Howard. *Bernini.* [Baltimore]: Penguin, 1966.

Hitchens, Christopher. *Arguably.* New York: Twelve, 2011.

Hitchens, Christopher. *God Is Not Great: How Religion Poisons Everything.* New York: Twelve, 2007.

Hitchens, Christopher. *Letters to a Young Contrarian.* [New York]: Basic, 2001.

Hitchens, Christopher. *The Missionary Position: Mother Teresa in Theory and in Practice.* Twelve Books. April, 2012.

Hitchens, Christopher. *The Portable Atheist: Essential Readings for the Nonbeliever.* Philadelphia, PA: Da Capo, 2007.

Hitchens, Christopher. *Thomas Jefferson: Author of America.* New York: Atlas / HarperCollinsPublishers, 2005.

Hitler, Adolf, and Ralph Manheim. *Mein Kampf,.* Boston: Houghton Mifflin, 1943.

Hobbes, Thomas, and Richard Tuck. *Leviathan.* Cambridge [England: Cambridge UP, 1991.

Holy Bible: The New King James Version, Containing the Old and New Testaments. Nashville: T. Nelson, 1982.

Hugo, Victor, and Victor Hugo. *Les Miserables.* New York: New American Library, 1987.

Hume, David, David Hume, A. Wayne Colver, and John Valdimir. Price. *The Natural History of Religion.* Oxford [Eng.: Clarendon, 1976.

Joshi, S. T. *Atheism: A Reader.* New York: Prometheus, 2000.

Kalat, James W. *Biological Psychology.* Pacific Grove, CA: Brooks/Cole Pub., 1998.

Khalifa, Rashad. *Quran: The Final Testament : Authorized English Version, with the Arabic Text.* Fremont, CA: Universal Unity, 2001.

King, Ross. *Michelangelo and the Pope's Ceiling.* New York: Penguin Books. 2003.

Kittel, Rudolf, Wilhelm Rudolph, and Hans Peter. Rüger. *Biblia Hebraica Stuttgartensia.* Stuttgart: Deutsche Bibelstiftung, 1983.

Krakauer, Jon. *Under the Banner of Heaven.* Anchor Books, 2004.

Krueger, Douglas E. *What Is Atheism?: A Short Introduction*. Amherst, NY: Prometheus, 1998.

La, Vey Anton Szandor. *The Satanic Bible*. New York: Avon, 1969.

Lamott, Anne. *Grace (eventually): Thoughts on Faith*. New York: Riverhead, 2007.

Lewis, C. S., W. H. Lewis, and Walter Hooper. *Letters of C. S. Lewis*. San Diego [Calif.: Harcourt Brace, 1993.

Loftus, John W. *The Christian Delusion: Why Faith Fails*. Amherst, NY: Prometheus, 2010.

Lucretius, Carus Titus., Ettore Paratore, and W. H. D. Rouse. *Lucretius, De Rerum Natura,*. Cambridge, MA: Harvard UP, 1959.

McAfee, David G. *Disproving Christianity: And Other Secular Writings*. Great Britain: Dangerous Little, 2011.

Mills, David, and Dorion Sagan. *Atheist Universe: The Thinking Person's Answer to Christian Fundamentalism*. Berkeley, Ca.: Ulysses, 2006.

Miller, Arthur. *The Crucible*. New York, NY: Penguin, 1996.

Miller, William. *Evidences from Scripture and History of the Second Coming of Christ about the Year A.D. 1843, and of His Personal Reign of 1000 Years*. Syracuse: T.A. and S.F. Smith, 1835.

Newman, John Henry. *History of My Religious Opinions*. London: Longman, Green, Longman, Roberts, and Green, 1865.

Newton, Isaac, I. Bernard Cohen, Robert E. Schofield, and Marie Boas Hall. *Isaac Newton's Papers & Letters on Natural Philosophy and Related Documents*. Cambridge, MA: Harvard UP, 1958.

Northbrooke, John, and John Payne Collier. *A Treatise against Dicing, Dancing, Plays, and Interludes. With Other Idle Pastimes*. London: Reprinted from the Shakespeare Society, 1843.

Omar, Khayyam, and Edward FitzGerald. *Rubaiyat*. New York: Crowell, 1964.

Pospielovsky, Dimitry. *A History of Soviet Atheism in Theory and Practice, and the Believer*. New York: St. Martin's, 1987.

Rancour-Laferriere, Daniel. *The Sign of the Cross: From Golgotha to Genocide*. New Brunswick, NJ: Transaction, 2011.

Ramachandran, V. S., and Sandra Blakeslee. *Phantoms in the Brain: Probing the Mysteries of the Human Mind*. New York: William Morrow, 1998.

Remsburg, John E. *The Christ: A Critical Review and Analysis of the Evidences of His Existence*. Amherst, NY: Prometheus, 1994.

Robertson, Pat. *The New Millenium: 10 Trends That Will Impact You and Your Family by the Year 2000*. Milton Keynes, England: Word (UK), 1991.

Robertson, Pat. *The New World Order*. Dallas: Word Pub., 1991.

Rushdie, Salman. *Joseph Anton: A Memoir*. New York: Random House. 2012.

Sagan, Carl. *Cosmos*. New York: Random House, 1980.

Shaffer, Peter. *Equus*. Harmondsworth, Eng.: Penguin, 1973.

Shakespeare, William, and W. J. Craig. *The Complete Works of William Shakespeare*. London: Oxford UP, 1943.

Shaw, Eva. *Eve of Destruction*. Lowell House, Los Angeles, 1995.

Smith, Ken. *Ken's Guide to the Bible*. New York: Blast Books. 1995.

Spinoza, Benedictus De, and Jonathan I. Israel. *Theological-political Treatise*. Cambridge: Cambridge UP, 2007.

Steigmann-Gall, Richard. *The Holy Reich: Nazi Conceptions of Christianity, 1919-1945*. New York: Cambridge UP, 2003.

Stenger, Victor J. *God and the Folly of Faith*. New York: Prometheus Books, 2012.

Stenger, Victor J. *God: The Failed Hypothesis: How Sciences Shows That God Does Not Exist*. New York: Prometheus Books, 2007.

Thomas, and Daniel J. Sullivan. *The Summa Theologica*. Chicago: Encyclopaedia Britannica, 1955.

Thompson, Damian. *The End of Time: Faith and Fear in the Shadow of the Millennium*. Hanover, NH: University of New England, 1997.

Totten, Samuel, and Eric Markusen. *Genocide in Darfur: Investigating the Atrocities in the Sudan*. New York: Routledge, 2006.

Twenge, Jean M., and W. Keith. Campbell. *The Narcissism Epidemic: Living in the Age of Entitlement*. New York: Free, 2009.

Wilson, A.N. *Jesus: A Life*. New York: W.W. Norton & Company. 1992.

Wright, Robert. *NonZero: The Logic of Human Destiny*. New York: Pantheon, 2000.

Recommended Viewing

2012: The Science of Superstition (Documentary) Director, Nimrod Erez. Disinformation Company, 2009. Film.

8: The Mormon Proposition (Documentary) Director, Reed Cowan. David v. Goliath Films, 2010. Film.

Collision: Christopher Hitchens vs. Douglas Wilson (Documentary) Director, Darren Doane. Crux Pictures, 2009. Film.

Deliver Us From Evil. (Documentary) Director, Amy Burg. Disarming Films, 2006. Film.

Dispatches: Return to Africa's Witch Children (Documentary—Television) Directors, Mags Gavan & Joost Van Der Valk. Channel 4 Distribution, 2008. Series.

Dispatches: Unholy War (Documentary—Television) Director, James Millar. Channel 4 Distribution, 2007. Series.

Dispatches: Beneath the Veil (Documentary—Television) Director, Cassian Harrison. Channel 4 Distribution, 2005. Series.

Dispatches: Women Only Jihad (Documentary—Television) Director, Fiona Stourton. Channel 4 Distribution, 2006. Series.

Fall from Grace. (Documentary) Director, K. Ryan Jones. Duopoly Films, 2007. Film.

God On The Brain (Documentary) Director, Liz Tucker. British Broadcasting Corporation, 2003. Film.

God's Next Army (Documentary) Director, Tom Hurwitz. Lumiere Productions, 2006. Film.

Hand of God (Documentary) Director, Joe Cultera. Zingerplatz Pictures, 2006. Film.

Jesus Camp. (Documentary) Director, Heidi Ewing. A&E IndieFilms, 2006. Film.

Lord, Save Us From Your Followers (Documentary) Director, Dan Merchant, Big Finish Media, 2008. Film.

The Assassination of Dr. Tiller (Documentary) Carrie Wysocki. MSNBC Network, 2010. Film.

The Most Hated Family In America (Documentary) Director, Geoffrey O'Connor. British Broadcasting Corporation, 2007. Film.

Religulous. (Documentary) Director, Larry Charles. Thousand Words, 2008. Film.

About the Author

Joshua Kelly is a Master of Arts student in Theatre and Performance Studies at Central Washington University. He graduated with honors with his bachelor's degree from the University of Montana in Missoula. Kelly has been working closely with many high-profile atheists, including the award-winning writer Dan Arel (*Parenting Without God*) on his *Patheos* site, Matthew O'Neil (*What the Bible Really Does [and Doesn't] Say about Sex*) and J. D. Brucker (*God Needs to Go*). He has had the privilege to work with Anthony Magnabosco (Street Epistemology) and Dr. Peter Boghossian (*A Manual for Creating Atheists*) on *Atheos*, the app for religious discussion sponsored by the Richard Dawkins Foundation for Reason and Science. He has also contributed a chapter on "The Philosophy of Atheism" to the book *666*, featuring writing from Dr. Lawrence Krauss, Dr. Richard Carrier, Douglas Wilson, and several others. More of Kelly's writing on current events can be found on *Patheos* at www.patheos.com/blogs/danthropology.